What Your Colleagues Are Saying . . .

Educators will find much inspiration and support in this book, which offers insightful and practical ways to support students' emotional health. It is our bodies that hold trauma, and it is through our bodies that we can find release and emotional rest. This compassionate work provides educators with easy-to-implement strategies and activities that use the breath and body to create change from the inside out. The goal of this comprehensive resource is not only to lower anxiety and challenging behaviors, but also to create learning communities that further joy, wonder, and happiness.

Hannah Beach
Co-author, *Reclaiming Our Students: Why Children Are More Anxious, Aggressive, and Shut Down Than Ever—And What We Can Do About It*

I am so excited to hear that *Cultivating Happiness, Resilience, and Well-Being Through Meditation, Mindfulness, and Movement* will be available to practitioners across K–12 settings. Christine Mason and her colleagues share practical, sensible, and you-can-do-today strategies in a beautiful way that adds a spirit of calm at a much-needed time in schools. Educators looking for a compassionate approach to supporting their students in a developmentally appropriate and engaging way need to look no further: You have found your resource.

Susie DaSilva
Superintendent of Schools
Ridgefield, CT

Learning, understanding, and using the Five Cs described in this book for social-emotional learning in my practice as a school principal have been game changers! Working with staff and having compassionate conversations has changed how we do business in school. Staff and students are definitely benefitting from being engaged in mindful movement and yoga.

Stacy Bachelder Giles
Principal
Bridgewater-Hebron Village School
Bristol, NH

As a parent, I know how strongly we hope our children will thrive and flourish. With the enormous challenges facing our world today, I am worried, as many are, about the world we will be leaving them. How can we best equip our children to navigate their challenges today and the world's challenges tomorrow? For centuries, meditation and yoga have provided a gateway to calmness and insights that can guide our actions and interactions as we strengthen our health and well-being. To protect and support them, and for our collective future, these teachings must reach our children. Christine Mason and her team of dedicated yoga-meditation teachers have written a manual to help schools implement practices that can make a profound difference for each and every child and for our planet. Filled with hundreds of photos and time-tested yoga sets, breathing exercises, and meditations, *Cultivating Happiness, Resilience, and Well-Being Through Meditation, Mindfulness, and Movement* provides a pathway to a better, brighter future as it addresses students' and teachers' immediate needs. This book will be useful for yoga instructors as well as public and private school teachers, school counselors, and administrators. I encourage you to read, practice, and reflect, watching in wonder at the significant improvements in your own happiness, resilience, and well-being as well as in all the children in your life!

Amrit Singh Khalsa
CEO
Kundalini Research Institute
Santa Cruz, NM

I have had the pleasure of working with Christine Mason and have benefitted from her expertise in engaging educators in much-needed reforms. We need more of the authors' vision and the holistic, human-centered approach described in this book in our work. As we move to prevent and alleviate the impact of trauma, we must build skills like mindfulness to best prepare current and future generations in our ever-changing world.

Jesse Kohler
Executive Director
Campaign for Trauma-Informed Policy and Practice

This is an excellent, informative, and well-researched book. It is a must-read for all future and current teachers, school counselors, and administrators and is without question one of the best books written on the topic. *Cultivating Happiness, Resilience, and Well-Being Through Meditation, Mindfulness, and Movement* is a valuable guide to improve teacher training, schools, and personal happiness and will be added to my classes' reading lists."

Sandra McElroy
Professor of Early Childhood Learning
Pine Manor Campus, Boston College
Chestnut Hill, MA

Too often we forget that our personal and professional well-being and health are directly related to our individual efforts to remain mindful, reflective, and balanced. *Cultivating Happiness, Resilience, and Well-Being Through Meditation, Mindfulness, and Movement* is an outstanding resource for all who wish to continuously learn, grow, and improve. The advantage here is that this work provides the reader with practical and replicable steps and skills to increase one's overall well-being. This is a must read for anyone interested in elevating and enriching both personal and shared experiences.

Joseph L. Ricca
Superintendent of Schools
White Plains, NY

The practice of using meditation, mindfulness, and movement should be in every educator's tool kit of strategies under the labels of self-preservation and decision making. *Cultivating Happiness, Resilience, and Well-Being Through Meditation, Mindfulness and Movement* is the workbook they need to learn these stress-reducing techniques. The book is situated on a stable foundation of theory and what theory looks like in practice. The authors provide validating research and align it with evidence-based activities educators can easily incorporate during their working hours, and they demonstrate how these techniques decrease the risks of empathic distress and burnout while increasing an educator's capacity to become more compassionate and impartial when making judgments about their students.

Victoria E. Romero
Educational Consultant and Author
Building Resilience in Students Impacted by Adverse Childhood Experiences and
Race Resilience: Achieving Equity Through Self and Systems Transformation

Cultivating Happiness, Resilience, and Well-Being Through Meditation, Mindfulness, and Movement

Cultivating Happiness, Resilience, and Well-Being Through Meditation, Mindfulness, and Movement

A Guide for Educators

Christine Mason
Jeffrey Donald
Krishna Kaur Khalsa
Michele M. Rivers Murphy
Valerie Brown

Foreword by Ruschelle S. Reuben

A Joint Publication

CORWIN

FOR INFORMATION:

Corwin

A SAGE Company

2455 Teller Road

Thousand Oaks, California 91320

(800) 233-9936

www.corwin.com

SAGE Publications Ltd.

1 Oliver's Yard

55 City Road

London EC1Y 1SP

United Kingdom

SAGE Publications India Pvt. Ltd.

B 1/I 1 Mohan Cooperative Industrial Area

Mathura Road, New Delhi 110 044

India

SAGE Publications Asia-Pacific Pte. Ltd.

18 Cross Street #10-10/11/12

China Square Central

Singapore 048423

President: Mike Soules

Associate Vice President and Editorial
    Director: Monica Eckman

Program Director and Publisher: Jessica Allan

Senior Content Development Editor: Lucas Schleicher

Associate Content Development Editor: Mia Rodriguez

Editorial Assistant: Natalie Delpino

Editorial Intern: Ricardo Ramirez

Project Editor: Amy Schroller

Copy Editor: Melinda Masson

Typesetter: C&M Digitals (P) Ltd.

Proofreader: Larry Baker

Cover Designer: Gail Buschman

Marketing Manager: Olivia Bartlett

Printed in Canada

Library of Congress Cataloging-in-Publication Data

Names: Mason, Christine Y. (Christine Yvonne), 1949- author. | Donald, Jeffrey, author. | Khalsa, Krishna Kaur, author. | Rivers Murphy, Michele M., author. | Brown, Valerie L., author.

Title: Cultivating happiness, resilience, and well-being through meditation, mindfulness, and movement : a guide for educators / Christine Y. Mason, Jeffrey Donald, Krishna Kaur Khalsa, Michele M. Rivers Murphy, Valerie L. Brown ; Foreword by Ruschelle S. Reuben.

Description: Thousand Oaks, California : Corwin, [2022] | Includes bibliographical references and index.

Identifiers: LCCN 2021036797 | ISBN 9781071852811 (paperback) | ISBN 9781071852804 (epub) | ISBN 9781071852798 (epub) | ISBN 9781071852781 (pdf)

Subjects: LCSH: Students—Mental health. | Teachers—Job stress—Prevention. | Mindfulness (Psychology) | Yoga—Psychological aspects. | Meditation—Psychological aspects. | School improvement programs.

Classification: LCC LB3430 .M38 2022 | DDC 371.7—dc23
LC record available at https://lccn.loc.gov/2021036797

This book is printed on acid-free paper.

21 22 23 24 25 10 9 8 7 6 5 4 3 2 1

DISCLAIMER: This book may direct you to access third-party content via Web links, QR codes, or other scannable technologies, which are provided for your reference by the author(s). Corwin makes no guarantee that such third-party content will be available for your use and encourages you to review the terms and conditions of such third-party content. Corwin takes no responsibility and assumes no liability for your use of any third-party content, nor does Corwin approve, sponsor, endorse, verify, or certify such third-party content.

MEDICAL DISCLAIMER: The exercise and lifestyle suggestions in this book come from ancient yogic traditions. Nothing in this book should be construed as medical advice. Always check with your personal physician or licensed health care practitioner before making any significant modifications to your lifestyle, to ensure that the lifestyle changes are appropriate for your personal health condition and consistent with any medication you may be taking.

Contents

PART I: INTRODUCTION   1

CHAPTER 1

CHAPTER 2

CHAPTER 3

CHAPTER 4

PART II: HEART CENTERED LEARNING: THE FIVE CS 105

CHAPTER 5

CHAPTER 6

List of Online Resources

For these and other resources related to *Cultivating Happiness, Resilience, and Well-Being Through Meditation, Mindfulness, and Movement*, visit the Corwin Resources page at **https://resources.corwin.com/CultivatingHappiness.**

Foreword

Mindfulness and self-care publications saturate shelves and online listings these days. There's mindful walking, mindful eating, mindful gardening, mindfulness for business, and even mindful quantum physics. With all the options, why should you take the time to read this particular book? Our experience in Montgomery County Public Schools tells the story. The practices that Jeff Donald and others in this book have recommended have truly uplifted students and faculty in so many of our schools.

Although several books describe the benefits and the importance of mindfulness for well-being and the efficacy of this science in schools, very few actually show you how to do it with a step-by-step game plan. This marvelous book answers not only the fundamentals of "what" and "why," but also the "how." You'll find, too, that stories from educators around the country add to our understanding of this work of heart; each story expands your motivation and courage moving forward in so many profound ways—on so many levels.

We have all heard the standard definition of mindfulness as a particular way of paying attention in a purposeful manner, staying in the present moment. Yes, this definition is true, but that is only half of the story. What is missing is a fully integrative reason for why we do it in the first place! Mindfulness practices can be better described as follows:

> Mindfulness is a science of self-development and self-awareness through the alignment of body, breath, and mind—a science of personal union. Mindfulness teaches us how to steady the mind and emotions while awakening the awareness of intuitive and peaceful qualities of the heart. Mindfulness is a universal approach to inner peacefulness, clarity, and courage. Compatible with all cultural traditions and religious faiths, mindfulness provides tools to experience inner balance and purpose.

Not only does mindfulness, through its focus on self-knowledge, create a deeper understanding of our inner selves; it also expands our interpersonal connection with others as we become more compassionate, empathetic, and aware.

As our understanding of self and others leads to multiple positive outcomes, we can easily draw the throughline to how cultivating this science in school settings benefits all participants in the learning process and ensures academic success. You would not be surprised to discover that researchers exploring the impact of mindfulness training on children and adolescents (as well as adults) have revealed a wide range of positive results including improvements in executive functioning, attention span, emotional and behavioral regulation, and immune function. Studies also show this science substantially reduces burnout and the negative effects of vicarious trauma. Not bad for a practice that essentially costs nothing but gives you everything from health enhancement to more satisfaction and purpose!

What's the catch? you may ask. This practice is called a "practice" for a reason. Like anything else in life, we get better at what we rehearse. Mindfulness requires motivation, intention, and action to cultivate this state in our lives. It is not a magic pill.

If you're anything like me, you most likely will feel more comfortable getting the motivation, intention, and action in place if you see the science and research beforehand, which is why the first chapters of this book systematically produce the scientific validation required to both understand and accept these practices as valuable and worthy of teaching our students and ourselves.

This book is a much-needed road map for educators who instinctively know that they must teach more than academics. It provides a wealth of self-help tools for teachers, students, families, and others. Most importantly, it engages us as educators to implement these practices ourselves, to meet the changing needs of modern education, even as we realize that all of us deserve a chance to learn more about ourselves and to experience the mind–body harmony that these practices support. This is all a part of the "joy factor," to shine—to feel the internal glow of being in sync with our breath, moment by moment, day by day, year after year, for a lifetime.

—Ruschelle S. Reuben
Chief of Teaching, Learning, and Schools
Montgomery County Public Schools

Preface

Cultivating Happiness, Resilience, and Well-Being Through Meditation, Mindfulness, and Movement is intended as a practical guide to help educators use mindfulness, yoga, and meditation with virtual, hybrid, and in-person classrooms. This book builds on the authors' collective experience in teaching yoga, mindfulness, and meditation, including Krishna Kaur's remarkable journey delivering Y.O.G.A. for Youth™ around the world; Christine Mason's 20 years of teaching yoga, and connecting to education through Heart Centered Learning®; Jeff Donald's experience designing and coordinating a districtwide mindfulness yoga program; Michele Rivers Murphy's use of mindfulness and Heart Centered Learning in schools throughout the United States; and Valerie Brown's experience in facilitating mindfulness leadership and coaching mindful leaders.

In *Visioning Onward* (2020), Christine Mason and coauthors Paul Liabenow and Melissa Patschke explain that "building a shared vision begins by seeing clearly and creatively. It involves painting an inspiring and clear picture of what you see and seek to create. . . . Engagement, sustained effort, and improvement are hallmarks of achieving an established goal through visioning" (p. 144). Creating a vision for a compassionate school takes time, energy, and effort. Staff, students, and families must be involved.

In 2019, in a blog on the Center for Educational Improvement (CEI) website, Meghan Wenzel said:

> By incorporating opportunities for students to develop emotional intelligence, resilience, and self-love, you are teaching them invaluable life skills that will serve them well inside and outside the classroom. When students feel understood and valued, they become more confident in their abilities and perform better. When they feel more comfortable in their own skin, they are more content—they are able to form deeper relationships and connections, which is crucial for healthy development. Fostering an open, welcoming, and accepting environment will lend itself to happy and healthy students who are ready and eager to learn. (Wenzel, 2019a)

Wenzel's article is one of many that CEI staff and interns have written describing how to create compassionate school communities. This work began in 2009, when CEI was first incorporated, and has continued with annual meetings of principals and other leaders, research projects, and

This book began as a vision for using tools to uplift students, promote and encourage self-care, and help students refocus to improve their ability to concentrate, engage in critical thinking, and make better decisions.

activities to further substantiate both the need and the process for developing compassionate schools. When Mason, Liabenow, and Patschke addressed visioning in 2020, they referenced compassionate schools, using the term *Heart Centered Learning®*, and referred to a "conscious effort to refocus our schools and school cultures so that students become immersed in environments that consider social-emotional well-being and the needs of self and others" (p. 1). Mason, Rivers Murphy, and Jackson (2020), in their book *Mindful School Communities*, described a heart centered school community as "a compassionate school community that balances well-being and learning" (p. 2). We see mindful breath, yoga movements, and meditation as integral components in building heart centered communities, communities engaged in Heart Centered Learning®.

Cultivating Happiness, Resilience, and Well-Being is a book that has been waiting in the wings for an audience. We knew we couldn't introduce it too soon, fearing perhaps school leaders would dismiss it as not related enough to education and learning. We also realized that, as with any new adventure, success usually doesn't happen overnight. In our earlier books we cautioned readers to practice first before sharing our strategies with others. The success we seek from mindfulness practice often begins with small gains—a student who is a tad more attentive, youth who smile as they reflect on *their* community, teachers whose worlds open up almost into a new dimension with longer breaths and greater connectedness between their heads and their hearts.

In 2020, the need for mindful breath work, yoga movements, and meditation was great. As so much of the world faced the gloom and doom of COVID-19, as so many educators truly wondered if their district's plan was really so wise, and as so many families struggled in their makeshift home schools, we realized the time for *Cultivating Happiness, Resilience, and Well-Being* was right. We knew that this book needed to transcend boundaries. It shouldn't be another yoga manual or another book on mindful classrooms. Instead, there was a serious need for a book that had (a) background research providing evidence of the importance of mind–body connections, yoga, and meditation; (b) practical suggestions that educators could pick up and follow to guide students through yoga and meditation activities; and (c) evidence demonstrating that schools can do this—that schools are beginning to implement what we are recommending.

RESILIENCE AND HEALING IN THE MOMENT: MINDFULNESS

With the disruption and tragedy of the COVID-19 pandemic, we all are experiencing much change, loss, and suffering. Educators are challenged to connect with students, facilitate academic learning, and give students meaningful educational experiences, even as we adapt to changing criteria for physical distancing.

Even in the best of times, reaching the diverse needs of many students requires skilled and talented educators. During 2020, however, the difficulties we encountered were multiplied tenfold. Schools had to find adequate online programs to teach academics, get equipment and virtual access to students, consider scheduling, and figure out what students could do independently. Many educators worked extra hours bringing food to families and seeking ways to help those most in need. Yet, with all the difficulties, we have uncovered an opportunity to help students and families heal and build resilience.

When under extreme or prolonged stress, individuals often become anxious, hypervigilant, distrustful, and uneasy. Children and adults alike who are impacted by trauma may experience nightmares, have difficulty sleeping, or become depressed or withdrawn (Lieberman & Knorr, 2007). Around the world today, we are seeing multiple examples of both acute trauma and posttraumatic stress disorders. In addition to the COVID-19 pandemic, in 2020 wildfires raged out of control, floods and hurricanes left hundreds homeless, and lives were lost not only to the coronavirus but to police brutality, racially motivated violence, violence occurring at peaceful protests, and accidental drug overdoses among those addicted to opioids as well. Stress and trauma surround us, not only in our own communities but also on our screens and in the media, day in and day out—without respite.

> Educators play a crucial role in promoting mental health and well-being. At the very heart of students' resilience is often an educator who plays a consistent, protective, and supportive role in their lives.

Educators and families can use the tools presented in *Cultivating Happiness, Resilience, and Well-Being* to maintain a healthy balance in the midst of the current chaos, uncertainty, and anxiety. During times of turmoil, educators are able to help students and families heal in the moment, assisting their transition from unhealthy or dysfunctional to healthy or functional coping and resilience (Figley & McCubbin, 2016; Vaughn-Coaxum et al., 2018). Whether we face a catastrophic pandemic or smaller and more localized tragedies, educators have an opportunity to foster the protective factors, and even to *be* the protective factors, that students and families need to become more resilient (Mason et al., 2021).

Both 2020 and 2021 have been challenging for all of us, and the impact on students has to be profound. They have had to adjust to receiving instruction in virtual settings. For those who have been able to return to face-to-face learning, the school setting and day look very different from the past.

TEACHERS PROVIDING CALM LEADS TO STUDENTS EAGER TO LEARN

Linda Cleary, a teacher for students with special needs at Fairfax County Public Schools, describes how she has used yoga and movement during the COVID-19 pandemic.

I teach in a public elementary school to a class of students with special needs in a designation called noncategorical. Along with two instructional assistants, I provide special education services to students with a wide variety of needs. We teach students with autism spectrum disorder, Down syndrome, and learning as well as physical disabilities.

During these challenging times, I felt it was important to provide a sense of calm and grounding for our students. Many of these students have a familiarity with yoga, so allowing for time within the instructional day provided a much-needed respite and restoration, which is important to learning.

I use yoga and movement each day when teaching in my classes. We use yoga not only to stretch our bodies but also to stretch our minds. Yoga helps us describe concepts like large and small, near and far, and up and down. It helps us learn and retain common sight words like *fly, go, see, and, stop,* and many more, by getting the movement into our muscle memory. We use our bodies to show letters, numbers, and shapes and to communicate feelings. Yoga is a fun way to assist students who are on the autism spectrum and those who have intellectual disabilities with imitation of movement and using visuals, providing a concrete guide to follow. Movement and hand signals are useful methods of expression for young students who become overstimulated with excessive use of words and language.

Many of these students have an aptitude for skills in the physical arena. They are eager to try new yogic positions, especially when paired with a vivid picture of the positions and movements. They are especially popular and inspiring when they align with animal stances and activity!

HOW TO USE *CULTIVATING HAPPINESS, RESILIENCE, AND WELL-BEING*

Teachers, therapists, and others can use *Cultivating Happiness, Resilience, and Well-Being* in their classrooms and schools in any number of ways. This book connects yoga, meditation, and mindfulness to the academic curriculum and serves as a tool to enhance student alertness, focus, and learning. The activities can easily be adapted or used for before- or after-school programs or in physical education classes. However, the activities also can be woven throughout the academic school day, with various yogic practices, breath work, meditation, and mindfulness skills inserted during key transition points, such as five fingers that point to key parts of the day: (1) transitioning into school for the day (virtual/in-person), (2) before morning academics, (3) after lunch, (4) before afternoon academics, and (5) before transitioning home/end of school day. *Cultivating Happiness, Resilience, and Well-Being* can also be used districtwide, as Jeff Donald suggests, as a resource for teachers to learn to implement the techniques we recommend.

In 2014, when the CEI published *Heart Beaming*, leaders at the CEI began talking with educators around the country about the possibility for brief "brain breaks," where students are given opportunities to get up and stretch, do some breath work, and/or engage in a brief meditation (Mason & Banks, 2014). We noticed that when schools implemented these and related practices, often students were less disruptive, more focused, and more engaged with their learning. So not only were students able to stay tuned in to teachers for longer periods of time, but they also participated to a greater degree, asking questions and sometimes even learning at a deeper level.

When we look at the neurobiology that supports techniques such as these brain breaks, this makes sense.

> The activities also can be woven throughout the academic school day, with various yogic practices, breath work, meditation, and mindfulness skills inserted during key transition points.

GLOSSARY

The following Glossary (Figure 0.1) was designed to help you understand some terms we will be using throughout this book.

Figure 0.1 • Glossary

Breath work: Breath work includes a variety of specific breathing techniques that are practiced to gain control over one's breath to help regulate emotions, increase lung capacity, and calm oneself.

Energy fields: Yoga-mindfulness-meditation impacts our awareness of energy both within our bodies and surrounding our bodies.

Equanimity: Equanimity refers to a balanced mental attitude or quality of mind, with neutral, unbiased reactions to things. With equanimity, an individual experiences all events with a calm and stable attitude and a sense of inner peace (Desbordes et al., 2015; Juneau et al., 2020; Wallace, 2010).

Executive functioning: From a neurological perspective, executive functioning is the aspect of brain function that involves the conscious control of thought, action, and emotion. The three main categories of executive functioning are working memory, cognitive flexibility, and inhibitory control. Often referred to as the "management system of the brain," executive functioning controls many of our everyday skills such as paying attention, starting and organizing tasks, and understanding another person's point of view. Executive functions are controlled by the frontal lobes of the brain, particularly in the prefrontal cortex (Zelazo et al., 2018).

(Continued)

(Continued)

Kriya: A kriya is a yoga set and includes a sequence of yoga postures with breath work and meditations incorporated into the set.

Meditation: Meditation is "a set of techniques that are intended to encourage a heightened state of awareness and focused attention. Meditation is also a consciousness-changing technique that has been shown to have a wide number of benefits on psychological well-being" (Cherry, 2020). With meditation, the mind is stilled, and a sense of relaxation and calmness occurs.

Mindfulness: Mindfulness is "the process by which we go about deepening our attention and awareness, refining them, and putting them to a greater practical use in our lives" (Kabat-Zinn, 1994). Mindfulness centers on the fundamental principle of being "awake" fully, with all senses attuned to one's surroundings and present state of mind. Mindfulness expert Jon Kabat-Zinn (1994) discusses the practice of mindfulness as "examining who we are . . . questioning our view of the world and our place in it . . . cultivating some appreciation for the fullness of each moment we are alive. Most of all, it has to do with being in touch." This practice involves a deep commitment to attention and awareness, requiring us to look inward to help us see more clearly.

Self-care: Self-care involves "providing adequate attention to one's own physical and psychological wellness" (Beauchamp & Childress, 2001). Self-care looks different for everyone—while one person might wind down by taking a yoga class, another might enjoy a spa day or simply a cup of tea and an early bedtime. While it may seem like a luxury to practice self-care, it is truly essential to one's well-being. When we are too wrapped up in work, family responsibilities, financial stressors, or anything else weighing on our minds, we tend to put our own needs last. This can cause more than just exhaustion. Neglecting our needs can have long-term mental and physical health complications. Establishing a solid self-care routine is not only good for one's health, but it might actually improve productivity in other areas of one's life.

Self-regulation: Self-regulation is the process of controlling one's behavior by self-monitoring, self-evaluation, and self-reinforcement (American Psychological Association, 2020a). Self-monitoring involves keeping a record of one's behavior, while self-evaluation consists of analyzing that information and assessing its value. Through self-reinforcement, an individual might reward oneself for appropriate behavior or for attaining a goal. Self-regulation is an essential skill in the social world, as it informs us how we relate to ourselves and others, and whether or not we are internalizing social norms (Berger, 2011).

Yoga movements: Krishna Kaur (2006) describes yoga as "a science of self-development and self-awareness through the alignment of body, mind, and sound—a science of personal union, balancing the body, mind, and spirit" (p. 1). Yoga is a holistic system of mind–body practices for mental and physical health. The practice of yoga includes eight limbs: (1) ethical standards and sense of integrity, including nonviolence and truthfulness; (2) self-discipline and meditation; (3) the physical postures; (4) breath and breath work; (5) inner growth, withdrawing from a reliance on the physical world; (6) focusing attention on a single point; (7) uninterrupted flow of consciousness with meditation; and (8) operating at our highest frequency and potential. Specific yoga classes or programs may focus on one or more of these limbs.

Many yoga programs for children share a common goal of teaching four basic elements of yoga: (1) physical postures, (2) breathing exercises, (3) relaxation techniques, and (4) mindfulness and meditation practices. The programs also teach a variety of additional educational, social-emotional, and didactic techniques to enhance students' mental and physical health and improve their behavior.

CULTIVATING HAPPINESS, RESILIENCE, AND WELL-BEING: THE BOOK

Cultivating Happiness, Resilience, and Well-Being is designed for teachers, therapists, and yoga teachers who are collaborating with schools and district-level mindfulness coordinators. It will also be useful to behavioral health therapists, community health and mental health providers, and other members of educational support teams.

As you start to read through *Cultivating Happiness, Resilience, and Well-Being*, remember it is one thing to *read* about yoga-mindfulness-meditation and another thing to actually *do* the recommended practices.

It may take several months to work your way through the chapters, implementing practices as your comfort level grows.

> Give yourself time to read, reflect, practice, and gain a sense of comfort with the exercises and activities.

Cultivating Happiness, Resilience, and Well-Being is organized into three major sections: the Introduction, the Five Cs, and Leadership. The Introduction (Chapters 1–4) includes, in addition to an introductory overview, a few basic recommendations to get you started, information on teacher stress and teacher practice, and strategies to organize space, materials, and instruction. In the introduction to the Five Cs (Chapter 5) and each of the Five Cs chapters (Chapters 6–10)—focused on consciousness, compassion, confidence, courage, and community—we describe yoga, meditation, and mindfulness activities that support the individual components. In the Leadership chapters (Chapters 11 and 12), we bring you ideas for leadership, mindfulness coaching, and collaboration, whether you are leading from within a school or a district or through regional, national, or international involvement.

Each chapter refers to related activities for academic learning for the Five Cs and Heart Centered Learning, with references to in-classroom, virtual, and hybrid learning. High-quality photos and graphics are included throughout the book, and/or readers are provided online access to these.

Incorporated into *Cultivating Happiness, Resilience, and Well-Being* are each of the following:

- Teacher notes, suggested yoga sets, breath work, mantras, meditations, and home practices, as well as explanations around the connection to the Five Cs and Heart Centered Learning.

- Recommendations to help teachers guide student exercises, including how to help students improve postures and common accommodations that can increase student buy-in and engagement, keeping advanced students interested while helping students who may struggle with an exercise.

- Suggested resources and apps that support our recommendations.
- Activities (yoga sets, meditations, and breath work), with a discussion of appropriateness for various age levels (pre-K to high school) and circumstances.
- A suggested "curricular context" and suggestions for integrating yoga-meditation-mindfulness into the school day.
- Examples of how the authors and others have applied these practices in their lives and in their instruction.
- A description of options for teachers, teacher preparation, or coordination with local yoga and meditation teachers.
- Suggested references for online apps and videos that can complement activities in each chapter.
- Data on implementation in Maryland and elsewhere, including information on number of teachers trained, impact on students, student and teacher opinions of effectiveness, and practical hints for infusing aspects of the program throughout the school day.

To guide your reading, look for the following features:

1. Key Principles
2. Story Boxes
3. Info Boxes
4. My Practice Boxes
5. Online Resources

Additionally, within each chapter is a graphic organizer that gives users ideas to guide lessons in that chapter and recommended adaptations, as well as a space to record any notes the user may wish to consider when implementing the suggested activities. The Curriculum Integration Planner, available online with a sample shown as follows in Figure 0.2, includes blank rows so you can insert your own material.

Figure 0.2 ◆ Sample Curriculum Integration Planner

LESSON	GRADE LEVEL	SUBJECT/ CONTEXT	ADAPTATION/NOTES
SAMPLE			*Place a stuffed animal on each child's belly.*
Compassion/ Posture and Movement	*Pre-K*	*Story time*	*The child gives the animal a "ride" so that the stuffed animal moves like a roller coaster as the child inhales and exhales.* *A useful activity before nap time; a good calming activity.*

online resources ⌖ Available for download at https://resources.corwin.com/CultivatingHappiness

KEY PRINCIPLES

Chapter 1: Teaching and practicing mindful breath work, yoga movements, and meditations in schools can strengthen self- and community care. Their efficacy in schools is supported by substantial neuroscientific research, an understanding of anatomy and physiology, and a growing body of knowledge demonstrating their value in alleviating stress, enhancing executive functioning, and advancing happiness and well-being for children and adults.

Chapter 2: Metacognition, focus, learning, and healing will be accelerated when mindful breath work, meditation, and yoga are infused throughout the day.

Chapter 3: Teacher stress can be alleviated through mindfulness, yoga, and meditation.

Chapter 4: Yoga and meditation can bring a sense of peace and calmness to your classroom. A few strategic considerations will enhance the yoga-mindfulness-meditation experience for you and your students.

Part II: The Five Cs: consciousness, compassion, confidence, courage, and community are foundational to cultivating happiness and well-being.

Chapter 5: To build consciousness, compassion, confidence, courage, and community takes intentionality, perseverance, and collaboration.

Chapter 6: Conscious awareness is the basis for understanding self, others, and our world.

Chapter 7: An open heart can bring healing and compassion to ourselves, each other, our communities, and our world.

Chapter 8: Confidence is the key to sustainable success.

Chapter 9: True courage comes from grit that is integrated into our psyches in a healthy way. It is found in a willingness to embrace challenges and face our vulnerabilities and in accepting the vulnerabilities of others.

Chapter 10: We are a part of many communities: our school community, neighborhood, nation, and global community. Individual and collective self-care is essential for our well-being, sense of purpose, and sustainable future.

(Continued)

(Continued)

Chapter 11: Mindfulness supports development of the "inner faculty" of leadership. Leadership is more about emotional intelligence skills of self-awareness, self-regulation, motivation, empathy, and social skills, such as fostering trustworthiness, and less about positional authority. As leaders face growing complexity, mindfulness supports greater calm, stability, and responsive decision making.

Chapter 12: To effectively grow a mindfulness program, schools or districts must invest in mindful leadership.

ONLINE RESOURCES
Visit https://resources.corwin.com/CultivatingHappiness

Online Resource 0.1   Curriculum Integration Planner Blank Form

Acknowledgments

We are teachers. Although we may be researchers, consultants, executives, authors, and administrators, above all, we teach. In these days, after the darkness that we have endured, we are honored to be counted among those who teach.

As we teach, we listen, listening deeply to understand beyond words what is in our hearts and the hearts, minds, and actions of others. We are guided by listening deeply, and we are grateful for our inner journeys.

We know that trauma, grief, suffering, and pain are constant companions for many around the globe and that healing is needed. We are grateful for the healers among us.

We live in busy worlds, full of actions and reactions, with people clamoring for results, yet we take time to tune in to our breath, to slow down our breath, to be still. We are grateful for our breath, and for the peace and clarity that come from stillness and quiet.

We think, we talk, we persuade, and we proclaim, yet we know that not all is solved by thinking and talking. We learn from our hearts and from our bodies. We are grateful for heart–mind–body consciousness and practices.

We are each many people—mothers, fathers, daughters, sons, wives, husbands, sisters, brothers, neighbors, citizens, employers, employees, thinkers, artists, musicians, laborers, gardeners, scientists, volunteers, speakers, teachers, writers, and learners—and yet we are one: one humanity for this time on this planet. We are grateful that we are together, joined by invisible bonds of compassionate caring.

From Chris

For many years, I spent one to three weeks each summer in New Mexico, in meditation for peace and for this planet. I would step off the plane and into another realm, camping out in the desert mountains, rising early, walking the land, challenging myself, and being with friends and the teachings we practiced with a powerful energy—this was no small campout. Typically, 1,700 to 2,000 people gathered from around the world. My deepest gratitude extends to all the teachers at this camp, for their wisdom and expertise, and for the strong bonds of friendship that emerged as we camped, cooked, cleaned, moved, sang, danced, sweated, and laughed together. In this same breath, I acknowledge my coauthors, their greatness, their insights, their understanding of the need for this book, and their willingness to commit and contribute according to their passionate leanings, with incredible synergy. To my students, I am grateful for all I have learned from them, and as always, thanks to John Wilhelm, my husband of 28 years—for his deepening love, wisdom, patience, compassion, and friendship.

From Jeff

I would like to acknowledge the Sikh community of Herndon, Virginia, for showing me a lifestyle and philosophy of service that has transformed my life for the better, in particular the guidance and mentorship of Satwant Singh Khalsa on my journey. I would like to thank my students over the years who were willing to stretch themselves by trying yoga and mindfulness with me, and allowing me to perfect a student-based practice that works every time. Above all, the support of my wife and best friend Claudine has been instrumental not only to this project but also to a fulfilling life of joy and purpose.

From Krishna

I want to first acknowledge my appreciation for the Y.O.G.A. for Youth Board of Directors for supporting me in making available to this project the kundalini yoga tools that have served youngsters for many years from elementary to high schools around the country and indeed around the world through Y.O.G.A. for Youth. I am grateful to my kundalini yoga teacher, Yogi Bhajan, whose wisdom and dedication has given me the skills and motivation to keep going no matter what life may bring. I deeply appreciate the support of my team, especially Shama Davis, who patiently gave me the space to work on this book; Kiyoka Akimoto, who sorted through the Y.O.G.A. for Youth manual for the most appropriate kriyas and meditations to be included here; and to KRI, the Kundalini Research Institute, for allowing the use of these yoga kriyas and meditations. I appreciate Christine for inviting me to contribute to this important and much-needed work, and though at times it has been a challenge to meet the deadlines, it has been a pleasure to be a part of this group effort to make these highly effective tools of yoga and mindfulness available to our youngsters at a time when they need it more than ever.

From Michele

In simple terms, Zen master Thich Nhat Hanh explains, "When we are well, our wellness spills onto others. And when we are unwell, that too spills onto others." This becomes a gentle reminder to me of the daily importance of taking time to take care to be well so I can be at my best. Mindfulness, meditation, and yoga are wellness pieces that I have naturally woven into my life as easily as the air I breathe. I am grateful to Chris Mason for our journey and our shared love of "the practice"—I have learned much from you, so thank you. Much gratitude goes also to my family, husband Tom, and two girls, Julia and Abigail, who practice mindfulness and understand the importance of being fully present. You ground me most by your unconditional love and affection.

From Valerie

Gratitude is a declaration of the heart. It is a state of mind that gives our lives meaning and purpose. No matter how competent, a book cannot be written alone. Joining this community to write this book is an act of gratitude, faith, and trust.

This book could not be written without the wisdom and teachings of Zen master Thich Nhat Hanh and the Plum Village community, Parker J. Palmer and the Center for Courage & Renewal, Georgetown University's Institute for Transformational Leadership, and Transformative Educational Leadership (TEL).

I am grateful to my teachers and mentors, Zen master Thich Nhat Hanh, S. S. Mahan Rishi Singh Khalsa and S. S. Nirbhe Kaur Singh Khalsa of Khalsa Healing Arts, Parker J. Palmer, Pendle Hill—a Quaker retreat and study center—and Plum Village Dharma teachers Lyn Fine, John Bell, Kaira Jewel Lingo, Sister Peace, and Joanne Friday. And deep gratitude goes to the inspiration of the mesas, arroyos, and canyons of northern New Mexico that nurtured and supported me.

From All of Us

On a practical note, rounds of appreciation go to all those who have helped with the research and production of *Cultivating Happiness, Resilience, and Well-Being*, including Meghan Wenzel, Dana Asby, Alison Sumski, Lauren Kiesel, Jackson Sims, and Whitney Becker; staff from Maryland public schools: Carrie Viera, Karen Tulchinsky-Cohen, and Judy Weiskopf; Amrit Singh and Siri Neel Khalsa at the Kundalini Research Institute (we are delighted that this book is copublished with KRI!); and the staff at Corwin: Jessica Allan, Ariel Curry, Mia Rodriguez, Lucas Schleicher, Nancy Chung, Amy Schroller, and Melinda Masson. To our colleagues at Corwin, thank you for your interest and patience as we reviewed so many of the finer details of the yoga sets—this was an immense undertaking. We so value your understanding of the transformative potential that this book brings to educators at this pivotal moment in history.

A final note of thanks to you, our readers: May you be guided in love, and may you find teachings that lighten your load and give you grace, courage, and tools to reach and teach each student, for this year and for all time.

About the Authors

Christine Mason, PhD, an educational psychologist, is a nationally recognized expert in the areas of educational reform, visioning, trauma and mindfulness, teacher and principal mentoring, and special education. She is also a yoga, mindfulness, and meditation instructor who was trained in New Mexico and certified in 2001, with a Level II yoga certification in conscious communication in 2005. From 2005 to 2009, she was chair of the Education Committee for Miri Piri Academy, an international yoga boarding school in Amritsar, India. In 2009, she served for five months as the interim principal at Miri Piri. Since being certified to teach yoga, Christine has taught two to five yoga and meditation classes weekly in local community centers and for the Fairfax County Parks and Recreation program. She is a member of the International Kundalini Yoga Teachers Association and is also certified in Radiant Child Yoga.

Christine is the founder and executive director of the Center for Educational Improvement, an intentional collaborative of educators and researchers actively engaging to create a transformational system of education focused on collective healing and holistic learning. We identify, curate, develop, and scale up sustainable practices, such as Heart Centered Learning and student-led reform, that nurture family and community connectedness, well-being, equity, and justice.

Christine is also the chief advisor to the Childhood-Trauma Learning Collaborative, with Yale University's New England Mental Health Technology Transfer Center. Her time as chair of Miri Piri's education committee and her multiple visits to India, as well as her experiences networking for transformative educational change and researching exemplary educational programs, serve as the foundation for her beliefs and efforts to bring compassionate practices to all aspects of education.

Early in her career, Christine was a classroom teacher and a professor, teaching courses in curriculum, inclusion, social-emotional learning, educational assessment, and educational research. She has also served as associate executive director of research and professional development at the National Association of Elementary School Principals (NAESP);

director of professional development for the Student Support Center in Washington, DC; and the senior director for research and development with the Council for Exceptional Children. Christine is lead author of several books and articles, including *Mindfulness Practices: Cultivating Heart Centered Communities Where Children Focus and Flourish* (with Michele Rivers Murphy and Yvette Jackson, 2019), *Mindful School Communities: The 5 Cs of Nurturing Heart Centered Learning* (with Rivers Murphy and Jackson, 2020), *Visioning Onward: A Guide for All Schools* (with Paul Liabenow and Melissa Patschke, 2020), and *Compassionate School Practices: Fostering Children's Mental Health and Well-Being* (with Dana Asby, Meghan Wenzel, Katherine T. Volk, and Martha Staeheli, 2021). She is also the primary author and developer of an innovative process for developing compassionate school cultures: the School Compassionate Culture Analytical Tool for Educators (S-CCATE).

Jeffrey Donald, MS, has served as an educator and instructional leader for the past 16 years. He is currently the mindfulness coordinator for Montgomery County (Maryland) Public Schools. Jeffrey holds a master of science degree in educational administration and supervision from Hood College as well as being a certified 500-hour master yoga and meditation teacher and Reiki master. Jeffrey has held international wellness retreats in Mexico and Costa Rica, has been featured on national news programs such as *PBS NewsHour*, and has co-authored two school-based mindfulness books.

As an advocate for social justice and systemic change, Jeffrey believes that the fundamental application of yogic practices and philosophy is essential to lifelong success and satisfaction, and therefore everyone is deserving of free access and opportunity to these practices and lifestyle. To this end, he serves on several yogic-based boards of directors, serves regularly in restorative truth and reconciliation commissions, and, most importantly, consistently teaches the science of kundalini yoga, Vipassana Meditation, and mindfulness to populations who historically have not had free access or opportunity.

Krishna Kaur Khalsa—When California and several other states passed the "three strikes" law in 1994, being a Black woman in the United States, I knew that it meant that many men and women of color, especially Black men and women, would be corralled in prisons even for something as simple as stealing a candy bar if it was their third strike. I also knew that our prisons were up for sale around the same time and that lots of money could be made from owning a prison. The two situations—the three strikes law and the privatization of many of our maximum-security prisons—were a match made in heaven. These two possibilities sparked in me the determination to do everything possible to help prevent our youngsters from getting that third strike. It was then that Y.O.G.A. for Youth was born.

I was initially called to teach high school youth in a program called Upward Bound. These low-income youth had strong desires to go to college but were not being exposed to the kind of education from their low-income schools that could support that vision to become a reality. I taught kundalini yoga to a group of inner-city youth in collaboration with Upward Bound for four summers. These youngsters, boys and girls, Black and white, were being housed on a beautiful university campus learning higher math, college-level sciences, and other college prep courses. That hope-filled program ended unceremoniously when our government passed what was called the No Child Left Behind law, but what, in reality, left millions of young Black and Brown boys and girls behind. They were devastated. We were frustrated. I then received a call from the director of a juvenile detention center for incarcerated boys. That is when it became obvious that I needed to create a Y.O.G.A. for Youth teacher training program. What was easy for me was not easy for many who wanted to help make a difference in the lives of our youth.

Training yoga teachers in the most effective ways to engage teens and preteens in the art and science of yoga and meditation was critical to the success of our organization. The trainings grew from 9 to 40 hours, where they have been for over 20 years. The increase in hours for the trainings was imperative as the need for our teachers to understand more deeply the issues surrounding trauma, anxiety, and fear grew in intensity. These triggers to youth's behaviors are chronic in our inner-city schools and homes today. Our teachers must be able to identify and respond effectively to the questions we are given on the spot by these youngsters. At the same time, it is precisely the yoga and mindful self-help techniques that empower them and give them hope and a belief in themselves that change their lives going forward. It wasn't long before I began receiving calls from places I never expected. It was eye-opening to realize that young Black and Latino kids were not the only ones who needed what we were teaching. The Y.O.G.A. for Youth training has been taught around the world, throughout Europe, Brazil, Chile, Germany, the United Kingdom, Mexico, and China and extensively throughout the United States and North America. Our children are everywhere and need these teachings to help them navigate through a very complicated world. Right now, there is very little else that makes sense to them.

During the past year, during the COVID-19 pandemic, Y.O.G.A. for Youth has served elementary and middle schools via Zoom in Los Angeles, North Carolina, and Maryland. These conditions are far from the best environments for youngsters at home trying to focus while siblings, pets, and other distractions prevail. Yet, in our experience, students enthusiastically engage for short periods of time as the memory of how they felt after the yoga classes at school is something they want to experience again and again. They say it helps them sleep at night. That might sound like a small thing, but when you haven't slept for three days, it can totally distort the way even the simplest of challenges triggers irrational thinking and undesirable behavior. There is a learning curve for sure, yet when it comes to our children, Y.O.G.A. for Youth wants all children to affirm their own greatness. That is more important than anything to us.

Michele Rivers Murphy, EdD, the Center for Educational Improvement's associate director of Heart Centered Learning, is a seasoned consultant, presenter, and educational leader. A change agent for over two decades, she has helped transform some of the highest-needs neighborhoods and districts by improving student engagement, school culture, and academic success.

Michele's organizational research specifically addresses the challenges associated with childhood trauma and stress that compromise learning and teaching. Through building compassionate, supportive school environments, educators learn to find balance between social-emotional health and well-being and academic achievement.

Michele has served as an educational leader at all grade levels. As an administrator, she created an innovative disciplinary approach as an alternative to in-school and out-of-school suspension, completely eliminating in-school suspension and decreasing out-of-school suspension by 75%. In addition, she expanded high-needs programming to a mainstream setting, with a focus on real-life practice, service, and connection to community. She also created a 21st-century school community model, which she presented to the Massachusetts secretary of education.

Michele is co-author (with Christine Mason and Yvette Jackson) of *Mindful School Communities* (2020) and *Mindfulness Practices* (2019), as well as co-developer and co-author (with Mason et al.) of the School Compassionate Culture Analytical Tool for Educators (S-CCATE). Michele obtained a doctoral degree in educational leadership (K–12) from Northeastern University. She also holds multiple certifications in both regular and special education.

Valerie Brown, JD, MA, PCC, transformed her high-pressure, 20-year career as a lawyer lobbyist, representing educational institutions and nonprofits, to human-scale work with leaders and teams to foster trustworthy, compassionate, and authentic connections. She is an accredited leadership coach, international retreat leader, writer, and chief mindfulness officer of Lead Smart Coaching, LLC (www.leadsmartcoaching.com), specializing in application and integration of mindfulness and leadership, and is a co-director of Georgetown's Institute for Transformational Leadership.

She holds the following degrees: juris doctorate, master of arts, and bachelor of arts. Her books include *The Road That Teaches: Lessons in Transformation Through Travel* (QuakerBridge Media, 2012) and the highly acclaimed *The Mindful School Leader: Practices to Transform Your Leadership and School* (Corwin, 2014).

Valerie has received extensive training from the Center for Courage & Renewal and Parker J. Palmer; the Institute for Transformational Leadership at Georgetown University; the Center for Mindfulness in Medicine, Health Care, and Society; the Center for Compassion Focused Therapy; the Ojai Foundation; the C. G. Jung Foundation for Analytical Psychology (New York City); Chestnut Hill College (Pennsylvania) certificate in holistic spirituality; The Leadership Circle Profile™; and Transformative Educational Leadership. Valerie is an ordained Dharma teacher in the Plum Village tradition founded by Thich Nhat Hanh and a member of the Religious Society of Friends (Quakers). As a certified kundalini yoga teacher, she helps leaders discover the wisdom of the body. She leads an annual transformational pilgrimage to El Camino de Santiago, Spain, to celebrate the power of sacred places.

THE AUTHORS' YOGA AND MINDFULNESS CERTIFICATIONS

Krishna Kaur was one of the first kundalini yoga students in the United States, studying directly with the Master, Yogi Bhajan, since 1971. She is a master teacher, and teacher trainer of kundalini yoga since 1975, and continues to teach and train around the world.

Christine Mason, aka Ravi Kaur, was certified to teach kundalini yoga in 2001 (trainers: in New Mexico, with Yogi Bhajan, Hari Kaur Khalsa, Gurucharan Singh, and others). She was certified as a Radiant Child Yoga teacher in 2001 (with Shakta Kaur) and received a Level II certification in conscious communication in 2005 (trainer: Gurudass Kaur).

Jeffrey Donald, aka Dharma Atma, was certified to teach kundalini yoga in 2017 (trainers: Darshan Kaur and Siddhartha Shiv Khanna). He received an award as a "Kundalini Yoga Luminary" in 2019 for the work he is doing in schools in Maryland.

Michele Rivers Murphy has received mindfulness certificates in mindful communications (2020), mindful educator essentials (2018), and mindfulness fundamentals (2017). She also completed the *Mindful Leader* course with Michael Bunting.

Valerie Brown, aka Inder Kaur, completed certification in kundalini yoga in 2000 (trainers: S.S. Mahan Rishi Singh Khalsa and S.S. Nirbhe Singh Khalsa). A Dharma teacher in the Plum Village tradition, she studied mindfulness training with Thich Nhat Hanh.

PART ONE

Introduction

Cultivating happiness, resilience, and well-being is an ambitious task. However, as we look back over our lives, we often ask, what matters most? We may find that we were happiest when we were helping others or had feelings of success and confidence that we were on the right track. Yet, when there is much heaviness in the external world, it becomes more difficult to be in a space of happiness and joy.

In the first few chapters of this book, you will learn about the background research supporting the yoga-mindfulness-meditation procedures we recommend. You'll also get some hints about how to use the techniques we describe to improve your own self-care prior to introducing them to others.

It is interesting, as Dr. Subagh Singh Khalsa states in *Healing Ourselves, Healing the World* (2012), that the slower we breathe, the quieter our minds become. So, to gain a greater sense of peace, breathe more slowly. Then, build from there. As he states,

> once you've begun your practice, maintain awareness of breath, posture, and mantra while riding your bike, painting the house, or carrying out the trash. Take your practice to work. (p. 17)

He goes on to explain the power of stillness:

> In stillness, something new, something transcendent, can happen . . . If you wish to live a life of happiness and freedom from emotional upheaval, the best thing you can do is daily practice. Practice every day, come what may. If possible, practice with others, as the synergy of the group can be most helpful. (p. 18)

So, in these times of stress and anxiety, here is a two-part prescription for educators:

1. Establish your own practice.
2. Bring your practice into your classrooms and give everyone the advantages of a communal experience.

1

The first few chapters of *Cultivating Happiness, Resilience, and Well-Being* provide you with tools to step onto your path toward wellness, joy, and a heightened sense of peace and calmness. Somewhat amazingly, with this will come improved mental alertness and energy, greater focus, and an enhanced motivation and ability to learn, be effective, and help others. However, have patience. We all grow and learn in different ways, at different rates. You may find yourself excelling in some places and taking a few deep breaths as you slowly build your ability in other areas. Remember, more important than perfection is the practice. The effort you make will impact your brain, body, emotions, relationships with others, and inner and outer world.

CHAPTER ONE

Research Support for Mindful Breath Work, Meditation, and Yoga Movements

KEY PRINCIPLE

Teaching and practicing mindful breath work, meditation, and yoga movements in schools can strengthen self- and community care. Their efficacy in schools is supported by substantial neuroscientific research, an understanding of anatomy and physiology, and a growing body of knowledge demonstrating their value in alleviating stress, enhancing executive functioning, and advancing happiness and well-being for children and adults.

The practice of mindfulness and yoga allowed me to find the powerful tool that was always there, my breath. I can use my breath to calm my body's response to anxiety and stressful situations. By sharing this practice with my students, I invite them to build their own capacity with stress management in the school environment as well as in other spaces. Mindfulness is a superpower!

—Angela Norwood, Middle School Teacher, Silver Spring, MD

Just as Angela Norwood, a middle school teacher, helped her students build their own capacity, you too can share a few basic practices to make a world of difference for your students. Imagine schools, whether they are virtual, in physical classrooms, or in a hybrid model, where children and adults are joy-filled, connected, and inspired by each other. In these schools, there is a balance between being, activity, and "absorbing the good," as psychologist Rick Hanson (2016) describes it—active learning, productive exploration, and serious efforts to increase our individual and collective knowledge and wisdom. Imagine schools where high achievement is not only possible, but probable; where students laugh, eagerly await the next mystery that will unfold in their day, and smile just knowing that this day belongs to them; where teachers can calm classes with a "deep breath"; where staff and families celebrate and problem solve together, taking time, as needed, to reflect and plan together; and where we can be authentic—our true selves. In these schools, as Mihaly Csikszentmihalyi (2013) says, we are in the flow, at one with the life stream we are in.

> Practical tools are needed to help educators transform educational practices—transforming schools and classrooms from systems that no longer work to ones that shine a spotlight on student and family strengths; transforming systems and lives to further joy, delight, happiness, and a sense of purpose.

We realize, however, that practical tools are needed to help educators transform educational practices—transforming schools and classrooms from systems that no longer work to ones that shine a spotlight on student and family strengths; transforming systems and lives to further joy, delight, happiness, and a sense of purpose. One of the practical tools is mindfulness—being fully present, in the moment, without judgment (Kabat-Zinn, 1994). Mindfulness also involves a conscious awareness of our own physiology—our breath, our sense of anxiety or well-being—and the use of tools such as yoga or meditation to help restore a sense of calmness.

REACHING FOR STARS

Emma Seppälä (2016), a researcher who has taught mindfulness to veterans returning from war, has reached for the stars with her ideas about how to help people impacted by severe trauma. Rather than focusing on helping them get by with incremental improvements in their lives, she has sought to bring happiness to them. As she says,

> happiness—defined as a heightened state of positive emotion—has a profound effect on our professional and personal lives. It increases our emotional and social intelligence, boosts productivity and heightens our influence over peers and colleagues. These are the very ingredients that allow us to be successful without having to sacrifice our health and psychological well-being. (p. 8)

In *Cultivating Happiness, Resilience, and Well-Being*, we too are aiming for the stars—not through wishful thinking, but through applying time-honored practices that have resulted in significant improvements in physical health and fitness, emotional health, neuroplasticity (how the brain adapts), and everyday functioning.

SIX KEYS TO HAPPINESS

Here are the six keys to happiness that Seppälä (2016) highlights in her book:

1. Live in the moment.

2. Tap into your resilience—train your nervous system to bounce back from setbacks.

3. Manage your energy—instead of engaging in exhausting thoughts and emotions, learn to manage your stamina by remaining calm and centered.

4. Do nothing—make time for fun, idleness, and irrelevant interests. You'll be more creative.

5. Be good to yourself. Instead of playing only to your strengths and being self-critical, be compassionate with yourself and understand that your brain is built to learn new things.

6. Show compassion to others. (pp. 11–12)

We invite you to take a deep breath, look around, and settle in a comfortable chair, with an open mind and heart. Then, with another deep breath—a breath that gets deep into your abdomen—read on, believing that you will find guidance in the pages that follow.

We begin with a simple exercise that you can easily use with your students during a transition time when you have three or four minutes.

REACHING FOR THE STARS

In *Heart Beaming*, Mason and Banks (2014) provide an exercise for teachers to use as one of several "mind" breaks as they teach:

• Sit in a comfortable chair, straighten your spine, gently close your eyes, and focus on the area between your brows. Hands are on your heart.

• Take a few deep breaths, getting the breath deep into your abdomen.

(Continued)

(Continued)

- Now, in your mind's eye, imagine a night's sky, with stars shining brightly.
- As you gaze at the stars, one seems to twinkle just a bit more brightly.
- You look more closely and see a picture of someone you love.
- Reach out with your hand and pull that image into your heart. Breathe deeply as you feel love for that person.
- Repeat one or two more times.

To End: Inhale deeply and relax.

RESEARCH BASE SUPPORTING MINDFULNESS, YOGA, AND MEDITATION WITH CHILDREN

Our recommendations for use of mindful breath work, yoga movements, and meditation in schools are research based. They are supported by a growing body of research that frames the importance of body awareness and movement, meditation, and mindfulness practices in alleviating trauma, sharpening cognitive skills, and enhancing attention and focus. These practices may be particularly helpful for developing executive functioning and self-regulation in students who struggle with attention problems (Cohen et al., 2018; Rabiner, 2013). David Rabiner's (2013) preliminary study with 10 first-, second-, and third-grade students provides an example of this research base. He reports that after doing three weeks of yoga, for 30 minutes, twice per week, students with attention problems improved their time on task in the classroom.

School yoga programs are prevalent in the United States, and their popularity is continuing to grow. Butzer and colleagues in 2015 reported on 36 school-based yoga programs that were being implemented in over 940 schools across the United States. Seventy-five percent of those programs offered yoga that spanned from preschool or kindergarten through high school, and the remaining programs focused on one specific age group. The majority of these programs shared the common goal of teaching the four basic elements of yoga: (1) physical postures, (2) breathing exercises, (3) relaxation techniques, and (4) mindfulness and meditation. Beyond these basics, most of the programs included didactic elements, such as ethics, philosophy, or psychology lessons. Many programs allowed the inclusion of non-yoga components, such as games, songs, arts and crafts, journaling, team building, and community-enhancing exercises. They also included activities that teach skills, such as lessons on social-emotional learning, bullying prevention, peer-counseling techniques, community action and outreach, leadership training, and character development. In most cases, these non-yoga elements were woven into the yoga lessons.

Psychologists Ingunn Hagen and Usha Nayar (2014), in a review of the mental health potential of yoga, describe the value of yoga in "training of mind and body to bring emotional balance," suggesting that "children and young people need such tools to listen inward to their bodies, feelings, and ideas." They reference other yoga teachers, such as Shakta Khalsa, who urges teachers "to meet children where they are" so that children experience yoga as fun.

In their review, Hagen and Nayar (2014) portray seven possible ways in which yoga can benefit children and youth (see Figure 1.1).

So, what evidence exists supporting the value of yoga for children and youth? What evidence supports using yoga and meditation in schools? Figure 1.2 includes a brief synopsis of 17 research reports published between 2010 and 2020 on the impact of yoga, meditation, and mindfulness.

Figure 1.1 ◆ How Yoga Can Benefit Children and Youth

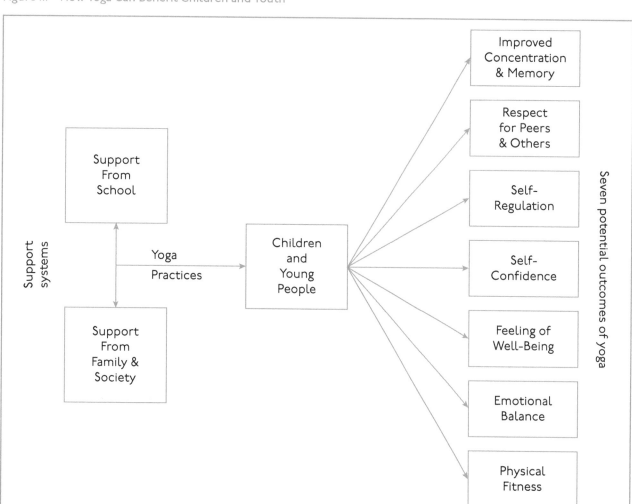

Source: Hagen & Nayar (2014).

Figure I.2 • Yoga Research

RESEARCH	PROGRAM	RESULTS
Overall Value		
Frank et al. (2017)	Transformative life skills yoga implemented with 159 students.	Students in the program showed fewer unexcused absences and detentions and increased school engagement. They also made improvements in the use of stress-coping strategies, emotion regulation, positive thinking, and cognitive restructuring.
Hagen & Nayar (2014)	Reviews the research-based results of yoga, summarizing common practices and benefits.	Yoga has a positive impact on focus and concentration, helping children with attention problems or special needs, as well as improving academic performance.
Sarkissian et al. (2018)	Measured effects of a 10-week Y.O.G.A. for Youth program with 30 youth in the inner city.	Yoga significantly reduced stress and increased resilience as measured on the Perceived Stress Scale, the Positive and Negative Affect Scale, and the Resilience Scale.
Impact on Behaviors and Mental Well-Being		
Matsuba et al. (2020)	Measured the impact of a culturally adapted version of MindUP (Hawn, 2011) for fifth- and sixth-grade children in post-conflict northern Uganda.	Over two years, children in the MindUP program demonstrated fewer depressive symptoms and more empathy for others. In a related study, the authors found significant decreases in anger, hostility, and rejection, as well as teacher reports of greater positive affect and empathic behaviors and improved academic grades for children using MindUP in comparison to children in a control group who did not use the program.
Viglas & Perlman (2018)	Studied self-regulation, prosocial behavior, and hyperactivity with 127 children in eight kindergarten classrooms with 20-minute lessons, delivered three times per week.	Children in the mindfulness group showed greater self-regulation, were more prosocial, and were less hyperactive compared to children in the control group.
Executive Functioning and Self-Regulation		
Mak et al. (2018)	Reported on the efficacy of mindfulness, including yoga, on attention and executive functioning in children and adolescents through a meta-analysis of randomized or quasi-randomized trials.	Thirteen studies met the criteria, and 5 of the 13 studies found statistically significant intervention effect sizes for at least one outcome measure of attention or executive functioning with medium to large effect sizes (0.3–32.03).
Rashedi & Schonert-Reichl (2019)	Studied self-regulation with the use of yoga and mindfulness with children.	The authors concluded that children were better able to connect their yoga experiences with their emotions when they were given the space to experiment with their yoga practices.
Zelazo et al. (2018)	Studied executive functioning in 218 preschool children in schools serving children from families with lower incomes in two U.S. cities. Looked at three conditions: mindfulness and reflective training, literacy training, and business as usual. The mindfulness and reflection group used calming activities and games followed by practice with reflection.	Executive functioning improved in all groups, with the mindfulness and reflection group significantly outperforming the "business as usual" group at follow-up (four weeks posttest). However, there was no difference between the mindfulness and reflection group and the literacy training group.

RESEARCH	PROGRAM	RESULTS
Impact of Mindfulness		
Janz et al. (2019)	Studied mindfulness-based interventions that were embedded in the curriculum in educational settings with Grades K–1. A total of 55 students participated in CalmSpace, and 36 students were on the waitlist control conditions.	CalmSpace students showed significant improvements on direct measures of executive functioning (obtained for instruments that were part of the National Institutes of Health tool kit) and on behavior (as reported by teachers on a Strengths and Difficulties Questionnaire).
Razza et al. (2020)	Examined the impact of mindfulness-based interventions, including mindful yoga, with preschoolers living in communities with high levels of trauma. Five classrooms (89 children) were randomly assigned to the intervention and control conditions.	There were significant increases in children's positive behavior and attention regulation during the times when they participated in the intervention.
Attention and Hyperactivity		
Chou & Huang (2017)	Implemented an eight-week yoga program with children with attention deficit disorders. Forty-nine participants were assigned to either a yoga exercise program or a control group.	Significant improvements in accuracy and reaction time were noted in the yoga exercise group on the Visual Pursuit Test and the Determination Test in comparison to results for children in the control group.
Cohen et al. (2018)	Examined the effects of a six-week yoga intervention on preschool children with attention deficit disorders, impulsivity, or hyperactivity.	Results for the ADHD Rating Scale-IV Preschool Version showed fewer distractibility errors of omission at the end of the six weeks for children who practiced yoga first. Yoga was associated with modest improvements on an objective measure of attention (KiTAP) and selective improvements on parent ratings.
Young Children		
Rashedi et al. (2019)	Investigated prekindergarten and kindergarten children's experience with yoga for 154 children in a randomized waitlist-controlled experiment with eight weeks of yoga. This qualitative-exploratory study relied on interviews and a grounded theory approach.	Children had positive emotions related to yoga and improved their knowledge of yoga and self-regulation. Children were often eager to share their feelings and knowledge about yoga.
Stapp & Wolff (2019)	Examined young children's experiences with yoga through observation and group interviews with 34 preschool children.	Children were overwhelmingly positive in describing their experiences with yoga and indicated that they would continue with yoga if given the opportunity.

(Continued)

(Continued)

RESEARCH	PROGRAM	RESULTS
Teachers		
Harris et al. (2016)	Evaluated the efficacy of the CALM program, consisting of gentle yoga and mindfulness implemented four days a week for 16 weeks.	The CALM program had a positive impact on teachers' stress and perceived stress with effect sizes of 0.52–0.80. Pre- and posttest measurements included self-report surveys of social-emotional functioning and well-being, blood pressure readings, and measures of cortisol levels.
Rashedi et al. (2020)	Explored the process of working with teachers over eight weeks to implement yoga in classroom settings.	Post-intervention teacher survey data showed that yoga was an effective pedagogical practice that enhanced children's positive behaviors.
In Comparison to Other Techniques		
Ross & Thomas (2010)	Compared research demonstrating that yoga is as effective as, or superior to, exercise.	Yoga has resulted in increased antioxidant status, reduced salivary cortisol (a physiological indicator of reduced stress), improved perception of stress, and enhanced moods.

ALLEVIATING STRESS

Yoga, combined with breath work, reduces stress, increases focus, and improves the capacity to learn. However, practice is required. Continuous benefits only come with practice.

What is the first sign that we are under stress? Many times, our bodies begin to react to the brain's decision that we are under threat before we even feel the emotion. These body messages act as an early warning system, and if we know how to pay attention, we can do many things to self-regulate.

Our bodies form what is called a body memory; everything goes on autopilot, and we are powerless to save ourselves from anger, rage, and bad decisions. For this reason, we utilize yoga to break that cycle. These exercises are carefully chosen to work areas of the body where we "hold" stress and anxiety, commonly throughout the length of the spine, to break "blocks" to our proper energetic flow.

In today's society, our bodies become so accustomed to daily anxiety and stress that eventually an imprint, or "body memory," is created that is extremely difficult and arduous to reprogram. When stress is inevitably presented, our bodies literally go on autopilot, acting out their learned method of survival. When this happens, we may shut down and close ourselves to compassion for self and others.

The physical movement and specific exercises used in Heart Centered Learning break the toxic cycle of the sympathetic nervous system's dominance over the body and return it to proper glandular equilibrium. Additionally, physical changes in adolescence can be quite difficult for students to navigate gracefully, which is another reason Heart Centered Learning employs physical exercise. Carefully chosen physical exercises and postures that enhance circulation and energy flow and unlock physical manifestations of stress are utilized to drastically lessen the negative effects of body memory and increase confidence. Posture and movement consist of all of the following:

- Physical exercises and postures that systematically work with the body, breath, and sound, enabling students to personally induce relaxation and mental tranquility.

- The cultivation of increased self-esteem and self-awareness through the achievement of specific stress-relieving exercises that help young people develop dynamic strategies for resolving internal/external conflicts before they escalate into inappropriate behaviors or reactions.

- Demonstrating alternative responses to psychological pressures and physical challenges with empowered self-control and peaceful creativity.

ANATOMY AND BODY ALIGNMENT

Yoga supports posture and fitness. It also helps reduce stress, increase alertness, and improve our mindful awareness of self (our body, mind, and emotions) and others. There are a few basic ground rules that will make your practice more successful:

- Practice breath work.

- Engage in warm-ups prior to settling into practicing a yoga set (a series of exercises specifically organized and sequenced to obtain the greatest benefits).

- As you practice, challenge yourself. However, yoga is not a competitive sport—the idea is to improve your own practice. So, push yourself, but not to the point of injury. Modify the set or adapt a posture as needed.

- Throughout a yoga practice, continue to work with your breath, so that you are moving with your breath.

- Consider following your yoga practice with relaxation and then meditation.

START WITH BREATH

Basic breath work and diaphragmatic breathing can improve your health and well-being. In deep breathing, the diaphragm, a jellyfish-shaped muscle above the abdomen, moves up and down. As it moves, the lungs expand and contract. Deep breathing stimulates lymph nodes to remove toxins through lymph drainage (see Figure 1.3).

As we naturally inhale, our chest expands, our lungs fill, and our diaphragm moves downward. When we exhale, our chest contracts, our lungs empty, and our diaphragm moves upward.

With deep, yogic breathing, we breathe deeply into the expanding abdomen on the inhale. As we slow our breath, we can more easily sustain the breath before exhaling deeply, pulling the navel point to the spine.

Figure 1.3 • Position of the Diaphragm When Inhaling and Exhaling

Source: istock.com/wetcake

SO, HOW DO WE PRACTICE DIAPHRAGMATIC BREATHING?

To begin, it is helpful to start by lying down on your back.

1. On your back, place one hand on your lower belly and one hand on your rib cage.

2. Begin by slowing down the breath and relaxing the mind, closing the mouth to use the nostrils to breathe.

3. Then inhale, sending the breath down into the lower belly, feeling the hand rise and fall with the inhale and exhale. Keep inhaling and fill the rib cage with air, feeling the sides of the ribs expand. Finally, feel the top of the lungs, and the upper chest, fill with air.

4. Exhale, reversing the flow. So, the upper chest empties, followed by the side ribs, then the lower belly.

5. If it's helpful, imagine filling a balloon. Inhale, sending breath down to the bottom of the balloon, filling the lower belly, then the side ribs and up to the top, a full balloon. Exhale, emptying the top of the balloon, deflating the chest, then contracting the side ribs and finally the lower belly, squeezing the last of the air out.

6. You can begin with a four-second inhale count and a four-second exhale count. As your lung capacity increases, you can gradually lengthen each count, keeping the length of the inhale the same as the exhale.

As the diaphragm moves up and down, it also stimulates the vagus nerve, a major nerve that runs from the lower internal organs to the brain and houses many of the parasympathetic nervous system's fibers. It supports health, growth, and restoration (see Figure 1.4).

Figure 1.4 • Parasympathetic Nervous System Including Vagus Nerve

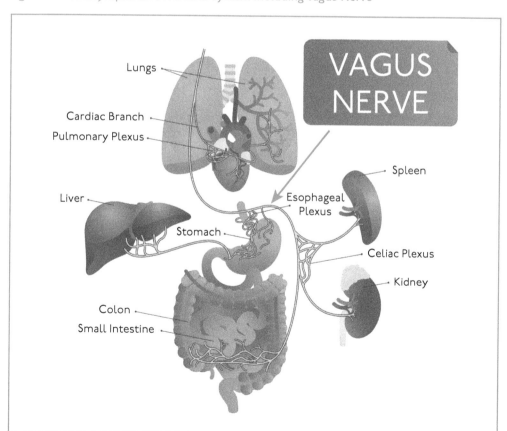

Source: istock.com/vectormine

The vagus nerve is a critical nerve connecting our hearts and emotions to our brains and our intellect. We devote the second chapter of our book *Mindful School Communities* (Mason, Rivers Murphy, & Jackson, 2020) to describing the importance of head–heart connections. In that chapter, we discuss the benefits of achieving a balance between the two, as well as some of the research supporting the efficacy of deliberately using breath, yoga, and meditation to alleviate the impact of trauma and increase vagal tone.

Stress can impair functioning of the vagus nerve; however, vagal tone, responsible for regulating the body during stress, can be strengthened. High vagal tone is related to coping and social engagement, including self-monitoring and control (Geisler et al., 2013; McCraty & Zayas, 2014; Reynard et al., 2011). According to Deepak Chopra, "breathing is one of the fastest and easiest ways to enhance vagal tone" (see Allen, 2017). Singing, humming, and chanting also stimulate the vagus nerve by activating the vocal cords and the muscles at the back of your throat.

IMPACT OF YOGA-MINDFULNESS-MEDITATION ON THE ENDOCRINE SYSTEM

The positive effects of yoga-mindfulness-meditation on the body are numerous. In addition to their positive impact on the vagus nerve, yoga and meditation can enhance and bring into balance the functioning of the endocrine system, which includes the glands that produce hormones that help control mood, growth and development, the way our organs work, metabolism, and reproduction.

Let's look at how stress impacts the body. When a person experiences stress, signals are sent to the hypothalamus, which is the brain's control center and is largely involved in maintaining homeostasis through creating or controlling hormones that regulate the body. The hypothalamus notifies the pituitary gland, which then notifies the adrenal gland to produce cortisol, the stress hormone. Cortisol travels through the blood to "wake up" a person's body parts (Bezdek & Telzer, 2017). While the body waking up to handle a stressor is important in the fight, flight, or freeze physiological response for, say, escaping from a bear, it can be detrimental when stress and anxiety occur too often (duration) or are too impactful (intensity), because cortisol has a strong negative impact on the prefrontal cortex.

The prefrontal cortex is the central processing unit of cognition and affect (Mason, Rivers Murphy, & Jackson, 2019). It is essential for cognitive thinking (learning) and strong executive functioning. A healthy functioning prefrontal cortex is needed to be fully attentive and engaged in learning. It regulates emotions, thoughts, and actions, and is the most sensitive brain region to the detrimental effects of stress. Even mild acute stress can have a strong negative impact on prefrontal cognitive abilities, and prolonged stress can cause architectural changes to the area with long-lasting negative impacts on function (Arnsten, 2009).

Prolonged periods of high levels of cortisol (released under acute stress) can have detrimental effects on memory. Prolonged periods of fear can also produce fatigue, depression, and hypertension and overstimulate the amygdala, leading to oversusceptibility to post-traumatic stress disorders, phobias, panic disorders, depression, and schizophrenia.

THE ENDOCRINE SYSTEM

Within the endocrine system are the hypothalamus, the pituitary gland, and the pineal gland, among others (see Figure I.5).

- The hypothalamus is the brain's control center for emotions and the regulation of physiological functions such as temperature, thirst, hunger, sleep, mood, sex drive, and the release of other hormones within the body such as adrenaline, noradrenaline, and cortisol.

- The pituitary gland is often called the master gland, as it creates hormones that control many of the other endocrine glands. Some of these glands include the thyroid and the adrenal glands, which regulate metabolism and the immune system. It is about the size of a pea and sits at the base of the brain.

- The pineal gland secretes melatonin, a hormone that helps balance the sleep–wake cycle. It is another pea-size gland and is located in the middle of the brain.

Figure I.5 • The Endocrine System

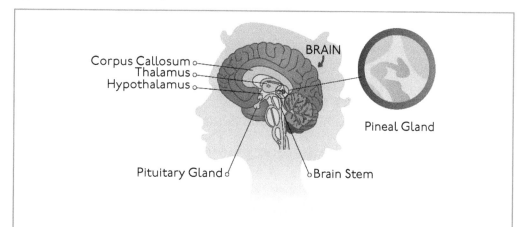

Source: istock.com/vectormine

The pineal gland, hypothalamus, and pituitary gland are all parts of the endocrine system and are housed in the brain.

Oxygen, Meditation, Relaxation, and Mood

Regular practice of yoga delivers more oxygen to all organs including the endocrine glands (Mahajan, 2014). Once more oxygen is delivered to the lungs, it is then carried to cells throughout the body. Over time, meditation impacts us on physical, cognitive, emotional, and psychological levels. It helps us relax and relieves stress, reduces pain, improves concentration, enhances self-monitoring and self-regulation, and contributes to positive moods, emotional stability, resilience, and overall psycho-emotional balance (Rubia, 2009).

Yoga: An Energizer

We often consider the value of yoga in aiding physical fitness and producing a sense of well-being and calmness. However, there are some yogic practices that result in amazing increases in energy. Several authors of this book, Krishna Kaur, Jeffrey Donald, Christine Mason, and Valerie Brown, have all been certified to teach kundalini yoga. With this type of yoga, there is a focus on impacting glandular activity, increasing oxygen, and moving energy from the lower body to the upper body (the heart, lungs, throat, and brain). The yoga kriyas (or sets) that we introduce in this book are designed to help move energy along this upward path—that is one of the key reasons we are taught to teach the kriyas in a specific sequence. With this approach, as we combine breath and meditation with movement, we often find that over the course of a yoga session we not only start to feel better physically, but we also seem both calmer and more alert. It is almost as if we are humming along on a superhighway that allows us to penetrate the layers of everyday garbage at a record speed.

> There is a focus on impacting glandular activity, increasing oxygen, and moving energy from the lower body to the upper body (the heart, lungs, throat, and brain).

YOGA POSTURES AND ALIGNMENT

The greatest benefits of yoga and meditation will be realized if one uses correct posture, which increases the energy flow throughout the body. Figure 1.6 shows the proper alignment of the spine for common yoga poses such as tree, easy pose, variations of warrior pose, and seated meditation. Note the body symmetry in many of the poses, and that the spine is in alignment with the head and neck. In most positions, the weight is evenly distributed side to side and front to back.

Yoga practices impact the mind, body, breath, emotions, self-regulation, and physical fitness. Butzer et al. (2015) suggest that "increases in mind-body awareness, such as becoming more aware of endogenous cues (e.g., satiety, need for physical activity), leads to positive behaviors and outcomes because of an increased awareness of the rewarding feelings and experiences that occur when one engages in positive behaviors" (p. 8). Figure 1.7 portrays the relationships they hypothesize between yoga and mental states, health, and performance. Note that the ultimate value reflects not only improvement in behaviors, health, and performance, but an ongoing state of enhanced self-care.

Figure 1.6 • Yoga Body Alignment

Source: istock.com/msdfuture

Figure 1.7 • Hypothesized Impact of Yoga

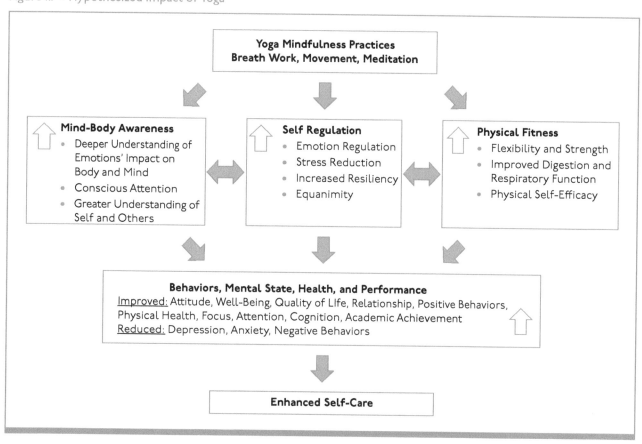

Source: Adapted from Butzer et al. (2015).

YOGA BRINGS HARMONY TO THE BODY

Krishna Kaur first developed her Y.O.G.A. for Youth program as a nonprofit serving predominantly marginalized at-risk youth, including many youth who had been incarcerated in detention or juvenile centers. In the *Y.O.G.A. for Youth Teacher's Manual and Curriculum Guide* (2006), Kaur explains that

> yoga brings harmony and balance to the body's circulatory, lymphatic, nervous, respiratory, muscular-skeletal, spinal, endocrine, digestive, immune, and genital-urinary systems, giving at-risk children and adolescents the emotional and physical stability to respond to life challenges with confidence and self-control. (p. 1)

She goes on to say that "meditation brings stillness, clarity, and focus to the mind, stimulating psychological and social well-being critical to living a successful life while mired in challenging circumstances" (p. 1).

Since 1993, her program has broadened its focus to address all youth. It has served over 16,000 youth in nine countries. As explained at yogaforyouth.org, the Y.O.G.A. for Youth curriculum

> addresses major components associated with diminishing fear, the root cause of anger, and increasing a belief in their own greatness. We are committed to alleviating violence, vandalism, substance abuse, obesity, eating disorders, teen pregnancy, sexual assault, bullying, suicide, poor grades and other self-defeating behaviors that are prevalent among today's youth.

HEART CENTERED MEDITATION

Meditative practices are an essential "upload" of positive affirmations that lead to greater well-being, confidence, and emotional clarity.

For thousands of years, people have used meditation to move beyond the mind's stress-inducing thoughts and emotional upsets into the peace and clarity of present-moment awareness. The variety of meditation techniques, traditions, and technologies is nearly infinite, but the essence of meditation is singular: the cultivation of mindful awareness and expanded conscious awareness.

Some begin meditating because of a doctor's recommendation, seeking the health benefits of lowered blood pressure, stress reduction, and restful sleep. Others come to meditation seeking relief from the fearful, angry, or painful thoughts that constantly flood their mind. Still others come to meditation to find greater self-understanding or to improve their ability to concentrate.

It is accurate to say that the purpose of meditation depends on the meditator. It is also true that anyone who meditates regularly receives profound benefits on all of these levels: physical, mental, and emotional.

Shakta Kaur Khalsa (2001a, 2001b) describes both the impact of meditating for different lengths of time and the stages of meditation in two books she has written on yoga.

> The purpose of meditation depends on the meditator. It is also true that anyone who meditates regularly receives profound benefits on all of these levels: physical, mental, and emotional.

STAGES OF MEDITATION

LENGTH OF MEDITATION	IMPACT
First 3–5 minutes	Circulation and blood stability are affected.
11 minutes	The pituitary gland and nerves begin to change.
31 minutes	Meditation begins to affect your whole mind, your energy field, and your body's internal elements.
62 minutes	Your subconscious mind and positive outer projection are integrated.
2.5 hours	Gains made are held throughout the day.

Source: Adapted from Khalsa (2001b).

According to Shakta Kaur Khalsa,

> when you first meditate, you will be drawn into the mind's drama; then you realize you have been drawn in. Little by little you begin to watch the mental activity. As would a benevolent observer you just watch your mind . . . With practice, your mind will eventually settle down and behave itself. By aligning the breath and inner focus, you experience one-pointed concentration . . . As you go deeper, you will open into a space of awareness that changes constantly, yet you are solid and sitting, aware of all your thoughts without being involved in them . . . The last [stage is where] you live as one who is grounded in what is often called higher awareness, or your higher nature. (Khalsa, 2001a, p. 203)

Yoga Can Be Taught as a "Secular" Practice

When we suggest implementing yoga in schools, we are recommending a "secular" version based on the art and science of yoga that is practiced by people all around the world. The yoga we are recommending is not tied to any specific religion, faith, or belief system. However, yoga will help students and staff find inner peace as it relieves stress, tension, anger, and fear. As Krishna Kaur (2006) says, "young people crave balance. It is essential to emphasize continuity and regularity in all your classroom dynamics so that each person feels safe, cared for and supported . . . Over time your students will learn to trust you" (p. 4).

In recent years, even as yoga has become more popular and more widely accepted, arguments against its practice continue. These arguments highlight reasons for schools and school districts to use care in how they discuss yoga-mindfulness-meditation. The authors of this book, based on our long-standing individual practices as well as our dedicated work with youth and adults, both recognize the value of yoga as a secular practice and caution against assuming that it is merely "a way to stay fit." We believe that when we consider yoga merely from a fitness perspective, we discount the neuroscientific results that are summarized in the first part of this chapter. Our individual practices, including yoga-mindfulness-meditation, affect not only our individual attitudes, beliefs, and sense of well-being, but also our relationships with others and the well-being of our community. The health of societies rests on the health and well-being of the children and adults within them.

ROOTS OF YOGA

In *Roots of Yoga* (2017), James Mallinson and Mark Singleton translate over 100 ancient yogic texts from Sanskrit with a focus on the practical, not theoretical or philosophical, origins. While they provide substantial evidence of the religious origins of yoga, they also recognize that yoga has evolved over the years, stating that "modern, global forms of yoga exist in a variety of complex and recursive relationships with 'traditional' yoga" (p. xxi). *The Allusionist*, a podcast about language from Helen Zaltzman, has a 2017 episode titled "Namaste" where Mallinson and Andrea Jain expand on concepts in Mallinson and Singleton's book and discuss the relationship between consumerism and the popularity of yoga. Mallinson and Jain also discuss the sense of peace and satisfaction that many yoga students feel from connecting to something beyond themselves.

Vicki Zakrzewski, the education director at the Greater Good Science Center, also describes the universal concern that humans have for "self-transcendence, in which the self is embedded in something greater than itself" (Benson et al., 2003, quoted in Zakrzewski, 2013).

She explains that while educators may consider the purpose of education as enhancing cognition, people are a bundle of thoughts, emotions, feelings, and beliefs, and they are impacted by culture, economics, and various other factors. She concludes that since we are teaching students who are more than their cognition, students will benefit from feeling a sense of meaning and purpose, being guided to have experiences of "awe," and participating in service learning and other activities that will give them opportunities to make worthwhile contributions in their local communities.

PRINCIPLES FOR SUCCESS

To help you build a practice and a program for success, we have developed six guiding principles. In this book, we will help you teach using these principles so that you will be in the "zone" or flow—successfully acknowledging student needs and not just teaching yoga, but teaching your students. That is, you will be paying attention to your students rather than just teaching the practices. You will find that each group is different, and that the practice schedule, the sequencing, and the pacing you use as you introduce postures, breath work, and meditations will vary as you teach with a conscious awareness of yourself and your students.

> **Principle 1: Practice.** One of the foremost ways to use yoga is as a "practice," which implies consistency. The benefits of yoga will be greater if it is practiced with regularity. In our years of experience, we have come to realize that its value rests with the practice. We will not be able to achieve heart–mind connections with sporadic efforts. The impact for schools will be greater if teachers and other staff practice yoga, meditation, and mindfulness, along with their students.
>
> As we have practiced yoga, we have come to have a greater understanding of the connection between our brains, our emotions, and our bodies. When we are stressed out, a few extra-long, deep breaths can bring us back to feeling centered. It was only through yoga that we realized that we can be open to life, to the flow of energy.
>
> **Principle 2: Breathe openly.** Breathe, not only to open pathways in the body, but also to open ourselves to understanding the present— to, in a sense, be more available to ourselves.
>
> **Principle 3: Yoga is not about competition.** A third basic principle is that there is no need to compete, only the need to self-assess, not in comparison to others, but in comparison to our own

ability, or skills. Some people are naturally more flexible, able to balance, or capable of deeper breaths. So rather than striving to be the best yogi, we strive to make some gains for ourselves.

Principle 4: Challenge, but do not injure, yourself. With yoga, we strive to stretch a little further, do a little more, and perfect our posture as best we can. However, we do not push ourselves to the point of injury. In Chapter 2, we discuss metacognition—our self-knowledge, which can help guide our practice.

Principle 5: It helps to have a teacher. Teachers are integral to yoga. They can help provide guidance, instruction, and feedback, ensuring that you have opportunities to learn more. With their guidance, you may come to understand more about your body and yourself. You might find these things out on your own, with apps or yoga videos, but being with a community—a teacher and other students—can provide you with a richer, more meaningful, and more impactful yoga experience.

Principle 6: Have a little fun. When learning or practicing yoga, it is important to focus. However, yoga also involves a wide array of emotions. It is wonderful when you take time to laugh, smile, and experience the sense of well-being that may arise. At times, you may even marvel at the fun you can have practicing a bear or elephant walk, hissing like a snake, or trying to balance in tree pose. Make sure that you are sharing the fun and excitement, and perhaps even your passion for yoga, with your students.

MINDFUL REFLECTION

1. What are you hoping to get out of implementing a yoga-mindfulness-meditation practice? For yourself? For your students? For your school?

2. What are you most excited about?

3. How will you use these guiding principles to support you in your journey?

ONLINE RESOURCES

Visit https://resources.corwin.com/CultivatingHappiness

Online Resource 1.1 Mindful Reflection

CHAPTER TWO

A Few Basics

KEY PRINCIPLE

Metacognition, focus, learning, and healing will be accelerated when mindful breath work, meditation, and yoga are infused throughout the day.

In Chapter 1, we reviewed a research base for yoga-mindfulness-meditation. In this chapter, we focus on mindfulness practices, metacognition, yoga games, and restorative practices, providing several examples of how the practices we recommend can be infused throughout the school day.

Meditation can improve cognitive function and focused attention, as can yoga, breath work, and mindfulness. However, meditation is often more effective if yoga movements and breath work precede it to prepare your body and mind to settle down into a meditation. Reflection is a critical component as well, and our metacognition, or thinking about our thinking, will be enhanced with yoga, mindfulness, and meditation. After all, the core of mindfulness is reflection, tuning in fully with all of our senses to the *here and now*, totally in the moment, with a heightened, conscious awareness of self, others, and our environment. With yoga games, in particular, we add a layer of fun to all that yoga-mindfulness-meditation brings to your students. And, with restorative practices, we add mindful discipline, furthering resilience and modeling conscious compassionate community building.

STRENGTHENING OUR OWN METACOGNITION THROUGH MINDFULNESS PRACTICE

Metacognition begins with us, as teachers. Our metacognition will be improved by building self-agency through becoming more "aware of our awareness." The metacognition of teachers involves our ability to monitor ourselves and ask, "How am I doing?" or "How did I do?" (Dawson & Guare, 2010; Mason et al., 2019). Mindfulness improves cognitive function and focused attention (Chambers et al., 2008) as well as metacognitive insight (Flook et al., 2010), leading to greater self-regulation and more positive academic outcomes for students. There is also a direct relationship between learning and behaving that stems from our ability to exercise self-control and reduce impulsivity, which is achieved through greater self-reflection, increasing our conscious awareness (Mason et al., 2019; Sodian & Frith, 2008).

TEACHERS CAN HELP STUDENTS MAKE THE CONNECTION TO SELF-AWARENESS

The ability to reflect becomes particularly important as teachers learn to navigate and respond to their own and also their students' increased trauma and stress during a time of worldwide pandemic. It is critical for teachers to be able to recognize their own triggers and antecedents to stress if they are to help students identify theirs. Modeling these strategies, instructing with heart, building relationships, thinking aloud, sharing ideas, practicing visible thinking, and cultivating more compassion toward peers, others, and the self all help to enhance our ability to reflect on how we are instructing, learning, and behaving.

The ability to self-reflect and ask "How am I doing?" helps us as teachers and as students recognize and understand through self-reflection, assessment, and correction *how* we can plan to best get there.

CONNECTING METACOGNITION TO HEART CENTERED FIVE CS AS MEDIATING FACTORS

Heart Centered Learning's Five Cs—consciousness, compassion, confidence, courage, and community (see next section) (Mason et al., 2019, 2020)—are naturally embedded in metacognition improvement and can easily help increase one's ability in this area. Teaching consciousness and how to develop a higher awareness of self develops an ability for "knowing something about how you, as an individual, think and learn" (Mason, Rivers Murphy, & Jackson, 2020, p. 53). The ability to self-reflect and ask "How am I doing?" helps us as teachers and as students recognize and understand through self-reflection, assessment, and correction *how* we can plan to best get there. This process also instills the "power of yet" (TEDx Talks, 2014) that helps inspire confidence that we all have the ability to control the plan to *get there*. The end result is the same for teachers and students to drive and empower their own learning, while building self-agency (courage) that fosters a growth mindset (TEDx Talks, 2014). As teachers, we have the remarkable opportunity to instruct through example and modeling; provide the support needed; share our own experiences, whether struggles or successes; and show our authentic selves to students.

Heart Centered Connections

Figure 2.1 • The Five Cs of Heart Centered Learning®

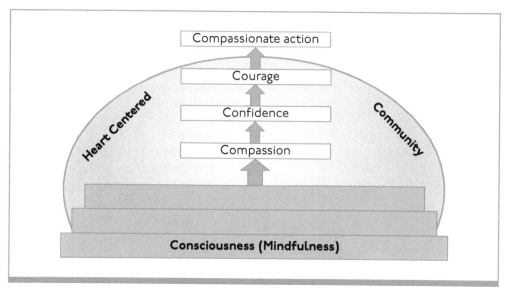

Cultivating Happiness, Resilience, and Well-Being is organized in part around the five elements of Heart Centered Learning. These are described in some detail in *Mindfulness Practices: Cultivating Heart Centered Communities Where Students Focus and Flourish* (Mason et al., 2019) and *Mindful School Communities: The Five Cs of Nurturing Heart Centered Learning* (Mason, Rivers Murphy, & Jackson, 2020). These texts provide the neuroscientific basis for our approach; a discussion of the importance of the heart center and vagal nerve; practical ideas for implementation; an introduction to mindfulness, yoga, and breathing; and practical academic exercises that can be used to support each of the Five Cs, including how exercises can be adapted for various grade levels. Each book also provides insights into communitywide implementation and leadership to support these factors (see Figure 2.1).

In addition, *Compassionate School Practices: Fostering Children's Mental Health and Well-Being* (Mason et al., 2021) provides another practical companion that supports practices recommended in *Cultivating Happiness, Resilience, and Well-Being* through further description of the impact of trauma and how schools and communities can better support youth who are most at risk. In that text, we provide another frame that is useful in considering where and when to implement mindfulness, yoga, and meditation. The Compassionate School Mental Health Model displays four major components that can help alleviate trauma, reduce the probability of serious mental health challenges, and improve the mental health and well-being of students (see Figure 2.2, a March 2021 updated version

You will see results sooner if yoga-mindfulness-meditation is interspersed throughout the school day.

of the model being used by the New England Mental Health Technology Transfer Center).

In *Cultivating Happiness, Resilience, and Well-Being*, we will show you how the practices we recommend can support student resilience and build positive mental health and well-being for students, teachers, and other school staff.

Figure 2.2 • The Compassionate School Mental Health Model

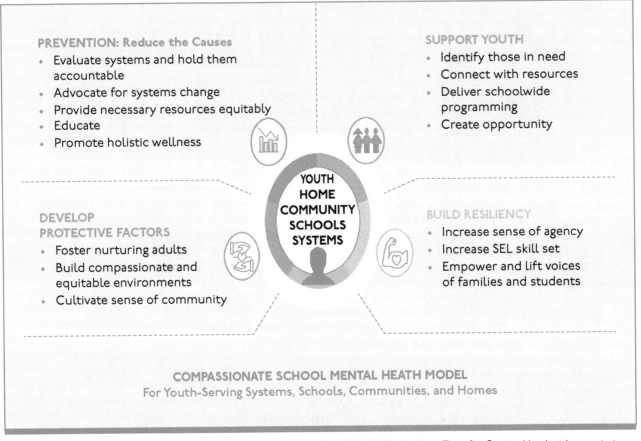

Source: Mason, Asby, et al. (2021) as adapted by the New England Mental Health Technology Transfer Center. Used with permission.

INTEGRATING PRACTICES INTO YOUR CLASSROOM

The words of Brian Aikens, an elementary resource room teacher in Pennsylvania, say it all:

This is not another thing for teachers; this is *the* thing! However, like anything, it takes time to integrate this into our classrooms or practices. It is important to me to share my personal stories with students about my practice, my struggles, and my success. It took me quite a while to fully integrate these practices into my classroom and make them a part of our classroom fabric. It started with my practice, sharing personal stories, using particular language in the classroom, using the bell of mindfulness, and integrating these practices into our academic learning. I start each school year with lessons on the brain and the impact our breathing has on our emotions. From there, we share some simple practices such as the bell of mindfulness, mindfulness jar, and bunny breaths. Throughout the year, we continue to add different strategies so everyone can find their three favorites that can support them.

Inviting the Bell and Mindful Breathing Script

When you are ready to introduce the bell to your classroom, it is important to introduce the practice of listening to the bell and teach students to invite the bell.

- Begin by sitting in a circle if possible.

- Hold up a bell and ask students if they know what the sound of the bell is for.

- Explain, "When we hear the bell, we can stop what we are doing and just breathe. We have a chance to rest, to take a break, to enjoy ourselves. We practice this by being aware of our in- and out-breath."

- Ring the bell.

- Now, invite students to count how many breaths they take during one sound of the bell. Tell them you will invite the bell, and when they can no longer hear its tone, they can raise their hand. Then they can share how many in- and out-breaths they took during the sound of the bell.

The "Three Mindful Breaths"

- Remain seated.

- Allow your breath to flow naturally in and out through your nose, trying not to control it.

- Say, "You can close your eyes for this, or if you don't feel comfortable doing that, kindly bring your gaze to focus on the ground. Bring your attention to your breath."

- Continue: "You can focus on the breath at your nostrils, noticing how the air feels cool coming in and it may be slightly warmer as it leaves your body. Or you can focus on your breath at your belly, feeling it rise and fall as the air enters and leaves your body. Stay focused, as best you can, on your breath. Just notice the air as it enters and leaves, enters and leaves your body. If your mind wanders, that's okay."

- "Simply bring your attention back to the in-breath and out-breath, breathing in and breathing out. Your mind will naturally wander off and get lost in its thoughts. That's okay—it's just what our minds do. Your job is to gently bring

(Continued)

(Continued)

> your attention back to your breath every time you notice your mind has wandered. Tell yourself 'good job' for noticing, and then continue to watch your breath."

- "Now I am going to ask you to take three normal breaths, and try and focus just on the breath for all three."

- Students open their eyes for discussion. Ask them open-ended questions, such as "What did you notice while you were doing this activity?" or "How does this sort of breathing compare with the way you normally breathe?"

Talk with the students about how a bell will ring randomly throughout the day. One bell can be found through a Google Chrome Extension at https://bit.ly/2sN0luW (see also Fitzgerald et al., 2021).

When they hear this bell or the bell on your desk, remind students that they can practice the "three mindful breaths." When they are done taking the three breaths, students raise their hands to respect others and so everyone knows they can go back to work. This brief moment of pause can help the brain relax and refocus. This practice, adapted from www.insightminds.com with permission, can be beneficial in the classroom to help students pay attention and regulate their attention as a mindful brain break.

Mindfulness Jar

A mindfulness jar is a clear glass jar filled with water, dish soap, and glitter.

It is a powerful visual metaphor for one's emotions. The glitter represents one's thoughts, feelings, and behaviors. When students are upset or angry, they can shake the jar and watch the glitter swirl around before gradually settling. The glitter's slow descent acts as a visual model that can unconsciously help slow their heart rate and breathing. These jars can also be used as visual timers for short mindful breathing exercises infused throughout the school day (Scott, n.d.).

Bunny Breaths

This breathing technique can help students feel calm, empowered, and self-regulated. Instruct students to breathe three quick sniffs in the nose and one long exhale out the nose. Invite them to have fun and pretend to be bunnies, sniffing the air for other bunnies, carrots to eat, or safety.

This breath can be cleansing or used when students are upset and can't find their breath. It helps them connect to their exhale so they breathe instead of spin out (B. Aikens, personal communication, March 2020; Your Therapy Source, 2020).

THREADING YOGA-MINDFULNESS-MEDITATION THROUGHOUT THE DAY

Here is what an academic school day might look like if yoga or "brain breaks" were inserted throughout the day.

- Begin with five to seven minutes of yoga. For younger students, this might include animal movements or movements to music. For older students, it could involve some engagement in practicing yoga postures of the students' own preferences. This could be with apps, virtual instruction, or in-class instruction.

- If a *morning academic lesson* is related to a particular topic, perhaps courage, yoga postures threaded throughout the morning might be related to courage as well. Consider lion's breath or warrior poses (see also Chapter 9 on courage).

- Students at some point during that *morning time* might work on their own self-affirmations, or "I can" or "I am" statements: *I can learn, I am smart, I am successful*, and so on.

- *Transition times* in classrooms or during virtual learning could include appropriate music. Often calm music is helpful. However, more upbeat music, such as music for marches, can also be used to help facilitate alertness and action.

- *For older students, transitions* might include a mindful minute—a short, simple meditation at the start of a new class. This allows students to "arrive" and quiet their nervous systems, readying them for learning. A *guided meditation* might also be used to help introduce or reinforce particular topics, such as a meditation on anticipating something new, getting in touch with nature, or letting go—perhaps with instructions to conduct a body scan (see page 242).

- *For younger students, transitions* might incorporate not only music, but animal movements and perhaps even opportunities to roar like a lion or buzz like a bee (see page 82).

- Meditations could be adapted for *history or social studies lessons*, for example, with a meditation for the well-being of medical staff or community workers. For older students, meditations could include those for the well-being of people in various countries or regions of the world.

- Rhythmic movements, games, and even singing could be incorporated into *celebrations*.

- For *reading and literature*, as the character traits of individuals are studied, appropriate yogic movements or meditations could also be used—that is, meditations for compassion, courage, or community.

Another example of implementation throughout the school day comes from Jessica Bazinet, a semifinalist for the 2022 Massachusetts Teacher of the Year. We encourage younger children to do their best. As shown in these pictures, their postures will sometimes approximate the postures we teach adults.

YOGA FOR SECOND GRADERS

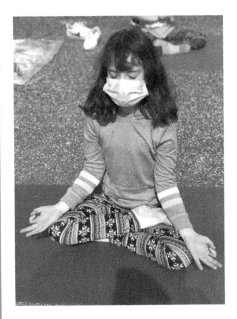

Source: Jessica Bazinet; used with parental permission.

Here is an example of a reflection writing exercise that Jess Bazinet uses with her classes.

> Challenges are things that are not as easy for us. Write a letter to your teacher to share something that is a challenge for you. Think about why it is a challenge and how you can get better!
>
> Dear mrs. bazinet. I want to get better at meditating its hard to sit still and think nothing I want to get better at meditating so I can get great at using the nature powers that mother nature and santa claws gave me and some people got so good at meditating that they can float a bit and that is why I want to get better at meditating.

You can hear Jess and others who work with the Center for Educational Improvement discuss the power of yoga, mindfulness, and Heart Centered Learning, including its impact on cognition and executive functioning, in videos archived at CEI's YouTube channel.

 Center for Educational Improvement. (2021b, April 16). *Executive functioning, mindfulness, and heart centered leadership* [Webinar]. YouTube. https://www.youtube.com/watch?v=puVHFCNbb_c; *also available on the Corwin Resources page.*

Hybrid and Virtual Instruction

With the COVID-19 pandemic, all of the authors have been teaching yoga, mindfulness, and meditation virtually. The techniques in this book are designed to be taught virtually or in person. In Chapter 4, where we discuss organizing space and materials for yoga, meditation, and mindfulness instruction, we give specific strategies to guide virtual instruction, including tips for lighting, cameras, and sound. We have found there are numerous advantages to "live" virtual classes, rather than simply calling up an archived recording. Primary advantages include:

- The sense of connection that is furthered by the introductory and closing discussion.

- The ability of the instructor to watch students when their cameras are turned on. As we watch students, we are able to provide additional guidance to help them with specific yoga postures and breaths.

- The sense of connection that is furthered by a teacher's laugh or smile, comments that are aligned to the specific needs of individual groups of students, and the powerful feedback students get by seeing their peers also doing a specific set or exercise.

 Also available, however, are many wonderful apps and websites that can be used to reinforce what you, and/or a yoga teacher, are teaching to your students (see Chapter 3, Figure 3.4).

Mindfulness Games

The introductory games described in this section, developed by Y.O.G.A. for Youth (Kaur, 2006), are excellent tools for introducing mindfulness techniques. They are specially designed to encourage a sense of safety, fun, and excitement with respect to practicing mindfulness. We recommend that you incorporate these games into your classes in whatever context is appropriate. They are time-tested, and they will work.

These games offer basic strategies for introducing mindfulness concepts and practices to students of all ages. They are particularly helpful when working with younger children with lots of energy and short attention spans. These games prepare all youth to learn mindfulness within their own personal comfort zone.

For many students, the biggest initial challenge is feeling safe and supported with their eyes closed. The act of closing one's eyes in a group can be threatening. However, in the context of these games, it becomes fun and challenging. If needed, an accommodation for all games for students who may have experienced trauma is to keep their eyes open, perhaps gazing down.

PASSING THE POSITIVE

Encourages self-esteem, self-expression, self-control, and positive affirmation.

Age appropriate: all ages

How to Play the Game

1. Have the group sit in a circle with their hands in front of their hearts, palms pressed together.

2. To start the game, point your joined hands toward any one person in the circle and say the number 1.

Note: The three games in this section are used with the permission of Y.O.G.A. for Youth (Kaur, 2006).

3. The person you pointed to now takes their joined hands and points randomly to any other person in the circle and says the number 2.

4. This next person then randomly passes the number 3 to a new student, and the following person passes the number 4.

5. Now comes the big challenge. At this point in the game, instead of passing the number 5, the person ready to pass the next number has to go back and say number 1, starting the cycle all over again.

6. In this way, the game continues with participants passing the numbers around the circle: 1-2-3-4, 1-2-3-4, 1-2-3-4, going faster and faster until someone makes a mistake and the rhythm is broken.

7. When the group is comfortable with the game, you can begin to incorporate positive messages to be passed (e.g., you-are-so-great).

Comments

This game is an excellent way of getting students to begin relating to rhythm and repetition as part of mindfulness practice. It is also a perfect vehicle for playfully introducing positive messages (mantras). One possible variation involves having the person who breaks the rhythm in one round stand up and leave the circle. This person is now given the official title of "Distractor," which means that they are allowed to gently walk around the players in the circle and, without touching anybody, try to distract people by whispering irrelevant numbers or words into players' ears. Do not allow the Distractor to get out of hand, yet understand that when done properly, this adds an exciting dynamic to the game and really teaches participants to learn focus and concentration skills.

The Spaceship Ride

Teaches visualization, deep relaxation, stress management, sustained focus, and creativity.

Age appropriate: all ages

How to Play the Game

1. Have the group sit in the perfect position or lie down comfortably with their eyes closed.

2. Tell the group something such as the following: "Let your bodies become very quiet, very still. Imagine that inside of your head is a big, beautiful spaceship. Notice its shape, its size, and what color it is. See the door of the spaceship open, and climb inside. Sit down at the controls because this is your spaceship and you are the astronaut. Prepare for take-off and turn the key: 3-2-1 . . . take-off! Up, up, up, out

(Continued)

(Continued)

of your head, higher than the breeze, higher than the birds, up through the clouds into the blue blue sky. When you are ready, go into space. Visit the moon. Visit the sun. Go up, up, up wherever you want to go. Feel yourself floating in space, light as a feather. Look out of the window. What do you see? When you are ready, let yourself come down, down, down, into the blue sky, through the clouds, down past the birds and the breeze, down past the trees until you come slowly and gently back into your head. Make a gentle and safe landing. Let the door of your spaceship open, and look all around you. Notice how good it feels to be back on earth. What did you see in space?"

Comments

Once again, give the students plenty of time to share their experience. Modify the visualization to include other types of journeys (e.g., magic carpet rides, riding into the ocean on the back of a friendly whale, flying to their favorite place in the whole world). Remind them that they can take themselves anywhere with this practice.

Superheroes

Introduces movement from one exercise posture to another, builds self-esteem, and explores the meaning of being heroic, powerful, and graceful.

Age appropriate: ages 3 to 12

How to Play the Game

1. Open the class with a discussion about the students' favorite superheroes. Engage their imaginations with questions about superhero qualities they admire and identify with. Let their excitement build.

2. Remind the group that "we are all superheroes" and that each of us has very special qualities and gifts to share with others.

3. Share with them your special "superhero" development exercises (i.e., exercise postures, breathing exercises) by playing the "Superhero Says" game, asking them to try out different yoga postures. You can rotate the superhero according to students' favorites (e.g., "Spiderman says do downward facing dog," "Wonder Woman says do child's pose").

Comments

This game works especially well with younger students. Remind them that practicing these exercises will help them to welcome their power. Children intuitively relate to the promises and responsibilities of being a superhero.

RESTORATIVE PRACTICES: BUILDING RESILIENCE, BUILDING COMMUNITY

As individual mindfulness and consciousness is enhanced, these tools can be used in many ways to further student skills and understanding. Along with its mindfulness program, Montgomery County Public Schools is implementing a restorative justice program. These programs work well together as both focus on conscious awareness of the self and others, and both are concerned not only about self-care, but about collective community care as well. Restorative justice, with a focus on active listening, peer meditation, and problem solving, rather than traditional punitive discipline, is part of the process that Jeffrey Donald and his colleagues use with opportunities for "community circles" and dialogues. These approaches help students to overcome feelings of inadequacy and trauma, and to feel heard and accepted.

The focus has to be on teachers themselves. It's the staff's mindset that really guides punishment. It really comes down to how the teacher chooses to respond. The punitive response is "What did you do?" The restorative response is "What's going on? How can I help?" However, the school administration makes a difference. Restorative justice works best in schools with full, enthusiastic administrative support. What is needed is a schoolwide approach, and different schools will vary in the extent of implementation of restorative practices.

IMPLEMENTATION IN ELEMENTARY SCHOOLS

There are many ways to implement restorative practices in the classroom. These tips are adapted from an interview with Sheila Wilson, a fifth-grade teacher and adjunct professor in Virginia (Ferlazzo, 2020).

- In daily morning meetings, teachers can build relationships with students, get a sense of their social-emotional mindset, and set the tone and focus for the instructional day.

- With goal setting, students set their own goals and determine realistic and actionable steps to achieve their goals. With individual goal conferences, teachers can monitor progress as students learn to self-check and refocus as needed.

(Continued)

(Continued)

- When an unacceptable behavior occurs, the teacher asks the offended students to share how the offense made them feel. This helps the offenders understand how their behavior impacts others. Mindfulness is a great tool for this inner reflection.

- There is also great restorative benefit when students reflect on their unacceptable behaviors in writing as they address questions such as "What choice did I make? How did my choice impact others? Is there a better way that I could have addressed this situation? If I had the opportunity for a redo, would I make the same choice? Why or why not?" Once again, mindfulness can help students understand more about themselves and others.

RESTORATIVE PRACTICES BUILD THRIVING COMMUNITIES

Insights from Jack Bonarrigo (personal communication, April 2020), an eighth-grade student at Dag Hammarskjöld Middle School in Wallingford, Connecticut.
(Note: This is a first draft.)

Schools everywhere have had students feeling unhappy and bottled up. They feel as if they can't express their feelings or thoughts about what is currently happening. A way to cope with these emotions is a technique called restorative practice, get a large group of people together and have them talk about things that are going on in their lives or any subject. Restorative practice doesn't only limit to a talking circle but the idea of someone getting their thoughts out of their head and into someone else's mind. The result of this technique is better thriving communities, less individualized focus and more teamwork.

The same technique can be applied in the court as offering a different path for convicts. This outcome is better for the person because they can talk about what they did wrong and try to fix it. It forces them to look back at what they've done and help them. However long it takes this will always be a better outcome than traditional prison sentences depending on the crime. Think about it, if there was a person that committed a crime would it be better to lock that person up or have them do therapy sessions with people with similar problems and find a resolve. If making a truly better society then removing people that have problems is not the answer, instead introduce this technique and bring those people back and add one more good person as opposed to take away a bad.

Centre for Justice and Reconciliation. (n.d.). Lesson I: What is restorative justice? In *Tutorial: Intro to Restorative Justice.* https://restorativejustice.org/restorative-justice/about-restorative-justice/tutorial-intro-to-restorative-justice/lesson-I-what-is-restorative-justice/

Wachtel, T. (n.d.). *Defining restorative.* IIRP Graduate School. https://www.iirp.edu/restorative-practices/defining-restorative/

Figure 2.3 provides additional information on implementation across all grade levels.

Figure 2.3 • Restorative Practices

SOURCE	TITLE	SUMMARY
AASA—The School Superintendents Association & Children's Defense Fund (2014)	Restorative Justice Overview	This report explores the benefits of restorative practices and provides examples, considerations, and resources for implementing them.
The Conflict Center (2018)	Restorative Practices Program	This page explains restorative practices and their benefits. They allow people to take responsibility for their actions while remaining connected to their community, and using these practices instead of traditional disciplinary methods can decrease student delinquency and improve academic outcomes and school climate.
Denver School-Based Restorative Practices Partnership (2017)	School-wide Restorative Practices: Step by Step	This guide provides implementation support and guidance for schools trying to reform their discipline system and adopt restorative practices. It answers a critical question: Where do we start?
June Naureckas (2019), Center for Educational Improvement	Restorative Justice in Schools: Benefits and Complications	This article explores the tenets, objectives, and outcomes of restorative justice programs, as well as discussing potential improvements.
Kaela Farrise (2021), Center for Educational Improvement	How Teachers Can Implement Anti-racist Practices in the Classroom	This article explains how educators can reduce bias in disciplinary responses by recognizing vulnerable decision points, implementing restorative practices, and giving more empathetic feedback.

(Continued)

(Continued)

SOURCE	TITLE	SUMMARY
Matt Davis (2015), *Edutopia*	Restorative Justice: Resources for Schools	This site provides examples of successful restorative justice programs as well as implementation resources for schools looking to adopt them.
Marieke van Woerkom (2018), *Edutopia*	Building Community With Restorative Circles	This site provides guidance and advice around facilitating meaningful discussion circles to build community.
Trackit Lights (n.d.)	Restorative Practice: 6 Questions That Improve Behaviour	This site discusses how restorative practices focus on addressing the root cause of behavior and repairing the damage the behavior caused. Asking questions can promote reflective thinking and empathy: "(1) What happened? (2) How were you feeling and what were you needing? (3) What were you thinking? (4) Who else has been affected? What do you think [they] might be feeling? (5) What have you learnt and what will you do differently next time? (6) How can the damage be repaired?"
University of Massachusetts Boston: Center for Peace, Democracy, and Development (2021)	Restorative Justice Project	UMass Boston's Restorative Justice Project provides conflict resolution, meditation, and restorative justice services to Boston's youth, families, and incarcerated populations. This page details the various projects and services they provide.

WHO CAN TEACH YOGA-MINDFULNESS-MEDITATION IN SCHOOLS?

Over the past 20–30 years of using yoga in schools, it has been introduced and taught in various ways: with certified yoga teachers from local community centers, by individual classroom teachers who have become certified as yoga teachers, by physical education teachers with backgrounds and training in teaching yoga, and by individual teachers without certification who have learned techniques as they have taken yoga classes for their own benefit. Some teachers have also learned specific yoga postures or techniques in in-service or pre-service classes and then taken these back to their classrooms.

SCALING UP YOGA-MINDFULNESS-MEDITATION FOR CHILDREN AND YOUTH

Krishna Kaur with Y.O.G.A. for Youth has taught thousands of classroom teachers about yoga practices as she has conducted workshops around the world. With Y.O.G.A. for Youth, yoga teachers are certified as they complete a standardized program of study over several months. One of the wonderful features of this program is that Y.O.G.A. for Youth certification connects certified teachers with other educators so that they can share practices, updates, and information within their Y.O.G.A. for Youth community.

Jeffrey Donald, a mindfulness coordinator in Maryland, has also established a program to virtually reach teachers throughout the district. Teachers receive many hours of program supports, including classes available online (https://news .montgomeryschoolsmd.org/staff-bulletin/mindfulness-videos-available-to-staff-students-and-families/) (*see also Chapter 12 on mindfulness*).

Jeffrey reminds us of liability concerns and district policies:

Teachers and districts should consider liability concerns when implementing any yogic practices that involve getting into and sustaining more complex postures. Districtwide training and supervision is ideal because it provides an avenue to get essential information to teachers, a venue for addressing teacher questions and concerns, and a way to formally check on teacher implementation and provide teachers with updates on best practices and preferred methodologies.

A teacher's ability to help students with yoga by suggesting adaptations, or simpler ways to complete specific exercises, can be helpful. Teachers will be more effective when they realize how to help students challenge themselves, without pushing themselves to the point of injury. For example, some students may be able to hold a yoga pose for a minute while others might be able to easily stay in that same position for three to five minutes. And with a teacher who coaches, "Keep going! You can do it!" students are likely to actually hold a pose for a few seconds longer—your confidence and your coaching can make a difference!

TEACHING MINDFULNESS AND MEDITATION

As we consider whether teachers without a network of supports or formal training can implement yoga, it is helpful to remember that teachers often introduce and teach body movements, particularly with young children, that are very similar to many of the yoga postures and activities. As with other activities, it may be that teachers' recognition of their own skills and competencies can be a valuable determining factor. As with teaching anything—whether it is art, photography, woodworking, or cooking—if you as the individual teacher have skills, background, and training, then you are better positioned to be effective. Certainly, over the ages, many teachers who have taken yoga classes have found ways to incorporate or adapt some of the yoga positions and techniques for their students.

When it comes to mindfulness and meditation, programs are available to provide certification and training for teachers. However, many teachers have studied mindfulness and meditation and found success in introducing them in their classrooms after completing introductory workshops.

As with yoga, there are a few precautions to consider with teaching meditation. Chief among these is that if an individual has experienced trauma, meditation can bring up negative memories. As one gets more deeply in touch with oneself—whether it is becoming more aware through one's breath, bodily movements, or meditation—traumatic memories that may have been repressed may surface. There are specific signs to watch for and strategies to use in these situations. Generally, starting with simple breathing exercises and movements will be helpful. If you have concerns, it is always best to discuss these with counselors or your district's mindfulness/yoga supervisor, and it is always helpful to use a calm, reassuring voice to help students in the moment. Teachers who are trained or certified to teach yoga and meditation to children and youth receive more specific guidance about this.

We also encourage teachers to get trained to teach yoga-mindfulness-meditation. Taking yoga classes can be valuable. Additionally, Y.O.G.A. for Youth offers online classes (see yogaforyouth.org).

RECOMMENDATIONS FOR THOSE WITHOUT FORMAL TRAINING

If you have not been formally trained to teach yoga, here are a few recommendations:

- Practice until you are comfortable.

- Consult online apps, websites, and videos for help.

- Remember that students do not need to be perfect in their practice and that in general, especially with younger children, we expect more approximations. Often with our youngest students it may be more a matter of movement and trying to imitate animal movements or sounds, rather than being more precise.

- If you feel any doubts about how to teach a certain posture or kriya, then check online or with a yoga teacher.

- Because of greater risk, if you are not a certified yoga teacher, then please refrain from teaching certain postures such as head or shoulder stands, back bends, or wheel pose.

Apps and Videos

 There's a world of apps and videos available for all different developmental age levels that can be used virtually or in person with students (*see also Chapter 3 and the Corwin Resources page*).

Adapting Yoga, Meditation, and Mindfulness

Common adaptations for yoga, meditation, and mindfulness include the following:

- Incorporating rhythm, music, stories, or games.

- Using a guided meditation or visualization with relaxation.

- Increasing the length of warm-ups to help increase flexibility and preparation for yoga and meditation.

- Using simple, clear, and easy-to-follow step-by-step directions.

- Demonstrating and practicing one step several times before going on to the next steps.

- Reminding students of correct postures (e.g., "Stretch your spine up").

- Adapting classes for students with special needs.

- Reducing the expected number of repetitions or length of time for a yoga set.

- Returning to easier postures or yoga sets.

For some of us, yoga positions will feel natural, and we will seamlessly move from one yoga position to the next. Others of us will find that over time, as we are able to stretch further, our flexibility increases; as our lung capacity increases, we can sustain our breath for a longer period of time; and after learning the yoga basics, we are able to move into more advanced poses.

In *Cultivating Happiness, Resilience, and Well-Being*, we connect common adaptations with specific exercises that are included in each chapter.

TRAINING AND RESOURCES

1. What training and experience will you draw upon when teaching yoga-mindfulness-meditation?

2. What additional training and resources could help you (online, in your district, etc.)?

3. Whom can you reach out to for support, encouragement, and guidance?

MINDFUL REFLECTION

1. What do you believe might be most exciting about implementing *Cultivating Happiness, Resilience, and Well-Being* in your classroom or school?

2. Where might you face the greatest challenges?

3. What resources do you have to support your journey, your practice, and your instruction?

ONLINE RESOURCES
Visit https://resources.corwin.com/CultivatingHappiness

Online Resource 2.1   Videos Available From the Center for Educational Improvement

Online Resource 2.2   Restorative Practices

Online Resource 2.3   Mindful Reflection

CHAPTER THREE

Teacher Stress and Teacher Practice

KEY PRINCIPLE

Teacher stress can be alleviated through yoga, mindfulness, and meditation.

Teaching can be incredibly rewarding and gratifying, but it is increasingly physically, mentally, and emotionally taxing. Shaping young minds and guiding students as they make sense of an ever-changing world is challenging work. Any teacher will tell you that the demands of the job extend far beyond the classroom walls. Teacher stress and burnout are significant issues facing schools today, and they affect not only the teachers themselves, but the students as well.

TEACHER STRESS AND BURNOUT WERE ALARMINGLY HIGH BEFORE COVID-19

Even before COVID-19, teacher stress and burnout were at troubling levels. A University of Missouri–Columbia (2020) study found that 94% of middle school teachers reported high levels of stress. In 2017, the American Federation of Teachers (AFT) conducted a quality-of-life survey with 830 educators who reported their work was "always" or "often" stressful 61% of the time, which was double that of workers in the general population (30%). One teacher lamented, "This job is stressful, overwhelming, and hard. I am overworked, underpaid, underappreciated, questioned, and blamed for things that are out of my control" (AFT, 2017).

Teachers reported having poor mental health for 11 or more days per month, twice the rate of the general U.S. workforce. They also reported lower-than-recommended levels of health outcomes and hours of sleep per night. Chronic stress and poor mental health can negatively impact

"This job is stressful, overwhelming, and hard. I am overworked, underpaid, underappreciated, questioned, and blamed for things that are out of my control"

teachers' job performance and thus student outcomes. Chronic stress can increase irritability, mood swings, exhaustion, depression, and anxiety, in addition to compromising the immune system and increasing educators' susceptibility to illness, which may result in more absences over time, all of which can disrupt student learning, behavior management, and relationship building (Ansley et al., 2018).

COVID-19-Related Stress

COVID-19 has exacerbated existing stressors while adding on brand-new ones. Educators now have to deal with workplace and global uncertainty; health and well-being concerns for themselves, their families, and their students; and challenges adapting to remote learning and mastering new technologies.

Overnight, teachers have been asked to adapt their courses to online learning, requiring them to work double time to record instructional videos and learn new tools (Ellis, 2020). Many educators are teaching students in person during the day and then turning around and teaching remotely in the afternoon for students who have chosen distance learning. "The days where it's 13-plus hours at school, you're just exhausted, hoping to make it to the car at night," a teacher shared. "We're seeing an extreme level of teacher burnout" (Singer, 2020).

> "The days where it's 13-plus hours at school, you're just exhausted, hoping to make it to the car at night," a teacher shared. "We're seeing an extreme level of teacher burnout"

The additional burden from the pandemic is threatening to break the already overburdened system, with long-lasting ramifications. Experts and teachers' unions warn of a looming burnout crisis that could lead to a wave of retirements. According to a recent survey by the National Education Association, the coronavirus made 28% of educators more likely to leave teaching or retire early (Singer, 2020).

 Additional information on teacher stress is available on the Corwin Resources page at **https://resources.corwin.com/ CultivatingHappiness**.

YOUR OWN DAILY PRACTICE

The good news is that there are proven strategies you can use to alleviate stress for yourself, your students, and others around you. But before you can alleviate the stress and trauma of others, you will first need to develop a regular self-care practice for yourself. During times, such as COVID-19, when stress is extraordinarily high, you may find that you will need to double or triple the amount of time you dedicate to your self-care practice to maintain inner stability and calm.

> Before you can alleviate the stress and trauma of others, you will first need to develop a regular self-care practice for yourself.

While many of us experienced fear during 2020, those fears did not just evaporate as we moved into 2021. Even now, we continue to experience doubts about our future, our well-being, and the health and safety of youth. Even if you haven't begun a yoga-mindfulness-meditation practice, you may have certain routines that you count on for your own health and well-being. This might include a regular exercise routine, trips to a gym or spa, time playing sports, walks outside, or swimming. Some of us also have certain foods we count on for energy, for feeling balance, or for the right nutrient–vitamin combinations. We might have learned to eat greens, to go light on sauces, and to watch our carbs, sugar, and salt. We also may have certain practices that increase our own comfort—herbal teas, warm baths, aromatherapy, listening to soothing music, or spending time gardening, playing an instrument, reading, or sharing time with friends.

In 2020, even as yoga and meditation teachers, we found we needed to reach deep within our treasure trove of practices to maintain a sense of positivity and optimism.

HOW I CHANGED MY ROUTINE TO ALLEVIATE STRESS IN 2020

Christine Mason relays some of the changes she made to alleviate her own stress in 2020:

The first few months. The initial impact. In March 2020, when news of the devastating spread and impact of COVID-19 was first announced, I was on my way back from New Orleans, and not feeling all that great. I wasn't sure what had hit me, but because of the potential for COVID-19, I self-isolated for two weeks and began a routine of significant bed rest, increased breathing exercises, and inclusion of yoga movements to support my lymph glands and immune system. Since I was not displaying a cough or prolonged fever, I was not able to be tested. However, it took me about six weeks to regain my strength and begin to again feel a sense of body tone.

Another major change for me occurred a few weeks later, when in April my adult yoga students requested that I teach yoga online. While I was well versed in using Zoom, it took considerable practice to learn how to use a Zoom camera while moving around, and to adjust to all the changes that were necessary to teach yoga online. One advantage of this request: I had to regain a certain physical fitness in order to instruct online.

Months 3–6. A shifting mindset and shifting routine. As we followed all of the protocols that were recommended—physical distancing, handwashing, mask-wearing, and limited visits to stores and take-out restaurants—COVID-19 continued to impact family, friends, and coworkers. As trips were canceled and dining out was replaced by delivery, teachers were telling us how students and families were suffering. We realized that *mindset* was important—that our attitudes and our sense of well-being were dependent in part on our own perspective. It was a time for gratitude.

In many ways, staff at the Center for Educational Improvement were very lucky: We had gone through the adjustment related to working from home many years ago, we were early Zoom users, and we understood the value of having a disciplined physical practice.

(Continued)

(Continued)

We had jobs and little need to risk exposure to COVID-19. I immediately understood that when it came to mindset, I needed to be in a position of positive influence. Because of my work as a yoga teacher, author, educational leader, and presenter, I had experience staying optimistic and hopeful, even when others were uncertain. With COVID-19 breathing down our necks, I understood the value of learning about the best international educational practices and finding support for educators who were on the front lines.

However, sometimes we were not even aware of the changes in stress levels for ourselves and others, until we noticed an increase in our anxiety and a reduced ability to perform at consistently high levels under pressure.

When we became more consciously aware, and monitored our actions and productivity, we recognized that our ability to reason and make logical decisions about how to tackle problems as they arose was diminished after months of attempting to do our best with COVID-19 constantly hovering in the streets and in the air. We started to consciously be more aware (see Chapter 6 on consciousness) of the stress of others and to consider our response through a "stress reducing" lens. We saw that the quality of my/our work, and our ability to meet deadlines, was endangered. In essence, to escape the COVID-19 mindset, we increased our "mindfulness"—including our mindful consideration of everyday life events. With this awareness, we adapted to some new routines, pushing back deadlines and giving ourselves and others additional time to process changes. As an executive director, I found it helpful to slow down my decision-making process to be more reflective prior to making decisions. During this period, patience took on additional meaning, as we practiced patience and consensus making with a new vigor and tenacity.

> **In essence, to escape the COVID-19 mindset, we increased our "mindfulness"— including our mindful consideration of everyday life events.**

Also, around months 4–5, I realized that I needed to change some of my newly formed habits. As an author, I was used to sitting in front of the computer for many hours a day. However, perpetual Zoom meetings were exhausting, and COVID-19 put a halt to my habit of visiting the gym every two or three days. While I had replaced this with neighborhood walks, in July when the humidity increased, these began to fall off.

Months 6–10. **Evolving lifestyle changes.** As it became obvious that COVID-19 was here to stay, and that I needed to up my practice, I relied on the discipline I had learned as a yoga instructor. To be an authentic instructor, I needed not only to teach, but to have my own yoga practice. Here are changes I made starting at about month 6: (1) I increased my yoga, floor exercises, and meditations so that on days when I was not walking, I devoted about 60–75 minutes to active physical yoga, and I also maintained at least 15–20 minutes for a sitting meditation; (2) I added more reps with free weights I had been using periodically and increased the pace of my floor practice to elevate my heart rate; and (3) I increased the lengths of my walks to 50–60 minutes, three times a week.

I provide this example to say that over the course of a few months, it became clear that due to the level of global stress, I needed not only to be more mindful, but also to alter the way I used the physical tools I had to enhance my personal practice. I gained significant insights during this time as I discovered that the yoga and mindfulness tools I had at my disposal were essential to maintaining balance and improving my decision making. During this period, I not only adapted to COVID-19, but I also used my yoga tools to push forward, with more creativity and improved problem-solving skills.

WHERE ARE YOU?

After reading about how Christine changed her practice during the pandemic, follow the steps in Figure 3.1 as you reflect on your own needs and practice.

Figure 3.1 • My Stress Reduction Starting Point

Step 1. Review your experience with COVID-19 and write your own story, reflecting on your changing levels of stress, how you coped, what worked well, and what you could improve.

Step 2. Identify stress-reducing practices and goals. Then identify a few of your most valued practices.

PRACTICE	CURRENT STATUS (TIMES PER WEEK)	GOAL (TIMES PER WEEK)
Activity		
Sleep/Nutrition		
Self-Care		

(Continued)

(Continued)

Step 3. Review your story and the practices and goals you listed. Select at least one practice that you may want to increase: _____

- **Consider when, where, why, and how you will implement your practice. Here are a few goal statements from teachers with whom we have worked:**

   ○ *Activity.* Implement 12 minutes of vigorous exercise daily. This may include walking or aerobics. The goal is to increase heart rate and movement.

   ○ *Sleep/Nutrition.* Increase intake of vegetables and reduce use of white flour, sugar, and artificial sweetener.

   ○ *Self-Care.* Implement aromatherapy by using a diffuser with lavender essential oil as part of my daily routine.

 Available at https://resources.corwin.com/CultivatingHappiness

OBSERVING YOUR PROGRESS

At the Center for Educational Improvement, we have established HeartMind Communities that include HeartMind Adventures involving four steps that can be used to help deepen your understanding of the relevance and importance of your practices and goals. These four steps can easily be used to reflect on and monitor your progress with your implementation of self-care mindfulness strategies.

- Observe

- Reflect

- Journal

- Deepen Your Understanding (see Figure 3.2)

As you implement practices to reduce your stress, reflect on changes in your mood, attitude, happiness, or well-being. You may want to include such things as how you shifted your actions and attitudes, how you felt physically, and what was easy or difficult about your new practices.

Figure 3.2 • The HeartMind Adventure

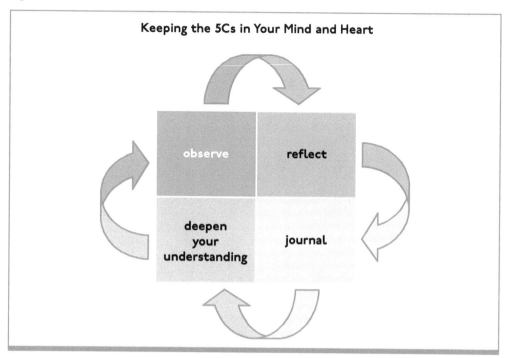

Source: Center for Educational Improvement (2020).

 Additional information on how to begin a HeartMind Journal is available on the Corwin Resources page.

CREATING A YOGA-MINDFULNESS-MEDITATION PRACTICE

The practices you identified in Figure 3.1 can take you far along a road to reduced stress and greater calmness. However, as we explained in Chapter 1, both neuroscience research and research on the vagus nerve and heart centeredness support the value of establishing and maintaining yoga-mindfulness-meditation practices.

Additionally, when we have periods of acute stress, such as many of us experienced in 2020, we may find that our regular go-to wellness practices simply aren't enough. Moreover, many of our normal health routines were disrupted as closed gyms ended our normal fitness routines abruptly. A personal mindfulness and yoga practice can strengthen our ability to access inner calm and maintain inner wellness, even when the world around us is in chaos. It can help us remain balanced and centered when the world is in flux, and it can help us find hope when the world around us is in fear.

Complete the following exercise to begin to plan for what you might do with your own mindfulness practice.

MY YOGA-MINDFULNESS-MEDITATION STARTING POINT

- Identify your level of expertise.

    ☐ Beginner

    ☐ Intermediate

    ☐ Advanced

- How much time do you want to devote to your practice?

    ☐ 5–10 minutes daily

    ☐ 20–30 minutes daily

    ☐ 40–60 minutes daily

    ☐ I am not sure if I can find time daily but will aim for 2–4 times a week.

- Where will you conduct your practice?

    ☐ I have a dedicated space (room, corner of a room).

    ☐ I can easily make space.

    ☐ I will practice at a studio or my school.

- Do you prefer to use music as part of your practice?

    ☐ Yes

    ☐ No

    If Yes, see Chapter 4 for more information on suggested music and apps.

- What will your practice be?

    ☐ A combination of breath work, yoga, mindfulness, and meditation

    ☐ Primarily breath work

    ☐ Primarily yoga

    ☐ Primarily mindfulness

    ☐ Primarily meditation

If you find one of the following sets appealing, make a decision to practice it for 40 days. If you are an intermediate or advanced yoga-mindfulness-meditation practitioner, review options for practices here, perhaps considering first a focus on consciousness (see Chapter 6).

If you are a beginning yoga practitioner, here is a recommended introductory set.

A Beginner's Practice

We suggest beginning with a few minutes on each step and increasing the length of time as you are comfortable.

See Chapter 4 for additional information on organizing your yoga-mindfulness-meditation practice.

Spinal Exercise Set

This set exercises the spine progressively and helps bring awareness to your breath and body while releasing excess energy and stress. These practices will be of immense benefit not only to you, but also to your students. The more comfortable you become with this sequence in your own personal practice, the more comfortable you will become in sharing these practices with your students as well.

When presenting these practices to your students, always remember to work within the group's zone of interest and comfort. Depending on the age of the youth, the exercises can be held longer for older students and shorter for younger ones. Over time, it is possible to increase the amount of time for each exercise. All breath is through the nostrils unless otherwise directed.

Note: This warm-up depicts our expectations and an acceptable response for each of the exercises. As we state in Chapter 4, this is appropriate for this developmental stage. With older students, we would provide additional guidance regarding each part of the sequence.

For this set, eyes can be open or closed. If closed, focus on the space between your brows. In the photos that follow, younger children are approximating specific postures and positions.

1. **Position:** Seated, hands on knees.

Movement: Rotate the middle of the body in circles around the sacrum, keeping the head still. Reverse directions.

Breath: Long, deep, slow breathing.

Time: 30 seconds–2 minutes.

2. **Position:** Sit on heels, palms on thighs.

Movement: *Spinal flexes.* Alternate arching to open chest forward and rounding to stretch the spine back.

Breath: Inhale, extend forward. Exhale, flex back.

Time: 30 seconds–1 minute.

3. Position: Sit on heels, knees together. Extend arms out to the sides, parallel to the ground, and bend the elbows to form a 90-degree angle, forearms and fingers pointing up.

Mudra: Gyan mudra (tips of forefingers and thumbs touching).

Time: 1 minute.

4. Position: Seated, hands on knees, elbows relaxed.

Movement: *Shoulder shrugs.* Shrug shoulders tightly up to the ears. Drop them completely to release.

Breath: Inhale, shoulders up. Exhale, shoulders down. Repeat.

Time: 30 seconds–2 minutes.

5. Position: Seated.

Movement: *Neck rolls.* Drop chin to chest and slowly roll head in circles, with shoulders relaxed. Reverse directions.

Breath: Long, deep, slow breathing.

Time: 30 seconds–1 minute.

Note: For this set, eyes can be open or closed. If closed, focus on the space between your brows.

Sensory Meditation

After practicing breath work and opening up the energy along the spine, the body is ready to settle into a seat for meditation practice. There are many different ways to define and practice meditation, but we will think of it here as an opportunity to bring our awareness to a single point. It is an opportunity to let go of distracting or anxiety-inducing thoughts, and practice nonjudgmental acceptance of whatever is here in the present moment.

Here is a good beginner's practice to try:

1. Sit comfortably with the spine long and tall. This can be sitting in a chair or on the floor.

2. Gaze down at the ground in front of you or close your eyes.

3. Take three slow, deep breaths.

4. Bring your attention to your ears and focus on the sounds you hear. Do not try to label, describe, or evaluate any of the sounds. Just listen.

5. If any other thoughts arise during the practice, notice them, and let them go. Return your attention to the sounds around you.

6. Notice that some of the sounds come from within you. Listen to those sounds.

7. Notice that some of the sounds come from the room or space around you. Listen to those sounds.

8. Notice that some of the sounds come from farther away. Listen to those sounds.

9. Allow all the sounds from within and around you to wash over your eyes. Breathe slowly and listen.

10. When you are ready, gently open your eyes.

REFLECTING ON YOUR PRACTICE

Use the HeartMind Adventure square (Figure 3.2) to reflect on the value of your practice and your progress. We recommend keeping a journal during the first 40 days. Here are some things to consider:

- Do you notice any changes in your flexibility, feeling of well-being, or mental alertness?

- What happened over the course of the 40 days? Did you lengthen the amount of time at each step?

- Did the quality of your meditation change?

- Did you notice any changes in your levels of stress or reaction to stress?

USING YOUR PRACTICE TO PLAN FOR TEACHING STUDENTS

As you engage in your own self-care and establish your own self-care routine, you can start to think about what and how to bring these practices to students. The beginner's practice described earlier in this chapter can be taught to students age 6 and up. Options for younger students can be found in Chapter 4.

As you continue, your practice will evolve, and you will be able to further not only your students' yoga-mindfulness-meditation, but also their self-care. You will find several examples of good self-care routines for teachers and students in this book; however, we wanted to insert an example of how teachers are teaching self-care to middle school students through mindfulness, meditation, and yoga.

YOGA WITH MIDDLE SCHOOL YOUTH

I have shared mindful breathing practices with middle school students experiencing a range of traumas, from experiencing abusive households, to witnessing gang violence on the neighborhood playground, to being expected to take on the role of a "caregiver" to younger siblings because of overworked or absentee parents. Students have told me that finding their breath has helped them feel calmer when everything around them feels out of control. As their counselor listening to their stories, I find that connecting to my own breath in the present moment helps me stay focused on their needs so that I can best help them navigate these challenges.

Krystle Kougias, Middle School Counselor, Bronx, New York

Helping Your Students Create Their Own Self-Care Practice

When you feel ready to begin bringing self-care practices to students, start with a lesson like the one outlined in Figure 3.3, which is intended to be used with elementary school students.

Figure 3.3 • Self-Care

OBJECTIVE		STUDENTS WILL BE ABLE TO RECOGNIZE THEIR STRESSORS AND CREATE SELF-CARE HABITS TO HELP REDUCE THEIR STRESS.
Introduction to Lesson/Ground Rules	1–2 minutes	Sample Rules: • We will support one another and create a safe space. • We will allow everyone to share their thoughts and feelings. • We will listen to how our bodies feel. • If something hurts or does not feel good, we will stop, knowing that each person and body is different. • We will focus on having a good time.
Breath Work	2–3 minutes	"Focus Ball Breathing" (Willard & Nance, 2018): • Sit with your legs and feet together. • Bring your palms together in front of your chest. • Keep your fingertips together as you pull your palms apart, forming a ball with your fingers. • Press your fingertips together until you feel the muscles in your hands and arms activating. • Close your eyes. • As you breathe in, inflate your ball. • As you breathe out, flatten the ball by pushing your palms together.
Setting the Stage	8 minutes	*My Incredible Talking Body* by Rebecca Bowen (Fagin, 2020)
Discussion	3–5 minutes	Define self-care and the different types with examples. Review info about the vagus nerve and its role in heart-mind connection. (See Chapter 1 for more information on the vagus nerve; see also Mason, Rivers Murphy, & Jackson, 2020, Chapter 2.)
Warm-Ups	2–3 minutes	Shoulder Rolls: • Sit up straight and get into a comfortable position in your chair. • Bring your shoulders up as high as you can. • Breathe in as your shoulders rise. • Breathe out as you let your shoulders fall back down. • Now move your shoulders in a circular motion.

(Continued)

(Continued)

OBJECTIVE		STUDENTS WILL BE ABLE TO RECOGNIZE THEIR STRESSORS AND CREATE SELF-CARE HABITS TO HELP REDUCE THEIR STRESS.
		• Lift them up and move them down. Continue to roll your shoulders. • Breathe in again as you bring your shoulders up as high as you can. • Breathe out as you let your shoulders fall back down. Neck Stretch: • Sit up straight and get into a comfortable position in your chair. • Gently let your head fall to one side. • Breathe in and breathe out. • Gently let your head fall to the other side. • Breathe in and breathe out. • Sit up straight and tall. • Let your head fall toward your belly. • Breathe in and breathe out.
Relaxation and Meditation	1–3 minutes	Get Your Grumpies Out (adapted from *Mindful Moments for Kids* by Kira Willey, 2016): • Tune into how you're feeling in this moment. Maybe you're grumpy, sad, or mad. Make a face to show how you're feeling. Today we talked a lot about finding activities and strategies that can help us feel better. We're going to try one today. • Take a really big breath in and blow any bad feelings you're having away. We're going to repeat that two more times, just to make sure we got them all out! Take a really big breath in and blow any bad feelings you're having away. Now, let's do it one more time. Take a really big breath in and blow any bad feelings you're having away. • You can use this any time you need to get any bad feelings out and help you feel better.
Discussion	2–3 minutes	Discuss the following questions as a group: 1. How do you know when you feel sad, mad, grumpy, or stressed? How does your body feel? 2. What activities make you feel better? 3. What did you learn today that can help you feel better when you are stressed?

Source: Adapted from Willey, (2017).

 Available at https://resources.corwin.com/CultivatingHappiness

Using Ancillary Apps

Teachers are the trusted adults in students' lives. Students will listen to teachers. Receiving a teacher's leadership and instruction is more personal and 100 times more impactful than relying on technology. So guided yoga and meditations from teachers are infinitely superior to those from apps. By leading the lessons, you affirm the importance of these practices in your own personal lives. Rather than press play for classroom instruction, listen to the app yourself several times, and then teach students directly. Having said this, apps, when used sparingly, can be helpful and also a good motivator. We have been in classrooms where teachers show a video of other children doing specific poses or exercises. It can be helpful for students to see other students doing these exercises. Just use care.

Some teachers use apps because they lack confidence or don't feel they have the required skills. If this is the case for you, use the apps as you begin to bring yoga and mindfulness into your classes, but don't end there. Get yourself prepared to instruct. Here are three key recommendations:

- Pick a couple of things to master so that you gradually increase your competence and confidence.

- It's okay to start with something simple and relatively easy.

- It's also okay to collaborate with other adults to share the instruction with teachers who have more experience or expertise.

Many online resources are available to assist with yoga, mindfulness, and meditation instruction. The resources in Figure 3.4 cover a wide range of mindfulness practices and strategies that educators can use for both their own personal well-being and the well-being of their students. Yoga and mindfulness apps such as Down Dog, Calm, Headspace, Happify, and Gaia mostly focus on the user (i.e., the person holding the device that the app is downloaded on). Educators can benefit immensely from taking the time to show themselves compassion and care through physical movement and mindfulness practices. These platforms offer many ways for educators to grow a more positive mind–body connection that will impact their own personal lives and, in turn, improve the lives of the students with whom they work. When educators prioritize themselves, they are better able to show up for their students and model self-compassion in a genuine way.

Apps and websites such as Smiling Mind, MyLife, Yoga Ed., and Breathe for Change offer explicit mindfulness instruction and curricula for educators to integrate into their professions. Educators can leverage the trainings and programs offered by these platforms to improve the health of students and staff in their school communities. Many of the programs in Figure 3.4 offer free subscriptions and resources for anyone working or learning in the K–12 environment, making mindfulness training easily accessible to all. Investing in mindfulness education will create and maintain safe and supportive learning environments—something that should be a priority in 21st century education.

Figure 3.4 • Mindful Yoga Apps/Programs for Teachers

NAME	DESCRIPTION	SOURCES
Down Dog App available on mobile devices	*Down Dog* is a yoga, high-intensity interval training, barre, and meditation platform that allows users to completely customize their practice to fit with their schedule, goals, level of experience, target areas of the body to work on, workout intensity, workout style, length of workout, and more. *Down Dog* provides different apps for different types of wellness practices, which are available to download on mobile devices (Stolyar, 2020). Cost: Currently offering free unlimited access to all of its apps for health care workers, educators, and students as a response to the COVID-19 pandemic.	www.downdogapp.com www.downdogapp.com/schools
Calm App/website available on mobile devices	Includes built-in guided meditations, sleep stories, and breathing exercises (Haug, 2017). Cost: An annual subscription (currently $69.99/year or $14.99/month), or the free version provides limited access to meditations, sleep stories, and music.	www.calm.com www.calm.com/freetrial/plans
Headspace App/website available on mobile devices	*Headspace* is a mindfulness, meditation, and sleep platform that provides many ways to engage in mindfulness for better overall health. Both the app and the web version of the platform offer guided meditations, wellness articles, and sleep support, as well as tutorials on meditation for beginners (Haug, 2016). Cost: Currently offering free premium membership for all K–12 teachers, school administrators, and support staff in the United States, the United Kingdom, Canada, and Australia.	www.headspace.com www.headspace.com/educators
Happify App available on mobile devices	Users start by answering prompts in a questionnaire that will lead them to a specific "track" through the app. These tracks correspond with different activities, games, and resources designed to help the users achieve their goals. All resources provided through the tracks are backed by psychological theory (e.g., cognitive-behavioral therapy, mindfulness, and positive psychology) and are developed by professionals (Belluomini, 2019).	www.happify.com
Gaia App available on mobile devices and streaming services	*Gaia* blends yoga, mindfulness, meditation, and spirituality for a mind–body healing experience (Chon, 2020). The platform offers over 8,000 classes, videos, and programs to cater to the unique skills and goals of each user. Users can log in on their mobile devices or stream on platforms such as Roku, Chromecast, and Amazon Fire TV. Educators working from home can enjoy chair yoga flows targeted for individuals who sit for long periods of time looking at a screen.	www.gaia.com
Smiling Mind App/website available on mobile devices	*Smiling Mind* (2020) is a mindfulness app designed by psychologists and educators based on research supporting improved mental health and performance in school with regular mindfulness practice.	www.smilingmind.com.au/

NAME	DESCRIPTION	SOURCES
MyLife App/website available on mobile devices	*MyLife* (2020) is an app that helps users develop emotional regulation skills to handle life's stressors and worries. This app offers guided meditations as well as opportunities to check in by recording thoughts/feelings as they arise.	https://my.life/mylife-for-schools/
Stop, Breathe, & Think App available on mobile devices	This app (Monticello Kievlan, n.d.) helps users track their progress and develop real skills for managing anxiety, backed by cognitive-behavioral theories. This app also offers a kid-friendly version ideal for youth ages 10 and up. *Stop, Breathe, & Think* also offers programs and trainings for educators in mindfulness/meditation and social-emotional learning.	www.commonsensemedia.org/app-reviews/stop-breathe-think-kids-focus-calm-sleep
Yoga Ed. Website, online courses, and downloadable resources	*Yoga Ed.* (2021) is designed for all members of the K–12 learning community, from children ages 3 and up to teachers and school counselors working with students every day. Cost: Free yoga and mindfulness classes to support and improve the physical and mental health of students and educators worldwide. Educators can use these classes to provide brain breaks during virtual or in-person learning days, model healthy coping skills, and teach the importance of physical movement to benefit physical and mental health.	https://academy.yogaed.com/p/yoga-ed-for-free-online-yoga-mindfulness-classes-for-all-ages
Breathe for Change Website, online curriculum, and downloadable resources	*Breathe for Change* (n.d.) is a yoga teacher training program designed for educators from a trauma-informed lens. These trainings blend social-emotional learning strategies and movement to create a safe and supportive learning environment. Educators who complete the training program can earn up to three graduate credits or continuing education units as well as a *Breathe for Change* Foundations Certificate, which certifies individuals to lead yoga, social-emotional learning, and mindfulness practices in their school community.	www.breatheforchange.com www.breatheforchange.com/foundations-course

online resources ▸ Available at https://resources.corwin.com/CultivatingHappiness

MINDFUL REFLECTION

1. How comfortable are you with your own yoga and mindfulness practice? Are you using it for your own self-care?

2. Review recommendations for breath, movement, and meditation from this chapter. Where will you start? Try to select one of each.

3. If you are a beginner, start with one to three things, do a daily practice for 40 days, then answer this question: Did you become more comfortable?

ONLINE RESOURCES

Visit https://resources.corwin.com/CultivatingHappiness

Online Resource 3.1   Causes of Teacher Stress

Online Resource 3.2   My Stress Reduction Starting Point

Online Resource 3.3   Begin a HeartMind Journal

Online Resource 3.4   My Yoga-Mindfulness-Meditation Starting Point

Online Resource 3.5   Reflecting on Your Practice

Online Resource 3.6   Self-Care

Online Resource 3.7   Mindful Yoga Apps/Programs for Teachers

Online Resource 3.8   Mindful Reflection

CHAPTER FOUR

Organizing Space, Materials, and Instruction

 KEY PRINCIPLE

Yoga and meditation can bring a sense of peace and calmness to your classroom. A few strategic considerations will enhance the yoga-mindfulness-meditation experience for you and your students.

In Chapter 3, the focus was on teacher self-care. In this chapter, you will learn about how to prepare to take what you have learned in your own practice to students.

While this chapter is about organizing and preparing to teach yoga-mindfulness-meditation, there is a critical difference between teaching yoga-mindfulness-meditation and teaching many other things. Meena Srinivasan, author of *Teach, Breathe, Learn* (2014), explains her dedication to teaching:

> I've always felt that teachers are a vital link in helping realize Gandhi's vision that "if we could change ourselves, the tendencies in the world would also change," [and] this is why I teach—to touch lives and help make the world a better place in some small way. (p. 21)

So, as you prepare your space to teach, consider Srinivasan's words, along with this statement by authors Andrew Harvey and Karuna Erickson from their book *Heart Yoga* (2010):

> Yoga was created by ancient sages of India to be a healing and transforming gift for the entire world. . . . Because of the indivisibility of consciousness and energy, there is a profoundly intimate correlation between the elements within our bodies and

the natural elements of the outside world. . . . When yoga is practiced with conscious knowledge of its vast original purpose, and its union with simple, luminous, and profound meditations, it awakens this joyful praise of existence within every cell of the body. (p. xvi)

We have experienced remarkable transformations in our lives from teaching yoga-mindfulness-meditation and from practicing these disciplines. To this day, we remain in awe of the teachings we share with you.

A note about terminology: Throughout this book, we refer to yoga-mindfulness-meditation. Elsewhere in the book (see Chapters 1, 2, 3, 11, and 12), we have said more about mindfulness. We find that mindfulness practices such as focusing on the breath and paying attention to sensations are becoming generally more accepted by public schools. However, teachers, even if they have taken yoga classes, may have reduced access to how to use yogic practices with their students. So, this chapter is intended to directly address that deficit by giving you comprehensive recommendations about a yogic approach to breath, movement, and meditation.

I. PREPARING TO TEACH: YOGA SPACE AND MATERIALS

Let's get practical. How you set up your yoga space will be impacted by several factors:

- Whether you are in the same classroom or whether you move from class to class

- The available "free space" in your classroom

- Available equipment and supplies

- Your intent to create a space for healing and transformation for students

Physical education teachers may have easy access to yoga mats and considerable space for students to spread out. If you are teaching in a dance studio, you may also have the benefit of mirrors to help guide learning. However, many classroom teachers have improvised. If you are in one classroom, you may be able to set up a "yoga or mindfulness corner." Some schools have a mindfulness meditation room. Students can also practice standing near or sitting at their desks. Each of these provides unique opportunities to be creative.

Here are a few yoga props and other materials to enhance your yoga instruction:

- Yoga mats and cushions for sitting

- Yoga blocks or bolsters to help students stay in position

- Yoga music and apps

- A screen or whiteboard for sharing yoga videos

- Calm lighting—perhaps some battery-operated candles

- A chime or a chime setting on an app to signal the end of a meditation

- Mat cleaner (use all-natural products or make your own with a mixture of white vinegar or witch hazel, water, and a scent such as lavender—using care in case students are allergic to specific scents)

While all of the above are helpful, none is absolutely essential.

 More information on using props is available on the Corwin Resources page at **https://resources.corwin.com/Cultivating Happiness**.

The Key: You, the Teacher

The key to successful yoga and meditative practices begins with your own preparation and insights. The most significant component is the teacher—your preparation, your enthusiasm, and your knowledge will have the greatest impact on the students' experience. Beyond space and time, yoga begins with your willingness to be led by the insights you learn as you practice.

Yoga can be conducted outdoors or indoors, in the heat of the blazing desert or the chill of a mountain pass. Most likely you will begin teaching yoga from your classroom or your home. You may or may not have an elaborate space with significant props. Our *Heart Beaming* (Mason & Banks, 2014) exercises, for example, are conducted from a standing position so that teachers can use them as yoga breaks, with students standing beside their desks *(available on the Corwin Resources page).* Younger students can participate as they do with circle time and exercises—from the carpet or mats.

To add to the ambience for your own practice and for your instruction, you might also consider a little aromatherapy with essential oils and a diffuser, but use caution as some students may have allergies or sensitivities to certain fragrances. Here are a few basic considerations:

- Let your own insights from your meditation, your practice, and your reflections guide you.

- When setting up yoga in a classroom, opt for adequate space between students so that they can stretch out without bumping into their classmates.

- Consider the comfort of students. Designate two to three students as your "yoga advisors" who help you make decisions about decorations, aromatherapy, and music, for example. You can also survey the class to get a sense of everyone's preferences. In addition to Spotify, YouTube, and Pandora, here are a couple of excellent websites for downloading yoga music:

   ○ Spirit Voyage (https://spiritvoyage.com)

- ○ Kundalini Meditation Experience: Chakra Practices for Yoga Workout and Energy Activation Music Awakening by Kundalini Yoga Music (https://music.apple.com/us/album/kundalini-meditation-experience-chakra-practices-for/981584969)
  - ○ Kundalini Music (www.last.fm/tag/kundalini)
  - ○ Kids Yoga Music Masters (https://music.apple.com/us/artist/kids-yoga-music-masters/986062133)
- Sometimes older students can be useful mentors or tutors to help with instruction and encouragement.

REFLECTIONS ON PREPARING TO TEACH YOGA-MINDFULNESS-MEDITATION

For the past 20 years, Christine Mason has taught adults in yoga and meditation classes, teaching two to five classes per week. Here are a few of her insights:

- I began slowly with a few minutes of a daily practice.

- I have learned a lot about my body, my breath, and my mind over the years. Sometimes, my experiences have helped me understand more about my students at a deeper level. I have a better understanding of grief, physical pain, the impact of sports injuries, feelings of inadequacy, and joy and happiness because of what I have learned, my reflection, and my teaching.

- As I teach, I learn from my students. I learn how to help them as they struggle to keep up.

- I have also learned from amazing teachers such as Krishna Kaur, our esteemed co-author. While I teach in an intimate setting, Krishna has taught thousands of students, filling tents to overflow. She has such a gift for inspiring students to keep up. Being in her presence as she teaches is truly one of the highlights of my yoga practice.

To keep things simple as she prepares to teach, Christine often follows a practice of practicing daily the yoga postures and sets, warm-ups, and meditations she will be teaching in her classes during the week. With this practice, she is able to integrate more deeply the benefits of the yoga sequence and to understand which specific warm-ups may help prepare students for a more difficult yoga session. This has worked for her, even as she is alert to variations that might be needed for one class or another. When she teaches, Christine sets her intention to be in sync with her students, and to be conscious of their needs and what she as a teacher needs to do to guide them as they learn.

MY YOGA-MINDFULNESS-MEDITATION READINESS TO TEACH

When it comes to your readiness to teach, we urge you to "begin where you are and do what you can." You can do much to help alleviate stress and uplift your students through your teaching.

Here are a few questions for your reflection:

1. I feel most prepared to teach which of the following?
   - ❑ Yoga
   - ❑ Mindfulness
   - ❑ Meditation

2. You can teach what you have practiced and what you love about the practices.
   - ❑ What have you practiced? Where is your comfort zone?
   - ❑ What do you love about your practice?
   - ❑ When you sit quietly, what insights do you gain about how to teach?

In-Person Instruction During a Pandemic

During a pandemic, such as COVID-19, certain precautions need to be taken when teaching yoga in a group setting. With the Delta variant, and uncertainty regarding vaccinations for children, it is important to be alert to guidelines that may shift to control outbreaks and keep all of us safe.

- Be sure to follow current Centers for Disease Control and Prevention (2019, 2021) guidelines regarding physical distancing and masks as well as district guidelines regarding the number of students and adults permitted in a classroom at one time.

- Teachers should wear a mask, and perhaps a face shield, and use a microphone to be heard.

- Keep students in their assigned cohort to minimize contact with large numbers of people.

- When possible, teach outside. When inside, open windows and doors to enhance airflow and ventilation.

- Students may bring their own mats or props so that these are not shared. Another option is to clean and disinfect equipment between classes or to practice without the use of props. Remember, students can always practice yoga and meditation seated in their chairs or standing near their desks.

- Do not touch students to adjust their postures. Instead, demonstrate the posture or provide verbal cues (such as "keep your shoulders down").

- Use special care during breathing exercises to reduce the spread of droplets. It might be best to save the more forceful exhalations for online instruction.

A Traveling Yoga Kit

Some yoga teachers visit several classrooms in a school or different schools during the day. For these teachers, a traveling yoga kit may be valuable. While many schools that offer yoga have a classroom or grade-level set of yoga mats and props, not all schools can afford these items. To increase equity by providing this service to all students, regardless of economic status, traveling yoga teachers can put together a kit to carry around with them wherever they teach. Consider applying for a grant to purchase a kit for your school or district if you have a traveling yoga teacher.

PREPARING YOUR OWN TRAVELING KIT

Here are some options for traveling yoga kits:

- *A Large Cart or Suitcase With Wheels.* This will be essential to carry large amounts of mats and props from place to place. Make sure the cart or suitcase you choose is light since you'll be lifting it in and out of your car and/or taking it up and down stairs.

- *Lightweight and/or Foldable Yoga Mats.* If you do an internet search for "travel" yoga mats, you'll find a variety of options at different price points for different qualities (e.g., Sol Salute, 2021). For example, two generic travel yoga mats from YOGAaccessories cost about $17, the Khataland YoFoMat® Kids is about $30, and the eKO® SuperLite Travel Yoga Mat from Manduka is $44.

- *Props.* You can easily fit a class or grade-level set of straps in your yoga kit, but blankets and blocks may be more difficult to take with you. You could include five or six sets of blocks for students who really need them, or you could ask students to bring four textbooks with them to class to use as blocks. Students can use coats and sweaters as blankets during the winter. Yoga towels can also be a thinner, lighter alternative to blankets for restorative poses that do require a blanket.

- *Cleaning Supplies.* Carry mat cleaner and reusable cloths or wet wipes to quickly sanitize the mats after each use. It can make students feel more comfortable to clean their own mats just before the practice, but make sure previous students also clean the mats after their practice before rolling them up.

- *Hand Broom and Dustpan.* When you're traveling, you can never predict what will happen in your yoga room before you arrive. Having a clean space helps students stay in the practice, so keep a mini-broom and dustpan set in your kit to quickly sweep up anything on the ground before rolling out the mats.

- *Watch.* Not every room will have a clock in it, so make sure to have a watch on your wrist or your phone nearby to check the time.

- *Wireless Speaker.* You may not have access to a sound system, so bring along a Bluetooth or Wi-Fi speaker to play music. Keep the charging chord with the speaker in case it runs out of batteries.

PLACES TO ACCESS YOGA SUPPLIES AND MATERIALS FOR SCHOOLS

Not every school or district can afford classroom or grade-level sets of yoga mats and props. Creative educators have found solutions to this problem, and many organizations have started programs to donate these items to students. One way educators can find funding to purchase yoga mats and props is by applying for grants available for social-emotional learning or physical education programs. You can also ask community members to donate gently used mats and props or do a yoga mat drive asking for new mats to be donated.

Additionally, you can reach out to one of the organizations listed in Figure 4.1, a local yoga studio, or other relevant nonprofits in your community to see if any of them can offer you mats, props, or other support for yoga programming.

Figure 4.1 • Yoga Supply Donations and Grants

ORGANIZATION AND OFFERING
Give Back Yoga Foundation (n.d.) offers yoga mats to teachers starting a new program.
Gaiam has offered yoga straps to nonprofit organizations (Gaiam Staff, n.d.).
YOGAaccessories (2021) has supplied mats and props to a variety of nonprofit organizations.
JadeYoga (n.d.) has donated yoga mats to many organizations, particularly to those that serve survivors of domestic violence or human trafficking, individuals experiencing homelessness, or children with special needs.
Yoga Activist (2013) offers grants of $300 for start-up yoga programs.

 Available at htttps://resources.corwin.com/CultivatingHappiness

Virtual Instruction

During the past year, teachers have learned to position cameras. We have had to consider lighting, background, using microphones, and sometimes even using webcams and external speakers. If you are teaching any movement activity at all, you have likely gone through phases of trying various camera angles. To prepare, practice with both close-up views that focus on the head and upper body and more distant shots where the camera needs to capture you standing, seated, and lying down.

Here are some things that teachers have done to enhance their virtual instruction:

- *Arrive at your space at least 15 minutes ahead of class* and turn on the web platform you are using to check how your space looks and sounds on camera before logging in to the class.

- *Consider using a microphone* or wireless headphones with a microphone to enhance sound. When teachers are far from their computers, sound can be difficult to capture.

- *Use a speaker or device not connected to your computer and remote control to manage music* so that you can start and stop background music without it overpowering your voice or requiring you to get up.

- *Get yourself into a place of calm before logging in to class.* Students can tell if you have just rushed to roll out your mat. Remember that your emotional state sets the stage for the emotional state of each student in your class.

- *Greet students as they arrive* and let them know you will start two or three minutes after the class time to give everyone time to log in and set up. Invite students to spend this time getting their space comfortable.

- *Invite students to keep their cameras on or off,* but to keep themselves on mute. Periodically scan the room to see if students are following instructions or to determine if you need to repeat a direction or offer accommodations. Remind the students that they can unmute themselves to ask questions and that it might be difficult for you to see the chat while you are teaching. *[Note: In some cases, as a classroom teacher, you may feel a need to request that students keep their cameras turned on. If so, please be sensitive to how students feel about this and consider what you can do to reduce their embarrassment. Sometimes it helps to start with smaller break-out rooms where students practice with a few of their peers, giving them exercises where they can have success. You can differentiate this instruction just as you do with academics. Or perhaps you can demonstrate, provide a handout, and then ask students to practice for a few days before returning to class with their cameras on.]*

- *Overemphasize the emotion you want to cultivate.* Expressing and understanding emotions via webcam can be more difficult, so add some extra pep if you are looking to energize through your yoga practice, or bring increased calm to your demeanor if your goal is to enhance relaxation.

- *Work with students* who can help demonstrate breath work and yoga poses and positions.

- *Ask students periodically to give you a "thumbs up"* if they can see/hear your instruction or to leave messages in the chat box.

- *Take extra time to focus the camera on your feet or hands* for specific positions.

- *Slow down the movements to practice new parts of a set.*

- *Take time to break down new techniques, positions, and practices.*

- *Offer a moment at the end of class for students to interact with each other* to build community. Students can share their favorite poses, offer how they feel, or engage in a brief team-building activity.

Using a camera provides an opportunity to develop a video archive; if you choose to do this, make sure you have signed parental permission.

The Extra Prep for Virtual Success

We recommend that you conduct a test run before your first virtual class so that you can make the following adjustments as needed. Record the test run and review:

- Adjust the volume and position the speakers close to your microphones. *[Note: Christine places a Bluetooth speaker only about 4–5 inches away from her webcam, which is attached to her laptop.]* Test out the sound at various distances from the microphone. Many newer computers have built-in webcams that work very well, and some instructors will use an iPod and their smartphone for recording classes. If you have a computer that is more than three or four years old, you may need an external webcam. Recent PCs have powerful cameras installed, and external webcams may not be needed. If you opt to purchase an external webcam, look for one that has a high-quality sound with stereo speakers.

- Practice going from seated to standing positions and adjust the angle of the camera so that you are visible in all positions. You may need to practice several times to become adept at quickly refocusing/repositioning the camera lens as you move from seating to standing to horizontal positions.

- Practice the "flow" of the set and instruction with minimal reference to your notes. *[Note: Christine places a few notes in large type or with photos or line drawings on the flow near the camera but out of range of the camera lens.]*

- Notice the appearance of your surroundings and whether the color of your clothing reduces or enhances students' ability to see your body movements. You may need to clear distracting clutter, put a sheet or blanket over a busy area, or bring a folding screen into your space. If you are wearing black clothing, for example, ensure that you are not blending in with a black TV set or piece of furniture behind you.

RESOURCES TO GUIDE YOGA INSTRUCTION

In addition to this book, many helpful yoga manuals and resources are available, a few of which are provided in Figure 4.2. Prices range from about $12 to $35. These can be used in group and individual activities. For example, cards from card decks can be placed at learning centers or in mindful moment rooms.

Figure 4.2 • Yoga Manual, Book, and Card Deck Resources

TITLE	AUTHOR	AGE GROUP	PURPOSE	EXAMPLE
Manuals				
Kids Yoga Class Ideas: Fun and Simple Yoga Themes With Yoga Poses and Children's Book Recommendations for Each Month	Giselle Shardlow (2018)	Ages 3–8	• Provides simple and convenient ways to add yoga into your curriculum, classes, or home life	Each of the 12 monthly themes includes five yoga poses for kids and five recommended children's books.
Create a Yoga Practice for Kids	Yael Calhoun and Matthew R. Calhoun (2006)	For adults to develop a practice for children ages 3–11	• Explains how to create a flowing yoga practice that holds kids' interest while providing the benefits of yoga • Also provides ideas for yoga games, yoga at a wall, more relaxation games, and five-minute classroom yoga	This book is broken down into various themes and the poses that fit into these categories. It guides you through various practices and how you can skillfully take a child through the various sequences.

TITLE	AUTHOR	AGE GROUP	PURPOSE	EXAMPLE
Picture Books				
Naiya in Nature: A Children's Guide to Yoga	Shazia Latif (2015)	Ages 4–8	• Teaches seven beginner yoga poses, to breathe, and to smile	This book is a narrative that goes through the daily life of a young girl, Naiya, who uses her yoga skills to manage her stress and emotions.
Dragon Yoga: Contact Your Inner Muse—A Children's Book	Roberta Berta-O Freedom (2019)	Ages 1–4	• Includes a creatively illustrated guide to take you through yoga poses	There is very little text in this book. It includes more illustrations that connect yoga poses to animals/shapes found in nature.
Calm Ninja: A Children's Book About Calming Your Anxiety Featuring the Calm Ninja Yoga Flow	Mary Nhin (2020)	Ages 3–11	• The new children's book series, Ninja Life Hacks, was developed to help children learn valuable life skills • Focuses more on breath work than active poses	This narrative follows Calm Ninja, who experiences frustration and anxiety until he learns how to find his inner peace by finding his breath and practicing the Ninja Yoga Flow.
Card Decks				
Yoga for Children—Yoga Cards: 50+ Yoga Poses and Mindfulness Activities for Healthier, More Resilient Kids	Lisa Flynn (2018)	All ages	• Designed for use by parents, teachers, and occupational therapists	Complete with full-color, easy-to-follow photographs and step-by-step instructions, this interactive deck includes more than 50 cards divided into four color-coded categories: Mindful Me mindfulness activities, Time to Breathe breathing exercises, Strike a Pose yoga poses, and Rest & Relax relaxation exercises.
Kids Yoga Adventure Card Deck	Jennifer Carter Avgerinos (2018)	All ages	• Includes three imaginary adventures at the beach, at the zoo, and through India, incorporating 42 fun yoga poses.	Each card presents a lively scene with easy instructions for the yoga pose on the back of the card.

(Continued)

(Continued)

TITLE	AUTHOR	AGE GROUP	PURPOSE	EXAMPLE
Card Decks				
Little Yogi Deck: Simple Yoga Practices to Help Kids Move Through Big Emotions	Crystal McCreary (2021)	Ages 5–9	• A colorful card deck featuring 48 simple yoga and mindfulness practices to help kids work through big emotions on and off the mat	The 48 cards are organized into eight color-coded categories—anger, worry, excitement, sadness, joy, jealousy, shame, and peace—to give kids specific practices for the variety of emotions they might be experiencing. Along with a practice, each card features a vibrant illustration to visually depict the pose or activity.
Trauma-Sensitive Yoga Deck for Kids: For Therapists, Caregivers, and Yoga Teachers	Kirsten Voris and Brooklyn Alvarez (2019)	All ages	• A deck of 50 yoga shapes was created for trauma-sensitive yoga facilitators and other counselors, social workers, and caregivers who work with children • Unlike a traditional yoga deck, this one is trauma informed, somatic focused, and ideal for use in a variety of settings including small groups, classrooms, and one-on-one	These cards do not feature any text, as the simple cards with no text encourage a more trauma-sensitive approach, and help kids focus on their own experience as they move through the poses.
Yoga Pretzels: 50 Fun Activities for Kids & Grownups	Tara Guber and Leah Kalish (2005)	All ages (some poses are more difficult so may be better for older children)	• Practice bending, twisting, breathing, relaxing, and more with this vibrant and colorful set of illustrated cards	This yoga deck features 50 cards that each include a pose, illustration, and written description of how to do it and its benefits. The poses are divided into nine categories: Breathe, Game, Balance, Stand, Forward Bend, Back Bend, Twist & Stretch, Partner, and Time In.

II. COMPONENTS OF YOGA-MINDFULNESS-MEDITATION INSTRUCTION

This next section of Chapter 4 presents information on explaining yoga-mindfulness-meditation to students, some basic considerations for using sound and music, the power of your presence and your voice, tuning in to and ending classes, and what to do as you teach. We begin with two examples of lesson plans on how to improve our ability to handle stress (see Figures 4.3 and 4.4).

Figure 4.3 • Lesson: Being Mindful of Stress

Lesson	Being Mindful of Stress
Length	20–22 minutes
Grade Level	Grades 6–12
Materials	• Copies of "Stress Can Feel Like a Roller Coaster" (activity adapted from Turner, 2021) • Pencils or pens
Objective	To practice using mindfulness to recognize positive and negative stress
Opening	Teacher says: • Our last lesson focused on recognizing when we're feeling stressed and noticing how different breathing strategies can be beneficial in reducing the stress and anxiety we experience. Remember that we all experience stress and it is a natural response that is giving a signal to our body. When we learn to recognize the signal, we can use strategies and tools, such as breath work, to reduce our stress and help us refocus. Today, we will learn a new strategy, which is using mindfulness to recognize stress and develop healthy habits to help reduce that stress. • We're going to begin by finding a comfortable seat. Remember that everyone is different and so you should focus on what feels best for your own body. • Feel free to close your eyes or gaze gently at what's in front of you. Now, focus on your breath. Begin by breathing naturally and notice what that feels like. Then, take three deep breaths. Inhale deeply and hold. Now, exhale slowly. Inhale deeply again and hold. Now, exhale slowly. Last time—inhale deeply and hold. Now, exhale slowly. • Tune into how your body is feeling now. Do you notice a difference between how you felt before and how you feel now?
Sequence	• Follow directions embedded in the "Stress Can Feel Like a Roller Coaster" article. This includes: • 5 minutes to read and reflect • 5–7 minutes of discussion with peers • 3 minutes of visualization • 5–7 minutes for closure (see the next row)

(Continued)

(Continued)

Closure	Teacher says:
	• We all experience challenges throughout our lives. Sometimes it feels like those challenges keep piling up, and other times you may just be experiencing a small challenge. While it may be difficult in the moment, remember that these times are only temporary. Similar to a roller coaster, we all experience ups and downs. When we're experiencing the downs, it may be hard to remember it in the moment. When we are focused on a stressor or worry, it may feel like we are stuck. However, we can use mindfulness techniques to reduce our worries and stress.
	• While it's important to recognize negative thoughts, you can use something called a positive affirmation to help you change your thinking. We're going to try one now. Being by lowering your gaze or closing your eyes. Listen to the affirmation and then repeat it to yourself silently: *I am resilient; I will get through this difficult time. I will inhale the good and exhale the bad.* (Repeat 3 to 5 times.)
Supplementary Resources	Journaling is one way to further reduce stress and worry. You can use the prompts available from Journal Buddies (2021).
	In addition, you can adapt these prompts and encourage students to express themselves creatively through other art forms such as drawing and music. Here are some examples:
	• Draw a picture of a something that brings you peace or joy.
	• Write a song about your worry or stress and what you can do to reduce it.

online resources → Available at https://resources.corwin.com/CultivatingHappiness

Figure 4.4 • Lesson: Using Visualization to Revise Negative Thought Patterns and Feel a Sense of Safety and Peace

Lesson	Using Visualization to Revise Negative Thought Patterns and Feel a Sense of Safety and Peace
Suggested Length	20–30 minutes
Suggested Grade Level	Grades 6–12
Materials	"Guided Imagery: Create the State You Want" (Allina Health, 2015a)
	"Self-Guided Imagery Activity" (Allina Health, 2015b)
Objective	To understand how guided imagery can be used to diminish negative thought patterns
Opening	Teacher says:
	• Sometimes we catch ourselves in a negative feedback loop. In other words, we keep replaying a negative thought or scenario over and over in our heads. When this happens, it can be tough to change our thought pattern into a more positive one. Today we're going to talk about using visualization, or sometimes guided imagery, to change the negative feedback loop into a more positive one that helps us take action to reduce the stress or worry.

Sequence	Teacher says:
	• Begin by remembering a time when you were stuck in a negative feedback loop. In other words, you kept replaying a negative thought about yourself over and over again in your head.
	○ What were you thinking?
	○ What was the experience like?
	○ How did you feel emotionally? What did your body feel like?
	○ Were you able to get out of the negative feedback loop? Were there techniques or strategies you used to help reduce the negative thoughts and move forward?
	• Maybe you already have some techniques and strategies that work for you. If so, great! Today we're going to add another tool to our toolbox. This tool is called visualization, and it is a strategy that can help you get rid of the negative thought patterns. Now, I'm going to walk you through the strategy.
	○ Begin by finding a comfortable position. It can be at your desk or finding a seat on the floor.
	○ Next, close your eyes or look down toward the floor.
	○ Think back to a time when you had a negative thought that kept repeating in your head over and over again and prevented you from thinking about anything else.
	○ We're now going to listen to a visualization. [The teacher will play the visualization from Shanti Generation (2013).]
	○ Take three long, slow, and deep breaths—in through your nose, out through your mouth. When you are ready, return to your surroundings and open your eyes. Complete a mind/body scan. Do you feel any different? How has your thinking changed? How does your body feel? Is it more relaxed?
Closure	Please leave 10–15 minutes for closure.
	Teacher says:
	• Your shelter can help reduce negative thought patterns and help your emotions and body to experience a sense of peace and calm. Using the paper provided to you, draw a picture of the shelter you visualized. Try to include as many details as possible. Then, discuss the following with a partner:
	○ Why did you choose to draw the shelter the way you did? What does it represent?
	○ How might this shelter be helpful in reducing negative thoughts in the future?
Supplementary Resources	Have students visualize an image of "stress" and "stress-free" environments using the "Create the State You Want" worksheet from Allina Health (2014). Students can share with a partner or in small groups.

 Available at https://resources.corwin.com/CultivatingHappiness

YOGA-MINDFULNESS-MEDITATION INSTRUCTION

In Chapter 1, we explained that we do not believe in an approach to teaching yoga-mindfulness-meditation as purely physical exercises. Research has shown that yoga-mindfulness-meditation not only helps to improve muscle tone and fitness; it also leads to improvements in executive function, aids in alleviating stress and improving mindset, and contributes to improving one's outlook. Similarly, as we teach students, we find value in

> Research has shown that yoga-mindfulness-meditation not only helps to improve muscle tone and fitness; it also leads to improvements in executive function, aids in alleviating stress and improving mindset, and contributes to improving one's outlook.

describing the *impact* of specific breathing exercises, yoga postures, yoga sets, and meditations.

You will see this book refer to what we as yoga teachers have learned. There are yoga postures and sets that help with posture, activities that relieve stress on our bodies, breaths that calm us, and breaths that increase our alertness. In a similar manner, we can turn to meditations that include affirmations to increase a sense of confidence and courage, meditations that lead to feelings of safety and security, and guided visualizations that increase our sense of hope, help us become more aware of our emotions, and increase our compassion for ourselves and others. As teachers, we take the time to explain this to students in ways that are developmentally appropriate.

BENEFITS OF YOGA FOR STUDENTS

Carrie Vieira, a mindfulness and yoga teacher in Maryland, describes the benefits of yoga for the students she teaches.

> Yoga is a journey of self-discovery. Students learn to be fully present to this moment as they breathe deeply and move their bodies in ways that can increase their energy, improve their mood, and help them find inner balance. Yoga is about experiencing the connection between the body, the mind, and the breath. Everything that happens in yoga can have effects at both the physical and emotional level.

- As students bring their bodies into balancing postures, they learn to better regulate their emotions and stay centered.

- As students build strength in their muscles, they find the inner strength to deal with life's challenges.

- As students increase flexibility in their joints, they learn to navigate change with greater ease.

Sound and Music

Sound and music play important parts in mindfulness and yoga practice. Incorporating music into a practice can enhance mood, create a calming ambience, and help students feel more comfortable turning their attention inward.

- In the yoga presented in this text, we have identified the music used in the classes as they were originally taught. When teaching specific sets, you may want to use this music, or it is also fine to teach a class without music.

- Generally speaking, you'll want to select music that matches the goal of the practice. For a more meditative mindfulness practice, you will want to use songs without lyrics and that are pleasing and relaxing to the ear.

- For an energizing yoga practice with a lot of movement, it may be more appropriate to play something upbeat or something with lyrics that help guide the students' movements.

- Since everyone has different preferences when it comes to music, you can poll your students to learn and integrate their preferences into the practice. YouTube, Spotify, Pandora, and Apple Music are just a few of the many different places you can go to find songs well suited for meditation and yoga.

While the use of music can create a beautiful experience for students, there will also be times when you want to balance the experience of sound and music with the experience of silent awareness. Consider building in a minute at the end of the practice where the music fades away, and where students can sit quietly with just the sound of their breath mingling with the natural sounds of the room around them. Invite students to relax into this space of stillness and to notice how they feel.

Use of Mantra and Chants

Vocalizations are also a powerful tool in yoga and meditation practice. Words vibrate when spoken and can have a palpable energy for both the speaker and the listener. Hearing someone say the word *peaceful* out loud has a very different effect on a listener than hearing someone say the word *bomb*. Reciting positive affirmations, repeating words with positive connotations, and using chants or mantra are all ways that students can tune into the restorative effect of sound vibrations.

Some people seem to fall in love with mantra and chants almost immediately. Others will find mantra or chants to be less appealing or valuable. These practices are rarely taught outside of a yoga-mindfulness-meditation arena, so many of us may have had no exposure to them prior to learning about yoga-mindfulness-meditation, and we may even be skeptical as to their value. Yoga-mindfulness-meditation can be taught with or without integrating mantra or chants. As you are comfortable, we encourage you to try a few chants, repeating sounds or words for even three to five minutes as you sit calmly with your eyes closed and focused on the space between your brows. Sometimes appreciation of mantra and chanting increases with practice. You may even want to try chanting with an instructor from a YouTube channel.

- *Har* (which is pronounced with the tip of the tongue flicking the roof of the mouth; the *r* is lightly rolled) is chanted at a somewhat moderate pace as you pull your navel point to your spine with your eyes closed, focused on the space between the brows or brow point. Chanting this can be useful in increasing your sense of energy or elevating your mood or thoughts.

- Mantra may improve your immunity, improve your circulation, or enhance your attention and focus. (Sadhana Yoga School, 2021)

SING SONG YOGA®

The Sing Song Yoga app, Version 2.0 (Sing Song Yoga, 2020), is designed especially for kids and uses song lyrics to teach students specific yoga poses. The program can be used to explore and practice individual yoga poses or can be customized to create a sequence of poses the group wants to practice together. The Thornapple Kellogg School District in Michigan has found success with this app in classrooms across grade levels. Kindergarten teacher Jasmine Koster said the app "reinforces concentration and gives students a brain break" and that she "always receives positive feedback from the families" who use it (Farrise, 2019; Thornapple Kellogg Schools, n.d.).

---

online resources ➤ More information about Sing Song Yoga available at https://resources.corwin.com/CultivatingHappiness

YOUR PRESENCE AND YOUR VOICE

> To prepare to teach a yoga session to students, it is helpful to take a few deep breaths, even perhaps finding a few moments to "center in" and let go of any of your concerns of the day.

One of the wonderful things about teaching yoga is how instructors learn to use their voice to help calm and reassure students—certainly, a useful tool in times of stress! To prepare to teach a yoga session to students, it is helpful to take a few deep breaths, even perhaps finding a few moments to "center in" and let go of any of your concerns of the day. Centering involves bringing ourselves to a place of stillness, one where we are not distracted and we feel a sense of balance and peacefulness. Yogis sometimes refer to this as a "neutral ground" where we are not unduly swayed by emotions, whether we are soaring high or experiencing depression or sadness.

As you practice chanting and instructing yoga, you may find that with the deep breathing and your focused awareness, your voice automatically takes on a calm, peaceful characteristic. Listen to a few yoga teachers online resources ➤ (*audio links are available on the Corwin Resources page*) and practice, perhaps even recording yourself or asking others for feedback, until you feel you have successfully achieved this state of being a calming presence.

Tuning In: Mental Focus

As yoga teachers, prior to beginning our classes, we focus on our intention to teach our students. We do this first by mentally thinking, "I am a teacher."

Tuning In

Your authors center or "tune in" individually and then later with their classes. One way of helping students tune in is by starting the class with a recitation or chant. For example, you can pick a word or phrase that you and the students recite or chant together to start the class on a positive note. Some examples of words you can use are *truth*, *peace*, or *love* or even a phrase such as *we are success* or *we are we*. Sometimes students chant their own names to center in. Sometimes classes choose a word to chant together, or students may tune in silently, anchoring their session with a moment of quiet reflection.

For the practices from kundalini yoga marked with an asterisk (*), it is traditional to tune in out loud using the mantra *Ong Namo Guru Dev Namo*, which translates to "I call upon the infinite wisdom that exists within and beyond us." This is typically repeated three times.

 Audio links are available on the Corwin Resources page at **https://resources.corwin.com/CultivatingHappiness**.

Krishna Kaur (2006) says in her Y.O.G.A. for Youth manual that by tuning in, we

> set the tone and create an open space for the young people to experience themselves. . . . Creating a repeated ritual establishes a code of conduct for the students, honoring themselves, each other, and the blessings of the ancient teachings. It allows a class to take on an organic sense of organization and cooperation from within each participant. (p. 9)

Your presence—undistracted and focused on being fully present for your students—tells your students you care, and that you are available to support them. If you are tuning in with students, it is helpful to sit or stand in a position of balance—a balanced spine with each side of the body symmetrical to the other. Close your eyes and focus your attention on the space between the brows or brow point—a place we often focus on with breathing, yoga, and meditation. With our eyes closed, focused on the space between the brows or brow point, we are drawing energy to the hypothalamus and pituitary glands, which are master glands that impact mood, metabolism, and thinking (see Chapter 1).

Ending a Class

Just as we have established a standard practice for opening a yoga class, we also have a routine for ending the class. This routine, depending on which components you include, may take from one to five minutes. Once again, we sit or stand, with eyes closed, in a position of balance and symmetry. We announce that we are ending the class with a mantra. As yoga instructors, we learned the mantra *Sat Nam*, which means "truth is our identity."

You may also select your own ending mantra. It might be *Peace be with you* or *Truth be with you* or *Peace, truth, love.*

 We also have followed a practice of singing a few lines from "Long Time Sun" (*audio available on the Corwin Resources page at* **https://resources.corwin.com/CultivatingHappiness**).

ADDITIONAL ENDINGS

Christine Mason adds a wish for the world that she was taught by one of her first yoga teachers. It is repeated by her students: "Bless this earth with peace, love, and healing."

Concerned about children around the world, for the past 15 years, Christine and her yoga students complete the ending to their class with a positive thought for their own lives, reflecting for a moment on current needs (for vaccines, for wise leaders, for safety) and then repeating together:

"For children around the world" (pause for repetition)

"May they be healthy" (pause)

"May they be happy" (pause)

"May they be safe" (pause)

"May they be loved" (pause)

We encourage you to either follow our suggestions or develop your own routine or ritual for ending the class.

WHEN YOU TEACH

When your authors were prepared as yoga instructors, they learned how to present an entire sequence to students. With this, we tuned in, taught our yoga classes in a specific sequence, and then ended our class. However, when you are teaching one breath, one movement, or one meditation, while you may choose to silently tune in, you may also follow the standard protocol:

- Becoming centered, taking a couple of deep breaths, mentally tuning in if you choose, and providing an instruction.

- Modeling the movement, breath, or meditation if needed.

- Guiding the students through a few moments of practice.

- Encouraging students to "keep up" to "challenge, but not injure, themselves."

- Finding ways to suggest modifications without embarrassing students who may be struggling. It might be helpful to say "Another way to do this is ____" rather than "If you are having difficulty, try ____."

- Following a sequence that is often used with a yoga session, including warm-ups, breath work, a yoga set, relaxation, and meditation.

Warm-Ups

Yoga often starts with warm-ups, which involves warming up our spine and limbs to prepare us for the more intensive work of getting into and maintaining specific poses. In Chapter 3, we presented the spinal flex series, which is often used as a warm-up. During COVID-19, when many of us are less active and are spending more time in front of screens, many are turning to some standing variations.

Consider the following sequence:

- *Hip rotations.* Stand up, with feet shoulder-width apart and hands on your hips. Begin hip rotations, inhaling back and exhaling forward. Reverse directions. Next, move your feet further apart so your stance is wider. Continue for 2 minutes.

- *Running or jogging* in place for 2–3 minutes.

- *Squats.* Arms are out in front of you. Exhale as you squat down and inhale as you come up. Continue for 1–2 minutes.

- *Frogs.* Begin in a squat position, low to the ground, like a frog seated on a lily pad. Inhale in this position. As you exhale, come to standing in a forward bend position, buttocks toward the ceiling and head toward your knees. Go back to the inhale position and keep going for 5–20 frogs.

- *Mountain pose.* Stand straight, arms hanging loosely by your sides, knees straight but not locked. Eyes are closed, focused on the space between the brows or brow point. Breathe long and deep. This is a standing relaxation position.

Breath Work

Breath work done at the beginning of class or after a transition can calm students' brains and bodies. This can be especially beneficial for students who experience anxiety before a big test or presentation. Students should sit comfortably with an upright spine.

- *Belly breathing:* Placing one hand on the belly, feel the belly rise on the inhale and fall on the exhale.

- *Bunny breath:* Take three rapid inhales through the nose followed by a long exhale.

- *Lion's breath:* Take a deep inhale through the nose and a "roaring" exhale through the mouth.

- *Straw breath:* Inhale and exhale through a rolled tongue.

- *Spider-Man/Elsa breaths:* Clench fists to charge up webs/ice as you inhale through the nose, and open the hands with the palms up to release the webs/ice as you exhale through the mouth.

- *Alternate nostril breathing:* After taking a full inhale through the nose, use the right thumb to plug the right nostril and exhale out the left. Inhale through the left nostril and then use your right pinky to plug the left nostril. Exhale out the right nostril, then inhale through the right nostril.

Demonstrating Positions and Movements

When introducing a new yoga pose to students, take extra time to break down the steps and demonstrate the pose. Many yoga poses are named after animals, and you can capitalize on this connection to engage your students, especially the younger ones, as well as to help them better understand the shape and feel of the pose. For example, in cobra pose, have the students imagine being a snake lying on its belly, lifting its head and chest up into the air as it hisses aloud.

When working with older students, you can incorporate more precise language to help them develop awareness of their bodies and find proper alignment. For example, with cobra, you can tell older students to roll their shoulders up and back and squeeze their shoulder blades together as they press their palms and fingers into the mat and lift their head and chest off the ground (Dunin, 2019).

Timing and Pacing

As you teach, you will learn to adjust your yoga session according to the available time, abilities, and needs of your students. For a 15- to 30-minute class, you may find the following agenda to be helpful—vary this as needed.

SUGGESTED AGENDA FOR A 15- TO 30-MINUTE SESSION

- Introduction: Provide a 1- to 2-minute statement about the purpose of the day's session. You might wish to tell a story of your experience with a component of the session.

- Brief physical warm-up (3–5 minutes).

- Breath work and tuning in (3–5 minutes).

- Movement (yoga set) (7–15 minutes).

- Meditation (2–7 minutes).

- Ending class (2 minutes).

Timing and Using Timers

Many yoga manuals will suggest that a particular part of a yoga set be practiced for a specified length of time. The rule we have learned is that the time listed represents the "maximum" length of time for practicing a certain part of the set. This can be adjusted according to available time and needs of the students. We recommend adjusting the time for each part of the set proportionately (e.g., you could adjust a set from 20 to 10 minutes by cutting the length of each part of the set in half). You can teach with timers, setting either a stopwatch or an alarm on a cell phone, for example. You can also simply watch the time and estimate.

As You Teach: Observing Your Students and Making Accommodations

One of the basic premises of yoga-mindfulness-meditation is that it is not about competition with others. Yoga provides us an opportunity to become more aware of ourselves, our breathing, our abilities, and our needs. It also provides an opportunity to *challenge ourselves*. This means stretching our capacity and pushing our own limits, but not to the point of injury.

> Yoga provides us an opportunity to become more aware of ourselves, our breathing, our abilities, and our needs. It also provides an opportunity to *challenge ourselves*. This means stretching our capacity and pushing our own limits, but not to the point of injury.

- We do this to build capacity, stamina, strength, and confidence, and to increase our metacognitive awareness of what we are capable of learning.

- We also stretch our abilities with a little stress during the safety of a yoga class, making it easier to apply skills we learn in yoga to more complex, and sometimes more difficult, situations that occur outside of class. For example, if we learn to shift from feeling anxious to feeling calm in class, we can generalize these skills and apply them in other situations. A part of the responsibility of the teacher is to observe students, and then to adjust the length of a session, the length of time a posture is held, or the number of repetitions according to the capabilities of the students. So, we want to teach so that the most advanced or capable yoga students feel inspired and interested, but also so others are not demoralized by a sense of frustration.

As you teach, you can help students figure out what works for them by using phrases such as these:

- "Do the best you can."

- "If you need to take a few seconds to relax, put your arms down/come to center and relax, then return to the activity."

- "Remember to challenge, but not injure, yourself."

As you teach yoga in school settings, never touch a student to make an adjustment or help a student understand a posture or position.

Keeping Students Interested and Engaged

As with other classroom instruction, teachers who have adequately planned and organized their yoga instruction are likely to experience greater success. Here are a few pointers:

- Ensure that you have practiced and know the material you will be teaching.

- Have materials close by.

- Plan out the sequence of activities ahead of time. Consider elements that you include in other lesson plans such as the introduction (and hook to get students' attention), modeling and demonstration, increasing student understanding, clearly stating directions, giving students opportunities to practice, and how to close the lesson.

- Ensure that the instructions you present are clear, consider when you will need to model or demonstrate a breath or pose, and have an idea of when you might need to provide greater detail and more specific instructions. Instructions for younger students will usually be brief—possibly even as brief as "hop like a bunny" or "hiss like a snake." For older students, it is often useful to provide more precise instructions, such as "sit straight with your navel point pulled back to your spine, and elongate your spine as you stretch upward."

- For older students, be aware of what might be embarrassing and consider whether at times it might be helpful to teach smaller groups of students.

- Plan instruction so students can have success. Challenge them, but stay in that "zone of proximal development" so that students are interested and challenged, but not to the point of frustration.

- Give students helpful feedback, cheering them on and encouraging their efforts.

Encouraging Students

As you teach, periodically give general praise and encouragement. Phrases such as "Way to go!," "Great work!," "Looks good," and "You're doing great! Keep going!" are all helpful. Other phrases such as "Come on, stay with it!" or "We are almost there!" are also helpful. Christine on occasion will tell her students, "Wow. That was wonderful. We practiced for 15 minutes!"

Remember that your interest and enthusiasm are contagious. Students often enjoy hearing about you or your family, or other students you have taught. For example, over the years, as yoga teachers, we have often engaged in 40-day practices, where we practice the same yoga set for 40 consecutive days. (According to yogic teachings, it takes 40 days to learn a new habit and for transformation to occur.)

A 40-DAY PRACTICE

Christine will often share that a particular set was "one of my 40-day practices" or that "as I practiced this over 40 days, I found that I perfected the posture and more fully appreciated the impact of the set." She often shares with her students when she is conducting another 40-day practice, saying "right now I am on day 20 of the set for the pituitary gland; what I most appreciate about this set is that not only is it becoming easier, but I continue to feel better and better each day." In preparing for instruction for the coming weeks, she may ask students about what they want to work on. For example, there are specific postures or sets for body parts (e.g., back or neck exercises), metabolism or energy, and a sense of safety or calmness; meditations to reduce brain fatigue and increase alertness; eye exercises to reduce eye strain; postures to improve balance; and breath work to eliminate toxins.

A few guidelines to make sure students are following along and being respectful of you and each other. As yoga teachers, we sometimes become so involved in our instruction that we may find that we struggle with how to handle students who are disruptive or inappropriate. If you find, for example, that students are talking over you, you can pause and wait until everyone is quiet to proceed. You might also reflect on what is happening. Is a student bored or feeling inadequate? Is a student talking out because it is really hard for that student to sit still? Or are directions too complex?

Yoga teachers often begin their reflection about disruptive behavior by tuning into their own inner processes and awareness, including whether or not, as the disruptive behavior began, they were able to make a shift in their instruction or be sensitive to student needs. We urge you to be aware that yoga or meditation will sometimes produce an increased awareness within students, including an increased awareness of a student's own trauma (see Chapter 6). When this happens, students may become uncomfortable or disruptive to escape unpleasant thoughts or feelings. Sometimes pulling a student aside for a private discussion may be helpful (see also *Mindfulness Practices: Cultivating Heart Centered Communities Where Students Focus and Flourish* [2019, pp. 103–110], where Mason, Rivers-Murphy, and Jackson discuss practices recommended by Paul Gilbert).

Consider also if there is something more you need to do. When you prepare, are you factoring in information on student attention span and interests? Reflect on what you love to teach and where you have had the greatest success. Do you need older students to help set a positive role model for your students? Or is it time to use additional props, incorporate music they like, or even consider how to structure classes for different groups of students? Can you use learning centers, for example, with a yoga center, a relaxation center, and a meditation corner with a guided visualization app?

To help you anticipate possible problems and how you will handle them, we recommend that prior to starting yoga, breath work, or meditation with your classes, consider how you will handle discipline issues that might arise.

The most important thing when encountering students' resistance is to meet that resistance with deep compassion and empathy. Yoga and meditation should never be forced on a student; instead, here are some ideas for what you can do when students are resistant:

- Work together with the students to find an alternative activity that they can do during yoga or meditation practice that *does not involve them leaving the room*. It is important that students stay in the classroom even if they are not engaging in the practice, so they can still benefit from the experience of the calming energy of the space. Staying with the class also conveys that the students are welcome and accepted in the community as they are, and it provides an opportunity for the students to grow more comfortable with yoga and meditation over time. Discuss some alternative activities these students may quietly engage in while the rest of the class is practicing yoga or meditation. Some examples include drawing, journal writing, reading, and quiet reflection. Let the students take the lead in identifying what would work best for them.

- Emphasize that if at any point they decide they want to give the practice a try, they are always welcome to do so.

- Periodically check in with resistant students to see what questions they may have and how their ideas about yoga and meditation may be evolving over time. Demonstrating your care can make all the difference.

YOGA CLASSROOM MANAGEMENT STRATEGIES

- How do you normally handle discipline issues with your students?

- Do you think those same procedures will work when teaching yoga?

- What issues are likely to arise?

- How will you handle them?

- Could these disruptions be opportunities for listening circles and even consideration of restorative practices (see Chapter 11)?

- Do you have someone in school to help you plan and make decisions and adjustments for students who may be disruptive?

Signs of Fatigue and Avoiding Injuries

Some adults (and children) need extra guidance about how much is too much. When Christine observes fatigue, she says in the middle of the part of an exercise, "Now come to standing (or sitting) and take a few deep breaths." She guides the students to do that together; and then she says, "Okay, back in position for 40 more seconds" (or whatever is appropriate).

When Christine scans a room (whether in person or online), some of the things she looks for are:

- Students who have already paused; when several students have paused on their own, it may be a good time to think of shortening the length of time a movement is practiced.

- Students whose form demonstrates difficulty keeping up (lack of alignment).

- Students whose facial expressions show signs of frustration.

As yoga teachers, we are interested in relieving stress, not adding to our students' concerns, regrets, or feelings of inadequacy. When we see any of these, we may add words of encouragement, reminding students to take a break as needed or suggesting a modification that may be useful.

Some useful modifications include:

- Continuing the same movement, but lowering the arms slightly.

- Doing an exercise from an alternative position. For example, instead of rock pose, some people find it easier to stay in easy pose (see Chapter 6 for a discussion of rock pose).

- For seated forward bends, move from the hips and keep the neck in alignment with the spine rather than bending the neck to try to bring the head to the knee.

As yoga/movement teachers, we want to use care, as we don't want to find out that a student has been injured. Common injuries may be pulling a shoulder muscle, wrist injuries created by putting too much pressure on our wrists, pulling back muscles by overextending during seated forward bends, knee pain from squatting for too long, or strain from using muscles that aren't used to a new position.

 Visit https://aaptiv.com/magazine/common-yoga-injuries for a site that discusses common yoga injuries (Dellitt & Barajas, n.d.).

You can also avoid injuries by not teaching headstands or other advanced yoga poses that require more strength, endurance, or specific alignment. Instruction of these postures should be reserved for a certified yoga teacher who has had specific training in anatomy and physiology and how to teach these poses. Even in these instances, save this instruction for students with more advanced skills.

Props can also be of assistance, although many yoga sets can be taught without them.

TEACHING MEDITATION

Students live in a world that overstimulates their senses and draws their attention to many different places all at once. Meditation has the opposite effect; it draws students' attention inward to a single point and helps them grow comfortable with stillness. However, because students are so unaccustomed to stillness and quiet, they may initially find meditation boring or too hard. Just like eating their vegetables, children may be reluctant to do something that is healthy and good for them because it's not as fun or as interesting as eating an ice cream sundae.

Two key practices will help teachers find success when teaching meditation: (1) start with a short practice and gradually increase the length over time; and (2) don't give up!

Start Small

Meditation requires students to build new internal habits. Students are simply not used to holding their attention on a single point for an extended period of time, so when you first introduce meditation, start with a practice as short as 30–60 seconds. By scanning the room, you can see which students are moving into stillness and which students are growing restless. Use these visual cues to help you gauge how long the practice should be. As you notice more and more students fidgeting, start bringing the practice to a close. The next time you practice, lengthen the time by 30 seconds, and again, scan the room for your clue as to when it is time to wrap up.

A great focal point for students when they first start out is their breath. Have students bring their attention to their breathing and quietly focus on the movement of the breath. Students might find it helpful to count the breath in and out to keep the attention focused. Gently prompt students to bring their attention back to their breath anytime they notice that a thought has brought their attention elsewhere.

Another great focal point for students is their sense of sound. Have students bring their attention to the sounds they hear and invite them to simply listen to those sounds, without any inner dialogue describing those sounds. Ask them to first notice the sounds that come from within their bodies; then they can shift their focus to the sounds that come from within the classroom; lastly, they can turn their attention to the sounds coming from beyond the classroom walls.

Don't Give Up

We have heard from teachers on a number of occasions that meditation "just doesn't work" for their students. These teachers have tried to incorporate mindful moments into their classes, but they see how restless or

> Students live in a world that overstimulates their senses and draws their attention to many different places all at once. Meditation has the opposite effect; it draws students' attention inward to a single point and helps them grow comfortable with stillness.

uninterested the students become, and they abandon the effort, thinking that meditation is not going to engage their students.

It's important to recognize that meditation requires students' brains to work in different ways than they are used to. It requires the creation of new neural pathways and the development of new habits. These shifts take time, and a period of discomfort and restlessness in the beginning is natural and to be expected. The key is to stay anchored in your own practice and to keep modeling steadiness and stillness. As we mentioned earlier, the students will eventually follow your lead!

Remember also—and explain this to students—that it is the *practice* of meditation that can be transformative. Even as we practice meditation, we are getting rid of some of the clutter and freeing up neuropathways to be more available for learning. Arriving at a place of bliss or an empty mind, while an amazing experience, is not the be-all-end-all, and even having these as goals can interfere with the value and intent of the meditative process. Remember that there are a thousand and one different meditations. We provide you opportunities to learn about many of these in this book. While one approach may not resonate with you or any particular student, it is likely that another meditation will. Meditating on an empty mind is a more difficult practice than some of the other meditations, so help to ensure that students have varying experiences. Over time, many of us have learned to love and rely on some very specific meditations (see Chapters 6–10).

STUDENTS AS CO-LEADERS

As students grow more comfortable with practicing yoga and meditation, you can begin inviting them to co-lead practices with you. Collaborating with students in this way not only empowers them and elevates their voice, but it also helps with getting some of the more reluctant students to buy in. It would be best for this practice to be strictly voluntary and not linked to any grades, incentives, or rewards.

Create a structure or process for students who are interested in co-leading meditation or yoga sessions for their peers:

1. Tell students how they can let you know if and when they are interested in serving as a co-lead. This could involve sending you a message via email, filling out a survey or form, or coming to speak to you after class or at lunch.

2. Work with students to identify the topic or practice they will focus on, and brainstorm ideas together for what the practice could look like.

3. Have students come in at lunch or after school to practice with you beforehand.

STUDENTS AS CO-LEADERS

Christine has often entered a school to provide instruction to students and arranged for two or three student volunteers to come up front with her and serve as co-leaders. It is amazing what students can do to help instruct yoga, even if they have never done yoga or a specific posture before. There is something magical that happens when peers see their fellow students helping to co-lead.

III: INTEGRATING YOGA, MINDFULNESS, AND MEDITATION WITH ACADEMIC INSTRUCTION

Teachers have many options for integrating mindfulness practices into their instruction. Some best practices include:

- Opening each class with a mindful moment to create a welcoming space and set the tone for the class.

- Incorporating mindfulness practices before taking a test or any type of educational experience that may create stress or anxiety.

- Using mindfulness practices to help students navigate turbulent times, such as when the school or the nation experiences a tragedy.

It is especially important to understand that mindfulness does not always need to interrupt the natural flow of the class. The more often you practice mindfulness with students, the more it will become an integrated part of the way your classroom runs. Here are some examples of what that could look like, regardless of the grade level or subject area you teach:

- Students apply the metacognitive skills they develop through meditation practice to notice distracting thoughts that cause them to lose focus in class. They apply mindfulness techniques to refocus their attention.

- Compassion and kindness serve as the foundation of the relationships between you and the students as well as among the students themselves.

- Classroom discourse is guided by respect, active listening, and empathy.

- Positive affirmations provide students with the motivation and confidence they need when working through challenging academic material.

Yoga-mindfulness-meditation can also reduce student stress; increase our conscious understanding of others; and open up our minds to take risks, be more creative, or delve deeper as we learn. As we will explain in Chapters 6–10, yoga-mindfulness-meditation can be paired with academic and extracurricular subjects to enhance learning and understanding. To provide one small example, if we are studying about courageous leaders, we could teach yoga-mindfulness-meditation exercises to enhance our own feelings of courage and resilience.

A MINDFULNESS INTERVENTION ROOM

More and more schools are setting up mindfulness intervention rooms as an alternative to punitive practices. These rooms are used for students "to chill out." They are often smaller, more intimate spaces, sometimes with cushions on the floor, soft lighting, and music. Sometimes students opt to self-regulate by asking for permission to go to the meditation room. At other times, a student sees a counselor to discuss an issue and get advice, and then a teacher who has been trained in breath work, yoga, and meditation may be available to advise the student about a specific breath or meditation.

Sometimes students are given a mantra or affirmation to repeat (see the section on music and sound in this chapter). Sometimes the mantra is repeated aloud, in a whisper, or mentally. Here are a few you may find useful. Some are coordinated with the breath.

- I am calm. I am at peace.
- I breathe in peace and love. I breathe out fear and anger.
- I am successful.
- I am caring.
- I am loved.
- I am strong and resilient.
- I am improving each and every day.

Students may be particularly anxious or emotional when they first enter a mindfulness meditation room. Remember that in moments of great angst, students may find it hard to calm themselves down and begin a meditation or affirmation. It may be good to engage in some breath work or physical yoga or activity first.

- A good breath to help get rid of anger is cannon breath. With cannon breath, we focus on a strong exhale, pulling in the stomach as we blow out a strong exhale. Cannon breath may be repeated a few times or for a few minutes.

- Get to know your students. Some students will quickly adapt as they learn to rely on the mindfulness meditation room to help self-regulate. These students may need to use it frequently, particularly during the first few weeks after it is introduced. Some students will feel better if they talk with a counselor or other caring adult before the breath work or yoga. Other students calm down more quickly when they start with breath work or yoga and follow this with discussions with a counselor.

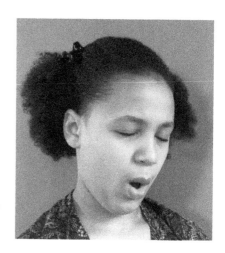

Counselors can use yoga-mindfulness-meditation, too, for their work with students.

INTEGRATING MINDFULNESS INTO COUNSELING SESSIONS

Alison Sumski, a high school counselor in Massachusetts, explains the benefits of using mindfulness in counseling youth (personal communication, March 2021).

As a high school counselor and former yoga teacher, I try to integrate mindfulness into each counseling session with a student. While the stressors of the school day can be unpredictable and overwhelming for students, I try to make my office as calming and unchanging as possible. The walls are adorned with encouraging and reassuring phrases and serene images, and a diffuser is always running with lavender and eucalyptus oils tracing the air. My desk "chair" is a yoga ball, and I typically have soft music or a white noise machine running throughout the day. I have a do-it-yourself gratitude bag front and center on my desk that I add to each day, and encourage my students to do the same. Taking control of the environment that I work in every day—and invite students into—is essential to both my practice as a school counselor and my own well-being.

I ground my counseling practice in patience, acceptance, and nonjudgment, all of which are central tenets to the practice of mindfulness. Approaching all students as equal helps me meet them where they are and lets them lead the conversation, something that I believe is essential in effective counseling. I also intentionally integrate mindfulness strategies into my sessions with the students that I meet with regularly. Many of these students suffer from anxiety and depression, disorders that take one away from the present moment. I like to introduce the concept of mindfulness early on when working with these

(Continued)

(Continued)

students, as it can take some time for beginners to feel ready to approach the practice with an open mind.

- I typically start with leading students through a deep belly breathing exercise so that students can feel the physiological benefits of mindfulness—in this case, reduced tension, lowered heart rate, and increased oxygen flow to the muscles and brain.

- For students that I have been meeting with more regularly, I might transition from breath work to a guided meditation to help them practice the process of slowing down and paying attention to their thoughts.

- When I assign "homework" or suggestions for counseling work outside of school, I like to lean into activities such as journaling, mindful eating, or mindful movement so that students can continue to develop their mindfulness practice on their own.

I've found that as sessions go on, students become more engaged in their practice. While mindfulness alone cannot solve mental illness, it can certainly be added to individuals' toolbox of coping skills and help mitigate their symptoms as they arise.

Listed in Figure 4.5 are some additional mindfulness activities that you can draw from when working with students in a mindfulness meditation room.

Figure 4.5 ◆ Mindfulness Activities

ACTIVITIES	DESCRIPTION
Mindful Games Activity Cards (www.susankaisergreenland .com/mindful-games)	This card deck invites parents, caregivers, and teachers to enjoy fun games to help kids develop their breathing, attention, concentration, and emotional identification and regulation skills.
Mindful Kids: 50 Mindfulness Activities (www.barefootbooks.com/ mindful-kids-deck)	This card deck (Stewart, 2017) includes creative mindfulness games, visualizations, and exercises to help children feel grounded, calm, and relaxed and practice their focus and loving-kindness. The cards and instructional booklet also include modifications to make each activity inclusive for children of all abilities.
Mindfulness Activities for Kids in the Classroom (www.teachstarter.com/us/ blog/classroom-mindfulness-activities-for-children-us/)	This article (Cassie, 2021) details quick and effective mindfulness activities you can do with your class, from breath awareness activities to body scans to mindful eating and walking exercises.

ACTIVITIES	DESCRIPTION
Meditation in Sports (www.youtube.com/ watch?v=E78y66GEPvs)	In this video from The Flow Station (2017), Phil Jackson discusses his emphasis on mindfulness so his team can build up their mental strength to focus, pay attention, work together, and reset their minds. Additionally, Kobe Bryant discusses how he meditates daily, which anchors him and sets him up for success.
Headspace for Sport (www.youtube.com/ watch?v=lbEat6qiumQ)	This video (Headspace, 2016) discusses the importance of mental preparation for professional athletes—being able to train your mind and drop outside concerns to be present in the here and now.

online resources   Available at https://resources.corwin.com/CultivatingHappiness

Note that some of these activities are most appropriate for specific age levels and that the YouTube meditations for sports and athletes may be of greatest value for middle and high school–aged students with interest in these areas.

ORGANIZING MY SPACE AND MATERIALS

- How and when will you implement yoga-mindfulness-meditation with your students?

- What do you need to do to organize your space and materials?

A Calming Corner

An alternative to a mindfulness intervention room is a classroom "calming corner," which works particularly well with younger students. This is usually a spot in the classroom where students can go to sit when they are feeling particularly stressed, upset, or otherwise challenged. The calming corner can have a bean bag, cushions, a lamp nearby with soft light, calming music, and headsets.

It may also include a few calming books such as the following:

— *A Handful of Quiet: Happiness in Four Pebbles,* by Thich Nhat Hanh

— *Anh's Anger,* by Gail Silver

— *I Am Peace: A Book of Mindfulness,* by Susan Verde

— *Listening to My Body,* by Gabi Garcia

— *Listening With My Heart: A Story of Kindness and Self-Compassion,* by Gabi Garcia

— *Mindful Monkey, Happy Panda,* by Lauren Alderfer

— *Sitting Still Like a Frog: Mindfulness Exercises for Kids,* by Eline Snel

— *You Are a Lion! And Other Fun Yoga Poses,* by Taeeun Yoo

Games and stories are particularly useful for engaging younger students (Rogas, 2018). Puppets and stuffed animals may be useful for helping younger students learn about their emotions. Scenarios can be acted out as teachers discuss how Kermit or another animal is feeling.

 Suggestions for additional games and stories are available on the Corwin Resources page at **https://resources.corwin.com/Cultivating Happiness**.

DEVELOPMENTAL STAGES AND APPROPRIATENESS

In Figure 4.6, we provide a few basic considerations for how to instruct students of different ages. Each grade level builds on guidelines from previous grades.

Figure 4.6 • Grade-Level Guidelines

Grades Pre-K–K	• Keep sessions short.
	• Use simple clear directions.
	• Use props such as breathing buddies (stuffed animals).
	• Encourage children to have fun with breath (buzzing bees, hummingbirds, a lion's roar).
	• Use imaginative stories with animal movements and circle activities.
	• Play "follow the leader."
	• Engage all senses and use play to support learning.
	• Rather than in silence, invite children to lie on the floor and relax with music.
	• Use routine for starting and stopping the yoga-mindfulness-meditation times.
	• Play "yoga games."
	• Teach students to be respectful, to listen, and that this is a safe time and space to relax and have fun.

Grades 1–3	• Focus more on breathing—holding breath, using specific breathing techniques.
	• Start to teach how to get into yoga postures and provide hints to students about how to improve what they are doing (e.g., "Stand straight, arms hanging loosely at your sides").
	• Remember that yoga games and mindfulness sensation experiences can be fun and still give students opportunities to practice.
	• Incorporate some partner work (e.g., "Join hands and stand up").
	• Begin using students as co-teachers to help lead sessions.
	• Use yoga breaks in classrooms to help keep students focused and attentive.
	• Encourage students to follow brief chants such as "I feel good!"
Grades 4–5	• Gradually increase length of sessions.
	• Give more specific and precise instructions.
	• Ask students to write about their feelings and experiences.
	• Teach students longer mantra or chants.
	• Extend meditation for longer periods of time.
	• Introduce guided visualizations.
	• Invite older students to help instruct younger students.
Grades 6–8	• Recognize that some students will appreciate more challenging poses and sets.
	• As directions for posture become more specific, use care not to embarrass students.
	• Lengthen meditations and chants and make them more involved.
	• Do not allow negative body talk directed toward self or others.
	• Consider after-school yoga clubs and yoga-based interventions.
	• Give more detailed explanation about the rationale for specific poses, breaths, and meditations.
	• Explain the benefits of yoga exercise.
	• Give students opportunities to use the internet and apps to support their learning.
	• Extend times for silence and reflection.
	• Incorporate opportunities for journaling.
Grades 7–12	• Build on student progress during prior years.
	• Realize that new students who come to your school may not have had prior experience and may need supplemental instruction in yoga-mindfulness-meditation basics. This could be an opportunity for peer mentoring or using videos you have archived.
	• Remember that some students will demonstrate advanced abilities and will want more extensive and advanced instruction.
	• Incorporate opportunities for students to build metacognition, particularly on their awareness of themselves, how they can regulate their emotions, and how feelings have impacted their lives.
	• Consider that some students may be interested in an after-school yoga club for intensive and extensive instruction and practice.
	• Know that students in these grades are often able to keep up with (and perhaps surpass) adults.

Sources: Adapted from Cook-Cottone (2017), Mehta (n.d.), Namaste Kid (2021), and Williams-Fields (2020).

ADAPTATIONS FOR YOUNGER STUDENTS

Yoga provides an opportunity for students to wiggle, stretch, laugh, and learn to follow a lead, responding to such prompts as "roar like a lion," "hiss like a cobra," or "fly your butterfly wings." Students enjoy moving into the poses of the downward dog, lion, butterfly, and cobra. These postures can strengthen the core and stretch the body into a more composed state (Center for Educational Improvement, 2012).

By incorporating breath work and yoga into preschool classrooms, children develop tools for practicing mindfulness as early as age 3 or 4.

SHAKTA KAUR DISCUSSES YOGA FOR YOUNGER STUDENTS

Shakta Khalsa, an author and yoga instructor who certifies yoga teachers, describes the importance of yoga for young students, including students with special needs. Following is an excerpt from a review of her book, The Yoga Way to Radiance (2016):

As a certified Montessori teacher and founder of a Montessori School and founder of Radiant Child Yoga, Khalsa has been instrumental in teaching schoolteachers how to adapt yoga into their classrooms, even in areas where traditional yoga isn't as commonly accepted.

"So in those cases, the teachers can simply have the children close their eyes and listen to the breath coming in sounding like waves on the ocean coming to the shore, and breathe out feeling that the waves are going back out to the sea. They can have children stand up and place their hands on the desk in a modified version of Downward Facing Dog, and stretch," says Khalsa. "And they never need to call it yoga at all! The effect is what is important, not the naming of the technique."

A teacher's internal state is just as important as a parent's internal state when engaging children. The book includes examples of teachers working with special-needs students, or as Khalsa prefers to call them, children with special intentions, having great success adapting yoga techniques to their teaching methods.

Khalsa's work with [children with special sensory needs,] such as those with autism, has reinforced her belief that children are more aligned with their own inner guide than adults. She says the challenges these . . . children face can instead be seen as learning moments to listen to our own intuition as parents and caregivers. (Williams-Fields, 2020)

The complete book review is available at https://resources.corwin.com/CultivatingHappiness.

The following material on staying calm is an example of how elementary school students can use a visual checklist as a reminder to help them stay calm or calm down when they become upset. The material is adapted from Wellemental (www.wellemental.co).

Name: _____

Date: _____

Things I Can Do to Be Calm:

MY CALM LIST
☐ Take 5 deep breaths
☐ Slowly count from 1 to 10
☐ Talk to someone I trust
☐ Take a sip of water
☐ Surround myself with a beautiful color in my mind's eye
☐ Do yoga
☐ Take another 5 deep breaths
☐ Count backward from 10 to 1
☐ Listen to music
☐ Sing a song
☐ Do something I like
☐ Squeeze every muscle in my body and then relax (do this 1–3 times)
☐ Visualize someplace that is peaceful
☐ Imagine being calm, feeling calm

Image source: istock.com/ VladGans

Yoga Before or After School

We encourage you to integrate yoga-mindfulness-meditation activities into the academic school day whenever possible. This might be through mindful moments, yoga stretches at your desk, or physical education classes. Or it may include a more extensive use of yoga-mindfulness-meditation throughout the school day. You may also consider making yoga available before or after school. Schools and districts have done this in various ways—presenting yoga as an optional experience. Sometimes it is offered for students, families, and staff. Sometimes it is offered as an elective or extracurricular activity. Other schools will make it a part of their after-school program and may even receive funds from Title IV or 21st Century Community Learning Centers, for example, to help pay for this. However you proceed, what we outline in this chapter and book will provide valuable guidelines.

If yoga-mindfulness-meditation is offered as an optional experience, please consider the implications: (1) Sometimes students most in need of yoga will lack access due to difficulties with scheduling and transportation, and (2) if yoga is offered outside school hours, what will teachers and other staff members do to reinforce its use at other times?

THE HAVE-MATS AND HAVE-NOTS

Karin Tulchinsky Cohen, a vice principal at Beall Elementary School in Maryland, explains the genesis for the after-school yoga class she teaches.

One of the highlights of my day is greeting students as they arrive at school in the morning. It's a tender time of transition when parents say goodbye to their children and release them to the care of the school. In that moment I feel the weight of my responsibility as an administrator in a public school. Our students come from all different places in the world and different strata in the economy. We have children who have stories of suffering that most of us can't comprehend. And some of our children come from places of abundance and ease.

Over the years I have noticed many things as I stand on the corner greeting my kids in the morning. I notice when kids sit in the front seat of the car even though they are much too small to comply with the laws of physics that determine safety. I notice when students are sad as they enter the building. I make sure to connect with them and remind them that they are loved. I notice students who eat their breakfast out of fast-food bags, and I notice when they get new shoes and new haircuts. I consciously create a container of warmth and belonging as I am their first contact with school when they arrive in the morning.

I began to notice an interesting phenomenon. There were students who brought yoga mats with them to school in the morning. They were always very enthusiastic, and they thoroughly enjoyed their after-school extracurricular activity. I then began to notice the children who never came to school carrying a yoga mat. And it made me think. Yoga is a practice that enhances everyone's lives. Yoga is a great equalizer. You don't have to be a particular size or come from any specific part of the world; just bring your true self to the mat. I thought about how wonderful it is to have the opportunity to begin practicing yoga as a young child. I continued to notice the children who brought yoga mats to school. I continued to notice the children who did not have yoga mats.

I decided that the only way I could bring about a change would be for me to start my own free-of-charge after-school yoga class for the children who did not have mats. I began to plan this initiative. I discovered many details that needed to be taken care of to actualize this idea. There were permission slips to be distributed to make sure parents wanted their children to do yoga. There were decisions to be made about which students would be invited to take the class. Would the invitation be based on the free and reduced-price meal service status that sets a definition for what it means to be in poverty? Would eligibility be based on more specific student needs? Could this yoga class serve as an opportunity to connect with children who might be having a hard time focusing in class for a variety of reasons with no connection to poverty at all? It ended up being yes to all of the above.

I worried that it would be very hard for the parents of my target population to provide transportation after school. I thought about the sibling structures of the students' families. If more than one sibling attended our school but only one of the siblings was able to join the yoga class, this would make it very complex for the parents to figure out transportation.

I worried about my inexperience and lack of preparation for the task of teaching yoga on a large scale. The past summer I had first ventured into teaching yoga classes for children in a mentor program. The children in that program experience similar circumstances to the ones I wanted to focus on in my school. I had gotten a grant to purchase 10 yoga mats to use with the children in the mentoring program. There were many more than 10 students in the mentoring program; the staff and I supplemented the number of yoga mats with our own mats. The summer yoga classes had gone very well. As I was preparing to teach yoga at my school, I got another grant from the wellness office to purchase a few more yoga mats. I was ready to jump into the unknown.

I set up weekly one-hour classes that had two sections of 30-minute sessions.

There was never a dull moment. My experience gave me the courage to offer more free yoga classes. Many of the kids loved the yoga classes.

- We opened the classes with a mood check-in, and then we did breathing exercises.

- Next we did a series of yoga postures that progressed in complexity and strength.

- The students had different preferences for the postures they enjoyed the most. Some loved the balance poses and laughed as we tried to sway like wind in the trees. Others enjoyed the dragon pose, something I made up for when we went into warrior I.

- I would have the students stretch their arms back and then lunge forward while making whooshing noises like fire-breathing dragons.

(Continued)

(Continued)

- We closed the classes with guided meditation and a final check-in to give them opportunities to develop self-awareness. I encouraged them to compare how they felt before class with how they felt after class. One of my favorite responses that I often heard at the end of class when I asked the students how they were feeling was "perfect." It was so satisfying to see their relaxed faces. When they saw me in the hallway or in the morning when I greeted them, they would ask me about the next yoga class.

I always had several yoga mats for the children to use during class. After a few weeks of classes, some of my students got their own yoga mats. Some of the mats had patterns, while others were solid colors; one child showed me where the word *breathe* was imprinted on his mat. On the mornings that we had yoga class, we smiled in anticipation of what awaited us at the end of the day. I noticed something. My yoga students looked proud and excited. They have become children who have yoga mats.

PROGRESS AND IMPACT

As you teach, we encourage you to find ways to measure students' progress and the impact of your instruction on their lives. Journaling, for both instructors and students, is beneficial. It provides an easy way to log progress, including changes in attitudes and thinking, as well as improvements in stamina by such measures as the length of time you are comfortable holding your breath or sitting in meditation.

As students continue with a regular yoga-mindfulness-meditation routine, as their stress is relieved, their cognition and academic learning may also improve. So, another measure may be improvements in academic performance.

We also encourage teachers to look for opportunities to ask students questions about whether any of the strategies are applied outside the yoga-mindfulness-meditation class. For internal tracking purposes within the school or district, simple age-appropriate surveys or journaling can be employed.

Other measures that can be important are indicators of improvement in student discipline (a reduction in referrals or behavior incidents), an increase in attendance, a decrease in suspensions or expulsions, and an increase in graduation rates. School climate and culture may also be improved.

The School Compassionate Culture Analytical Tool for Educators (S-CCATE) is one measure that is tied to the Heart Centered Learning and Five Cs that are reviewed in this book (Center for Educational Improvement, 2018; Mason et al., 2018). S-CCATE was validated on over 800 educators and provides data comparing your school to other schools in your district or state, and nationally. It is available online (www.s-ccate.org) (*also available on the Corwin Resources page at* **https://resources .corwin.com/CultivatingHappiness**) with options for receiving recommendations for activities to address concerns and build positive practices in your school.

The best method to collect data intended for use or sharing by your school district to the community (or other outside research purposes) is a validated research instrument that measures emotional growth. There are several freely available, and all require permission from the authors (nearly always they will grant permission provided they are cited).

MINDFUL REFLECTION

1. Consider what you need to do to prepare to teach. Do you need additional materials? How will you open and close your sessions? How will you help students stay engaged and handle possible disruptions?

2. What are two or three additional ideas or practices from this chapter that you would like to implement with your students farther down the road? What do you need to do, or how do you need to prepare, to build these elements into your yoga-mindfulness-meditation practice with students?

3. What is one challenge you anticipate encountering as you begin practicing yoga-mindfulness-meditation with your students, and how might you respond to that challenge?

ONLINE RESOURCES

Visit https://resources.corwin.com/CultivatingHappiness

Online Resource 4.1	Yoga Fun With Props! Got Props?! Find Out Kids Yoga Teacher Favorite Resources
Online Resource 4.2	Heart Beaming
Online Resource 4.3	My Yoga-Mindfulness-Meditation Readiness to Teach
Online Resource 4.4	Strategies for Protecting K–12 School Staff From COVID-19
Online Resource 4.5	Yoga Supply Donations and Grants Table
Online Resource 4.6	Yoga-Mindfulness-Meditation Instruction Lessons
Online Resource 4.7	Sing Song Yoga
Online Resource 4.8	Audio Recordings
Online Resource 4.9	Yoga Classroom Management Strategies
Online Resource 4.10	Six Most Common Yoga Injuries and How to Avoid Them
Online Resource 4.11	Mindfulness Activities Table
Online Resource 4.12	Organizing My Space and Materials
Online Resource 4.13	Yoga Games
Online Resource 4.14	S-CCATE
Online Resource 4.15	Mindful Reflection

PART TWO

Heart Centered Learning: The Five Cs

KEY PRINCIPLE

The Five Cs are foundational to cultivating happiness and well-being.

Part I of *Cultivating Happiness, Resilience, and Well-Being* laid the foundation for implementing yoga-mindfulness-meditation in classrooms.

Many adults and children have benefited substantially by implementing the foundational practices we provided in Part I. These practices can be life changers as they open up mind–body connections, even if they are practiced only a few minutes a day, several days a week. However, even greater benefits are possible if practiced daily.

TO OBTAIN THE GREATEST BENEFITS, PROCEED FORWARD

With Part II of *Cultivating Happiness, Resilience, and Well-Being*, we guide you further along a path to wholeness, wellness, and a renewed sense of calmness, clearer thinking, and increased "brain power." The authors have worked with many educators over decades to further implementation of the strategies we introduce in Part II.

In Part II, we provide a platform to help you integrate the yoga-mindfulness-meditation practices into the school day in ways that specifically support academic learning. Building on the strategies Christine Mason, Michele Rivers Murphy, and Yvette Jackson offered in their 2020 book *Mindful School Communities*, in Chapters 6–10 we connect specific breath exercises, yoga sets, and meditations to each of the Five Cs of Heart Centered Learning: consciousness, compassion, confidence, courage, and community. As Mason, Rivers Murphy, and Jackson (2020) remind us, "if you are like many educators, you think about how to help students improve not only their academic achievement, but also their self-esteem, self-regulation, and likelihood for lifelong success" (p. 12).

Linda Lantieri, director of the Inner Resilience Program, in *Building Emotional Intelligence* (2008) states,

> One way to make sure that children get the best lessons of the heart is to make them part of the school day as well as part of the children's home life. (p. 2)

To obtain the greatest benefits will take discipline. Each of the authors has our own *sadhana,* or daily discipline. This may be an early morning time that is set aside to practice, or it may be incorporating mindfulness as we eat, walk, and transition from one activity to another during the day. As Santokh Khalsa has explained,

> "The only way you can be an effective teacher is to be totally there for your students" . . . That, he adds, is why a daily practice is so important. "*Sadhana* is the means to let go of ego, personal agendas, and attachments." (Charnas, 2007)

WHY YOGA AND MEDITATION ARE SO IMPORTANT IN MY LIFE

Krishna Kaur describes how yoga and meditation gave direction and clarity to her and its potential to do the same for all of us.

I didn't grow up with a desire to practice or teach yoga, let alone to become a yoga teacher. I stumbled into it when nothing else I tried made sense. I grew up during the civil rights movement led by Dr. Martin Luther King Jr. I didn't march with him, nor did I go to the March on Washington that he led. But I believed in his words and the way he thought about the human spirit. My intention was to get strong and clear inside so I could recognize my purpose when it passed before me. It soon became clear that yoga was going to become a very important part of my life, my breath, and my way to stay healthy and be of service to others. After many years of teaching in South Central Los Angeles, I became officially certified as a kundalini yoga teacher in 1994. My personal experience with a daily yoga practice and a dedicated lifestyle gave clarity and direction to my life. It focused my way of viewing the world, and my ability to manage difficult situations. When I began teaching youth, it became clear that I had found my life's purpose and my profession.

What the world is experiencing now is not a total surprise to me. Fortunately, our social political structures are beginning to respond better to the minority concerns for justice and equality, as well as for ways to address the growing stress, trauma, and depression in our schools.

High levels of stress are a critical problem in our children from preschool through college. Something is seriously missing in the lives of our children that I believe can be more easily managed with the practice of yoga and mindful meditation. The gap between the wealthiest and poorest families in our country continues to widen, leaving our most vulnerable families too often faced with high-pressure situations that are at best overwhelming and certainly difficult for parents to manage. The coping mechanisms that I have experienced that have the best chance to narrow that gap are yoga and mindful practices. Together, these tools strengthen the immune, respiratory, glandular, and nervous systems and bring stillness to body and mind. When the body–mind connection is strong, and belief in oneself is supported with regular yoga and mindful practices, youth tend to make better choices.

From my many years of practicing kundalini yoga and meditation, I know the power it has to create stability and strength, mentally, physically, and emotionally. I want to see that our children have the opportunity to develop that within themselves. We talk often about educating the whole child, feeding the whole child, and nurturing the whole child, and as that commitment grows, so will the physical, mental, and emotional well-being of each child begin to awaken, both in our schools and at home. Now is a perfect time to evaluate our strategy regarding our children—our future—and commit to making the difficult choices regarding the direction in which our schools are moving.

Comments from Christine's adult yoga students who have consistently met with her one to three times a week, over 5, 10, and even 20 years, also reflect the benefits of our recommendations. As you read these, reflect back on statements about self-care (Chapter 3), knowing oneself, and mindfulness.

- "I haven't had a big revelation; however, I have experienced new and deeper levels of self-care."

- "Most important: being in the moment."

- "It allows me to check in with my body."

- "I see this as generosity to myself. I am rewarding myself. This is a luxury."

- "I appreciate you, your kindness, and caring."

STRESS AND CREATING A SENSE OF SAFETY AND WELL-BEING

- Consider the trauma we have all experienced with COVID-19.
- Reflect on how we have been overloaded with stress, worry, trauma, and heightened alertness as to danger.
- Reflect for a moment about what we know about the impact of all of this on our brains, our minds, and our bodies.
- Consider how your own stress impacts those around you.
- Consider people you know who are struggling the most. We even know that sometimes as stress accumulates, we disassociate from our experiences, our bodies, and ourselves. In a way, we become alienated from our true selves.

Being a Protective Factor. Now imagine ways to create a greater sense of safety and well-being, of being a protective factor for others, and of finding small experiences of joy.

One of the reasons it is so critical for schools to adopt the practices we recommend in this book is the sheer amount of suffering, trauma, and stress we have all experienced since early 2020. The Five Cs and the practices we introduce in this book will help you experience the instant joy of a small moment in time; they will also help lift the burdens you face, and lead you to a place of resilience, clearer thinking, better health, and greater ability to do what is needed.

MINDFUL REFLECTION

1. How have you used specific practices to achieve greater clarity and purpose?
2. How have you implemented those practices?
3. What practices are you implementing with students? How well are they working?

ONLINE RESOURCES
Visit https://resources.corwin.com/CultivatingHappiness

Online Resource PII.1   Stress and Creating a Sense of Safety and Well-Being

Online Resource PII.2   Mindful Reflection

CHAPTER FIVE

Overview of the Five Cs

KEY PRINCIPLE

To build consciousness, compassion, confidence, courage, and community takes intentionality, perseverance, and collaboration.

In explaining the value of the Five Cs, Mason, Rivers Murphy, and Jackson (2020) say,

> When we are **conscious** of our breath, of our emotions, and of those around us, we are more likely to act in **compassionate** ways and reinforce neural pathways that provide positive feedback about our lives. . . . As we feel a sense of calm and goodwill, we are more likely to feel **confident** about our abilities. Over time, this sense of confidence can strengthen executive functions . . . and our potential to be **courageous**— standing up to bullies, helping others in need, and considering someone else's feelings, thus strengthening a sense of **community**. (pp. 3–4)

With heart centered education, caring and compassion are embedded into instruction, curriculum, protocols, and policies, impacting not only students and staff, but also families and communities.

- With Heart Centered Learning, consciousness *improves the coherence* between our emotional experiences and our understanding of those experiences.

- For teachers, this understanding also *furthers our sensitivity* to the needs of students, providing a platform for making intentional, mindful decisions to further student awareness of self, compassion for others, self-esteem, confidence, courage, and resilience to make it through the difficult passages we all face in our lives.

- With conscious leaders, *teachers can act in concert, with strategic decisions for collaboration and support for each other and for our community.* Conscious, heart centered leaders not only inspire teachers, staff, students, and communities; they network with others to reach out to other communities to build support for equity, fairness, and justice as well.

- In heart centered communities, *students are presented with intentional exercises to build their consciousness, compassion, confidence, and courage.* Over time, these exercises not only build neural pathways and alleviate stress; they also increase the probability that, even under the most challenging circumstances, students will act with compassion in support of others and the greater good.

PRACTICES FOR LIFE

In the introduction to Part II, Krishna Kaur explained the life-altering value of the practices we recommend. To consider the wisdom of maintaining a practice, think of other accomplishments. Bill Gates and Steve Jobs didn't stop designing technologies after their first inventions. They were both caught up in the stream of activities that emerged from their initial successes. And so it can be with our careers, hobbies, and fitness routines. Just as runners who have toned their bodies don't one day say, "Enough! I have won the marathon, so I no longer need to run," so it is with many great achievements. Maintaining the benefits takes discipline, effort, and commitment.

Let's reflect for a moment on running and review the implications for the yoga-mindfulness-meditation practices that you implement in your schools.

WHY DO I RUN?

Co-author Michele Rivers Murphy explains her passion for running.

I have often been asked, *Why do you run?* My answer is always the same: *Because I can.*

I have run a long time, over four decades. There are some days that are clearly easier than others, but I am gentle and compassionate with myself. On days that early mornings quickly distract my plan to run—or when my body doesn't quite feel like getting out there at all—my family or inner voice gently nudges me out the door, knowing we will all be better off if Mom takes her run.

Running is one of my most favorite, constant, and silent meditative practices because it takes me places outdoors never to be viewed again in that exact same moment of time, day, or season. When I go to that place called *nature* and breathe my first outdoor breath of the day, I feel most alive and well. Running outdoors is a time to increase my connection with *self* and the amazing world of nature around me. I have run in the sunshine and blistering heat of summer, the coolness and brilliantly colored foliage of a fall day, the blustering cold and wind of winter, and the freshness and beauty of spring and new life. When I was a teenager and diagnosed with a serious heart ailment, I ran. When I was excited about college, travel, or a new experience or opportunity, I ran. When I lost a close friend unexpectedly, I ran to church to attend mass. When I needed clarity, a boost in energy, or a new perspective, I ran.

When I run outdoors in the woods, deep on a forest trail, around a lake, or up a mountainside, I gain an almost immediate sense of well-being that reminds me *why* I do what I do. I run to stay grounded, stay balanced, and sing inner joy. I have learned that running is more about the *climb* or *journey* than reaching the top of the mountain or finishing the 5 or 26 marathon miles run in record time. I notice. I have learned to fully and completely appreciate, enjoy, and embrace the journey and the moment, with all my senses, *leaning and tuning inwardly*, discovering what I can endure and what I am capable of in that given moment. "Steady, strong, stellar," I repeat as I run, especially on the high climbs and long runs that take an extra bit of balanced breath and focus. I stay in the moment, noticing and relying on my repetitive cadence, my foot strokes touching the earth to firmly ground me. I then shift any discomfort I may experience to the anchoring of my breaths as my breathing changes from slow and deliberate, sometimes labored, breath as I climb and begin a long ascent to the top to an effortless, easy breath as I float and descend as if flying down the mountain on the other side. I am also compassionate with myself, recognizing that some days I will be stronger and other days I will be challenged, but every day I am guaranteed the amazing beauty surrounding me if I only choose to notice.

Building Inner Capacity

For Michele, running is less about its many obvious physical benefits (cardio and circulation) and more about building her inner capacity and reserve of psychological and emotional resilience as well as keeping a sense of balance, calm, and equanimity in her life. As Michele explains,

> *Hitting my stride* in runner's terms means releasing the feel-good *endorphins* (hormones), followed by the post-run feeling of

endocannabinoids, a biochemical substance that is naturally produced by the body. Running is a self-care gift to *me*, it is a healing agent of sorts, it is a stress reducer and a positive mindset enhancer, and most of all, running is a gratitude builder. When I miss a run, I am not my best self.

What is most encouraging is that with regular exercise, the part of our brain associated with memory and learning called the *hippocampus* is found to increase in volume as well as improve our working memory and focus, our ability to switch tasks, and our mood. Regular exercise can help generate new blood vessel growth that nourishes the brain. Consistently committing to some form of exercise as part of our regular routine helps us to also produce new brain cells (neurogenesis) that may lead to overall improvement of brain performance and prevent cognitive decline.

Staying the Course

The practices we recommend are not for one day, one month, or one year. In fact, ancient sages have cautioned that we can sometimes experience such a sense of well-being that we are tempted to turn elsewhere and leave the practices behind. Your authors caution you not to be lured into a false sense of security or complacency, believing that now that you feel better, you can simply drop these practices. Plans for maintenance are needed. Hence, we recommend these practices for all grade levels, for each year, for every year. Part II will help you to develop your plan for this.

Yet, from experience, we know that you may, even with good intentions, find barriers along the way. In this book, we provide many practical examples of ways many of us have overcome obstacles to maintain our practice. We encourage you to keep reading and to keep practicing!

BARRIERS AND RESISTANCE TO YOUR PRACTICE

- Where are you likely to encounter barriers to establishing and maintaining a practice?

- Are the barriers you anticipate more directly related to available time, your general willingness, your uncertainty as to the value of yoga-mindfulness-meditation, or where this falls as a priority for you?

- Looking at other aspects of your life, have you established and maintained routine practices for other areas? (Consider health, diet, sleep, reading, hobbies, or time with family members.) What helped you to establish and maintain those practices?

Trauma and the Five Cs

One of your own barriers may be your own trauma. The following information is for all of us—those who instruct and those who are the learners.

During the COVID-19 pandemic, the many ways that global trauma impacts hundreds of thousands of us became the nightly news. The list is long and horrific. However, whether it is Trauma with a big *T* or the smaller, everyday traumas we face as we bump up against our own insecurities, trauma is ever present. Traumatic events affect individuals in unique ways. While some people with high levels of resilience are able to process difficult emotions associated with a trauma quickly and move back into their normal emotions and activities, others can be left numb, hurt, or in crisis by these same events. In the same way, each person's healing journey from trauma is unique.

While some people who have experienced trauma may find yoga, meditation, breath work, and other mindfulness practices calming and helpful, others may become triggered and turn away from these practices. We have taught seminars on trauma and stress, where tears have welled up in the eyes of educators, social workers, parents, and others as we discuss the prevalence of trauma and how it has a pervasive long-term impact on our lives. Please keep that in mind and be gentle with yourself.

THE FIVE Cs CHAPTERS

To guide teacher instruction and enhance student understanding and development of heart centered character traits, Chapters 6–10 include yoga-mindfulness-meditation activities that can be implemented or adapted across grade levels (see Figure 5.1).

Figure 5.1 • Organization of Each Five Cs Chapter

KEY PRINCIPLE: THE FIVE CS ARE FOUNDATIONAL TO CULTIVATING HAPPINESS AND WELL-BEING	
Components	
Teacher Notes	Ties specific aspects of each *C* to general principles for breath work, yoga sets, relaxation, and meditations
Introduction to the *C*	The rationale for inclusion of the *C*-relationship to student happiness and well-being
Curricular Context	Suggestions for where to insert the practice during the academic year, noting special considerations for various age groups and curriculum content

(Continued)

(Continued)

KEY PRINCIPLE: THE FIVE CS ARE FOUNDATIONAL TO CULTIVATING HAPPINESS AND WELL-BEING	
Components	
Warm-Ups Breath Work Yoga Set Relaxation Meditation	
Curriculum Integration Planner	A graphic organizer to help you plan and adapt material from the chapter.
Mindful Reflection	Three questions to help frame what is working best for you and how you might be able to enhance your practice and your instruction

Each chapter contains yoga kriyas, breaths, postures, warm-ups, and meditations that have been adapted from several sources. However, the primary sources are from texts published by the Kundalini Research Institute and other KRI-approved texts. These are noted with an asterisk (*), and the source for each is identified at the back of this book.

CURRICULAR CONTEXT

Just as consciousness is the first step for Heart Centered Learning, yoga-mindfulness-meditation exercises for consciousness are designed to be introduced early in the year.

- This can be done as part of an annual approach to the Five Cs.

- Or the Five Cs can be taught over two years, with consciousness and compassion in Year 1 and confidence and courage in Year 2. Community building can occur in both years, as follows.

	PRE-K	K	1	2	3	4	5	6	7	8	9	10	11	12
Consciousness	x		x		x		x		x		x		x	
Compassion	x		x		x		x		x		x		x	
Confidence		x		x		x		x		x		x		x
Courage		x		x		x		x		x		x		x
Community	x	x	x	x	x	x	x	x	x	x	x	x	x	x

With a two-year plan, Year 2 will include some review exercises from the Year 1 cycle. In this progression, over 14 years, students will receive 7 years of focus on consciousness and compassion and 7 years of focus on confidence and courage.

In terms of relevance to the academic curriculum, teachers at each grade level can examine their curriculum and make decisions about the relevance of any particular C for topics in social studies/history, literature, math, and science, as well as extracurricular subjects.

STUDENT MOTIVATION AND ACCOMMODATIONS

As you proceed in implementing your Five C practices with yoga-mindfulness-meditation, not all students will be equally motivated to participate. How a teacher handles motivation will depend on the circumstances and setting (after school, voluntary, or integrated into the school day). Participation is often increased with the use of student leaders who assist in teaching the sets and demonstrating the postures or movements. Sometimes, allowing students to quietly observe will help them gain confidence and increase their comfort level. (See also the sections in Chapter 4 on what to do when students are resistant, keeping students interested and engaged, and encouraging students.)

Accommodations such as smaller groups, lower lighting, and keeping the eyes closed for portions of the sessions can help students who are shy, uncertain, or easily distracted. Students who may be hesitant to circulate the energy generated with yoga by "standing up and shaking or dancing," for example, may be comfortable sitting crossed-legged in easy pose with their eyes closed and "swaying to the music."

When it comes to yoga postures, here are a few common accommodations:

- Shorten the length of an exercise.

- Find out what the student likes and plan to present that more frequently.

- Start small with yoga breaks, rather than 20-minute or longer yoga sessions.

- Teach only a part of an exercise, gradually introducing steps over a period of several days.

- Sometimes it is helpful to introduce more relaxation activities between yoga postures. Poses such as baby pose or a forward bend, seated on the floor and touching the toes, can be inserted for relaxation.

- Tight hamstrings are prevalent with athletes in particular, so more activities to stretch the hamstrings such as forward lunges can be helpful.

- Balancing can be difficult for some. Begin with simple balancing postures, such as raising a leg and twirling your foot, before introducing more complex balancing postures.

- Let students know that they do not need to aim for perfection—that over time, with practice, they will improve; however, this happens at a different pace for each of us.

- Remember to use prompts such as "navel point to the spine" or "shoulders down" to help students with alignment and to help them obtain greater benefits from the practice (see, for example, the "Anchoring Into a Position" section later in this chapter).

However, even as you make accommodations, remember to challenge students. As teachers, we want to help students take the next step forward. Sometimes, rather than finding an accommodation, it may be more helpful to be the cheerleader or motivational coach who spurs students on to greater accomplishments.

Trauma-Informed Yoga

Remember that sometimes students may show disinterest or resist yoga-mindfulness-meditation practices because of trauma in their lives. Importantly, teachers can learn trauma-sensitive tools and responses for when traumatic reactions occur for students. Exercises such as writing about chronic stress triggers might be too overwhelming for students who suffer from trauma, and students should never feel forced or pressured to participate. Instead, alternatives can be offered for students who feel uncomfortable or incapable as a result of trauma, physical and learning disabilities, or conflicting spiritual beliefs. Similarly, breath work and meditations may stir up memories that have been suppressed. If you sense that student avoidance is related to trauma, speak with a school counselor, and proceed with caution, using trauma-informed practices (see Chapter 4).

Note that while we are giving you many strategies for implementing yoga-mindfulness-meditation with children and youth who have experienced trauma, another important accommodation is the use of trauma-informed yoga.

Trauma-informed yoga emphasizes the impact of trauma on the entire mind–body system, instead of viewing symptoms such as troubling memories in isolation from the physical body (Omega Institute for Holistic Studies, 2017). It recognizes that trauma can impact someone physically, emotionally, socially, and mentally. Trauma-informed yoga can help strengthen the mind–body connection and help individuals develop a greater sense of ownership over their bodies again, promoting a feeling of safety, normalization, and validation regarding the feelings and bodily sensations that arise (Kirk Chang, 2020).

The goal of trauma-informed yoga is to help survivors experience internal sensations in a safe and healing way, rather than avoiding or numbing them. Using movement and breath work, yoga can help individuals face and overcome potential triggers in a slow and careful way. Yoga can be stimulating and soothing, on both the physical and the emotional levels. By incorporating both elements, teachers can help students develop balance in their nervous systems. Great teachers emphasize present-state awareness and grant students flexibility to notice and choose what brings them balance. Over time, as students practice this awareness and regulation, they will be better able to bring themselves to a balanced state in a variety of situations (Omega Institute for Holistic Studies, 2017).

 Ideas and resources around incorporating trauma-informed yoga into your practice and teachings are available on the Corwin Resources page at **https://resources.corwin.com/CultivatingHappiness**.

USING TRAUMA-INFORMED YOGA IN SCHOOLS

Dana Asby, the Center for Educational Improvement's director of innovation and research support and the New England Mental Health Technology Transfer Center's education coordinator, is also a certified trauma-informed yoga instructor. Dana explains the importance of considering trauma when instructing students:

> Because trauma changes the way our central nervous system, particularly our brain, processes physical sensations and emotions, many survivors of trauma have difficulty sitting with stillness and silence. Introducing more active mindfulness practices and offering choices may be a good place to start when using mindfulness with populations who have experienced trauma. A gentle flowing yoga practice that connects the breath to the movement can help trauma survivors slow down their nervous system, thoughts, and emotions and come into the present moment. When teaching yoga as a healing practice, focusing on alignment and touching students' bodies to adjust their poses can take away from the goal of better integrating the mind–body–spirit.

(Continued)

(Continued)

If a student does become triggered during a yoga session, remember that you as the teacher are the anchor and that your calm demeanor can help coregulate the emotions of all in the room. Remain calm, continue to use a soothing tone and cadence, and begin practices to bring everyone in the room back to the present moment. Rather than singling out the person who is currently in crisis, bring the whole class into a mountain pose or an easy seated pose where you can do a simple breath work practice with eyes open or use the five senses to notice the sounds, smells, sights, feelings, and possibly tastes around you. Ensure that triggered students follow up with a mental health professional as soon as possible after the yoga session so they can process these difficult emotions through talk therapy, artistic expression, journaling, or another integration practice.

MOTIVATION AND ACCOMMODATIONS

- What do you know about your students? Who is most likely to need accommodations? Why?

- How are you prepared to enhance student motivation to participate?

- Which accommodations are you most prepared to implement?

A FEW MORE YOGA-MINDFULNESS-MEDITATION BASICS

In Chapter 4, we provided you with guidelines for preparing for and implementing yoga-mindfulness-meditation. We include additional parameters here:

- Anchoring Into a Position
- Easy Pose
- Eye Focus
- Navel Point
- Breathing
- Mudra

- Venus Lock
- Strength Training With Yoga
- The Exponential Power of Coordinating Breath and Meditation With Movement
- Relaxation

ANCHORING INTO A POSITION

When teaching challenging positions, we often remind students to "anchor themselves in place by sitting in a 'good yogic posture.'" This refers to navel point to the spine, shoulders down and shoulder blades together in back, elevating the heart and the chest, and tucking the chin back slightly so the back of the head is in alignment with the spine. This position makes it easier to stay in position and enhances the energy flow within our bodies.

EASY POSE

Many of the yoga kriyas or sets refer to "easy pose," which is sitting on the ground, with the ankles crossed, spine straight, and shoulders down and back.

EYE FOCUS

If eye position is not specified, it is usually the student's choice. When the instruction is to close the eyes, unless otherwise directed, please focus on the space between your brows. Offer the alternative of finding a soft gaze at the tip of the nose for students not yet comfortable closing their eyes.

Between the Brows (or Brow Point). Often the instruction for eye position is to "focus between the brows." With this position, the hypothalamus and pituitary glands are more readily activated (see Chapter 1), and one's conscious awareness increases. As these glands are activated, other glands are in turn activated, and the

(Continued)

(Continued)

system receives in essence a "wake-up" call to be ready and in balance. With this eye position, it is easier to be "in the present" and to focus on the breath, sound, a word or mantra, or an image.

Eyes Wide Open. With the eyes wide open, we can reach a state of calmness and peace. Practicing with the eyes wide open also makes it easier to transfer the effects of meditation to our everyday lives.

Tip of the Nose. Closing the eyes so they are only one-tenth open and are focused on the tip of the nose can be challenging—especially when you try to maintain this position for several minutes. However, this eye position also brings us into present-moment awareness as it steadies, then locks, the mind into meditation.

Top of the Skull. With eyes either open or closed, gently roll your eyeballs up so the focus is at the center of the skull. This can be a very "elevating" experience. With this eye focus it is easy to feel a sense of weightlessness and achieve a blissful meditative experience. As Shakta Kaur Khalsa (2001b) relates, a focus on the top of the skull (sometimes referred to as the crown chakra) "elevates one into higher consciousness and activates the pineal gland, which controls the nucleus projection of every cell of the body" (p. 156; see also Chapter 1).

Center of Chin. With your eyes either open or closed, you can gently focus your gaze at the center of the chin. This position is particularly useful for focusing on memories.

NAVEL POINT

Throughout this book and in many yoga texts and classes, the term *navel point* is used, often in reference to "pulling your navel point to your spine." The navel point is the region of the body below your belly button. When you pull your navel point to your spine, you are using your abdominal muscles to tighten your core and strengthen the flow of energy through the central part of your body. One way to enhance your sense of well-being is to engage in activities that strengthen or balance your navel point. This can include lying on your back with leg lifts, spinal flexes, and cat-cow or even hip or body rotations (see Chapter 2) with the navel point pulled to the spine.

BREATHING

While many different breaths are used with yoga and meditation, unless a specific breath is specified, please assume that the breath will be through the nostrils on both the inhale and the exhale. (Other breaths that we introduce in this book are long deep breathing, Breath of Fire, alternate nostril breathing, the U Breath, cannon breath, Sitali breath, and even instances of inhaling through the nose and exhaling through the mouth—or its opposite: inhaling through the mouth and exhaling through the nose.)

MUDRA

Mudra refers to the position of the arms and hands that is used to facilitate the flow of energy in the body. The most common mudra is gyan mudra where the tip of the thumb and the tip of the index finger touch; other fingers are straight.

VENUS LOCK

The hand position is slightly different to enhance masculine and feminine qualities. For feminine qualities, interlace the fingers of both hands, with the little finger of your right hand on the bottom. Place the right thumb into the webbing that forms between the thumb and the index finger of the left hand. The left thumb pushes gently into the fleshy area at the base of the right thumb.

For masculine qualities, these two positions are reversed. The little finger of the left hand is on the bottom, and the thumb positions are reversed.

STRENGTH TRAINING

Front, back, and side planks provide excellent opportunities to strengthen the arms and torso without the use of free weights or dumbbells. Strengthening the arms, legs, and core (torso) will make it easier to hold other positions and will assist with alignment and energy flow.

Back Plank

Position: Place your palms, with fingers spread wide, on the floor slightly behind and outside your hips.

1. Press into your palms and lift your hips and torso toward the ceiling.

2. Look up at the ceiling, pointing your toes and keeping your arms and legs straight.

3. Keep your body in a straight (diagonal) line from your head to your heels.

4. Squeeze your core and try to pull your navel point back toward your spine. Hold the position for up to 30 seconds.

5. Come sitting into "stick position," an *L*.

6. Repeat three sets of 30-second holds, alternating between the back plank and stick position.

THE EXPONENTIAL POWER OF COORDINATING BREATH, MEDITATION, AND MOVEMENT

While each of the practices we suggest has value, the most powerful results will be achieved when you breathe with movements, and often with eyes in a specified position. With such intentional practice, you will find that you are "meditating" while practicing yoga movements and that you are able to stretch further, be more focused, and more powerfully impact your internal organs (digestive system), nervous system, glands, and brain.

- Often the instructions are to inhale as you raise your arms, legs, or torso and exhale as your limbs or body are lowered. Most often the breath occurs with each repetition.

- Another common instruction is to inhale as you rotate your torso and neck back, and exhale as you go forward. This is the breath that is used with spinal flexes (see Chapter 3).

- With neck movements or twists, the instruction may be to inhale left and exhale right.

- Typically, the body or limb is extended more fully on the exhale. So, the instruction might even be to inhale and then as you exhale stretch forward.

Other common instructions are to come into position, focus your eyes on the space between the brows or brow point, and begin Breath of Fire or long deep breathing (see Chapter 6 on consciousness).

RELAXATION

As we mentioned in Chapter I, teachers often insert a relaxation exercise between a yoga set or kriya and meditation. Relaxation can be done sitting up or lying down. If seated, students sit in easy pose, eyes closed and focused on the space between the brows or brow point, hands in gyan mudra, breathing long and deep. If lying down, students rest on their backs, hands palms up near their thighs. Relaxation provides a good opportunity to integrate the energy that was created during the yoga session. Relaxation times vary, but for a 20- to 40-minute class, you may want to include a 3- to 5-minute relaxation.

AS YOU TEACH: TIMING AND PACING

- As a teacher, when you demonstrate something with the left or right side of the body, turn to your left as you instruct students to turn to their left. (Do not attempt to teach by producing a mirror image.)

- As you teach a lesson, try to maintain a good natural flow and pace, smoothly proceeding from one exercise to the next.

- If you are teaching a longer set or kriya, you may want to split the kriya into three or four parts and teach each part separately before combining the steps during one session.

- When teaching a yoga set or kriya, do not insert additional steps in between the suggested poses or postures. The exception of this is the insertion of a relaxation pose (lying on your back or stomach, baby pose, or sitting upright in easy pose) with eyes closed. For beginning students, inserting these additional relaxation postures helps with integration of energy.

- Often, we end sets with a series of inhales and exhales, sometimes tightening the body and relaxing and letting go, and sometimes bringing our arms over our head and shaking our arms and hands as we inhale up and exhale down.

INFUSING PRACTICES THROUGHOUT CLASSROOMS AND SCHOOLS

When school leadership motivates staff and students to try the compassion-based breath work practices, exercises, and meditations during the academic day, over time there is a transformation into a compassionate school community. Practicing yoga-mindfulness-meditation consistently produces the greatest benefits; so, we suggest that schools introduce heart centered practices during routines that are familiar to all staff and students, such as morning announcements over the intercom, weekly/monthly school assemblies, or the student news program. Having the entire school do a meditation or breath work exercise together at the same time can be a powerful bonding experience.

Classroom teachers can use compassion-based heart centered techniques to strengthen the community bond within their room. Finding a regular time during the day—such as Morning Meeting, transitions between subjects, or at the beginning or ending of class periods—when students can expect to have time for practice comforts students, especially those who have experienced trauma. For younger students and students with disabilities, add "Heart Centered Exercise" to their visual schedules.

ARE YOU READY?

Co-author Jeffrey Donald reminds us that he has heard many teachers say that they "just aren't ready to teach this yet." His response: "Well, what does 'ready' look like?" He always reminds them of their first day of teaching. No one is prepared for this! Yet, they did it, and the second day was much easier. Remember, too, Carol Dweck's (2014) research on mindset and positivity, and her words "not ready, *yet.*" You can consider yourself a learner, even as you instruct. In fact, some of the best teachers wake each day with realization and gratitude that they are continuing to learn.

So, what are the steps to become ready? Let's go back to Chapter 1 and the principles for our work:

1. **Practice.** Have you begun your own practice? If not, what is holding you back? How can you begin? Several of us began with a few minutes a day, and 10 years later, we have our 30- to 50-minute daily practice.

2. **Breathe openly.** What do you know about your breath and breath work? Seeing improvements? If not, can you add a couple more minutes of practice? Many of us practice breathing for three to five minutes daily.

3. **Are you competing?** Do a self-assessment. What can you do? Work on improving two or three things, with the intent of introducing those into your classroom. Perhaps adopt a basic practice of practicing the warm-ups, breath work, and yoga sets you will be teaching, so that by the time you have introduced them to students, you will have practiced them at least three to five times.

4. **Challenge, but do not injure, yourself.** Some of us have been to yoga classes where we end up feeling incompetent and ashamed of our "lack"—what we *can't* do. Please, change your mindset. Look at yourself. As you practice, what are the small gains you are making? Over a few years, these small gains add up. By practicing the practice, your brain, your nerves, your digestive system, and your glandular system all improve. It doesn't take perfection to make tremendous gains!

5. **It helps to have a teacher.** Do you have one? If not, where can you look? Have you gone online? Have you looked at the apps we have in this book? Is there a teacher available at your school? Teachers are helpful!

6. **Have a little fun!** Is there one posture, set, meditation, or breathing experience that you particularly like? If so, do more of that one thing for a while. Christine Mason, who has taught yoga for 20 years, has found that over time her list of favorites has multiplied. She remembers that initially, she loved one breath because she felt so calm and grounded afterward, and she loved another because she felt such focus and energy! However, over time, she came to anticipate the newness and freshness of a new yoga set or routine.

MINDFUL REFLECTION

1. How ready are you to implement yoga-mindfulness-meditation practices?

2. Which of the Five Cs sounds most appealing to you? Is there one that might fit best with the curriculum you teach?

3. What plans do you have to make accommodations for students? How can you gauge whether these accommodations are successful?

ONLINE RESOURCES

Visit https://resources.corwin.com/CultivatingHappiness

Online Resource 5.1   Barriers and Resistance to Your Practice

Online Resource 5.2   Trauma-Informed Yoga Resources

Online Resource 5.3   Motivation and Accommodations

Online Resource 5.4   Mindful Reflection

CHAPTER SIX

Consciousness

KEY PRINCIPLE

Conscious awareness is the basis for understanding self, others, and our world.

TEACHER NOTES

1. We present several foundational breaths in this chapter. However, we encourage you to begin with long deep or heart centered breathing, and only advance sequentially as you and/or your students are ready.

2. Over time, as we become more aware of our breath, our minds, our emotions, and our bodies, we also become more conscious of our needs and the needs of others. Breath work, mindfulness, yoga, and meditation will all help staff and students become more consciously aware—or mindful of needs.

3. As you are teaching, it often works well to repeat one breath, warm-up, yoga posture or set, or meditation several times. This helps students improve their practice.

CONSCIOUSNESS AND SELF-AWARENESS

Conscious awareness of self, others, and our surroundings is foundational to all we experience—or fail to experience—in our lives. Consciousness means being alert and aware of what is going on around us, as well as being mindful and focusing our attention on the present moment. When we are consciously aware, we are better able to field our emotions, handle the stress that comes our way, and be more compassionate.

As Bidyut Bose, director of the Niroga Institute in California, and colleagues state in their book *Teaching Transformative Life Skills to Students* (2016),

> When we are consciously aware, we are better able to field our emotions, handle the stress that comes our way, and be more compassionate.

> learning to manage and reduce feelings of stress and anxiety when they come up can thus have a direct positive impact on learning readiness. . . . Self-awareness includes being aware of your body sensations, emotions, activities (including reactions), and thoughts. It is the essential difference between being subsumed by a powerful emotion and the ability to witness it. (p. 12)

Yet, as we explained in Chapters 1 and 3, when we are under stress, there is a tendency to want to escape or ignore our feelings. Our desire to end unpleasant thoughts and experiences can take over our lives, reducing our heart–mind–body connection and leaving us less able to respond compassionately or even appropriately to those around us.

Bose and his co-authors (2016) go on to explain the pervasive impact of our own consciousness and the value of mindfulness practices in improving our sense of well-being:

> Self-awareness affects our self-care, relationships and self-regard, and it affects every aspect of our lives. . . . The point of practice is to build awareness of our experience right now, without judging it or ourselves. . . . Assure students that however they are feeling is just fine and congratulate them for taking the time to notice. (p. 12)

In this chapter, we will explore active consciousness and mindfulness exercises to build our focus, awareness, attention, and breathing.

CURRICULAR CONTEXT

1. In the early grades, consciousness can easily fit with discussions of self and emotions.

2. In the upper elementary grades and beyond, consciousness activities can be directly tied to awareness of equity, justice, and sustainable living and environmental concerns.

3. By Grades 3–5, consciousness can be directly related to metacognition, which includes not only an understanding of self, but also awareness of one's emotions, moods, strengths, and challenges.

4. Across grade levels, metacognition includes students' awareness of how they learn best, with their preferences for how and when to complete assignments (e.g., in groups vs. individually, online vs. in person).

5. In social studies, consciousness helps us increase our understanding of communities around the world, including our awareness of how other people live, their culture, their traditions, and their concerns.

6. In literature, consciousness can contribute to our understanding of the characters in a story and of the dynamics among characters.

7. In science, technology, engineering, the arts, and mathematics (STEAM), consciousness helps us understand more about the nature of the universe, our observations, and scientific research, including why research findings may be rejected or questioned. With technology and engineering, consciousness helps us to focus on our growing awareness of the interdependence we have with technological innovations, or the adjustments we go through as we adapt to new technologies, and of the impact of new technologies on our lives, our work, and our future. The arts (art, theater, and music) help us to explore, discover, and express our feelings and ourselves in relation to the world.

Introspection or reflecting on ourselves can be useful for building our conscious understanding of our thoughts, feelings, and needs. The aim of introspection according to Daniel Rechtschaffen (2016) is

> to learn how to organize our inner world in a healthy way. Each part is there for a reason and cannot be expelled. Anger is a need to be valued and respected. Sadness is a need to feel authentic loss and grief. Fear is our protector, keeping us safe. What we can learn to do with mindfulness is to not get so enmeshed in shame or anxious feelings and witness the parts with presence and care. The intention is not to get rid of emotions but to experience them fully without getting lost in them. . . . [However], introspection is a vulnerable operation. As we slow down and look inside, we are forced to feel some of the stress and emotion that we have been postponing or defending against. It is vulnerable to see the imperfect, work-in-progress parts of ourselves. But that is who we are—beautiful and broken works in progress. (pp. 42–43)

Introducing consciousness to different grade levels involves helping students become more introspective and observant. It also involves helping them understand who they are and what is most important to them (personal values). The Four Questions About Self we pose in *Mindful School Communities* (Mason, Rivers Murphy, & Jackson, 2020, p. 42) begins with adapting these four core questions to an individual grade level. In the lower grades, for example, this involves drawing pictures and scribing for the students as they relay their stories.

1. "Who am I, really?"
2. "What do I value?"
3. "What do I know about the world around me?"
4. "What more do I need to learn?"

CONSCIOUSNESS WARM-UPS

The first warm-up is a fun one for balance. It can be used for all ages.

Balance Warm-Up

Part I. Leg to front, to side, and back.

Position: Begin in a standing position.

1. Put your right arm out in front of you, parallel to the ground and palm down. Raise your right leg up and forward toward your hand (almost as a kick but higher).

2. Move your right arm out to the right side, parallel to the ground and palm down. Raise your right leg out to the side and up toward your hand.

3. Return your right foot to the floor and then bring your right leg back behind you, with your leg straight, your foot on the floor, toes pointed forward. (There will be about 3 feet between your feet with the left leg in front of your body.)

4. Now bend your left knee and place your left hand on your left hip.

5. Then put your right arm straight out in front of you to the left and hold for a few seconds.

This is then repeated on the other side.

We suggest repeating this exercise two or three times. With practice, teachers can ask students to hold for a few seconds in each position.

Part II. Balancing with one leg raised and out.

Position: Begin in a standing position.

1. Extend your arms out at your sides.
2. Raise one leg out to the side (with the knee straight).
3. Hold and balance for a few seconds.
4. Repeat on the other side.

Over time, with both of these balance warm-ups, try to increase the length of time you are able to balance on one leg.

Cobra Pose as a Warm-Up

Sometimes it is fun and also helpful to take a posture and teach it separately to give students additional practice with a specific posture. When teaching cobra as a warm-up, plan your lesson to instruct students to come in and out of position several times.

Cobra balances energy and draws the breath from the lower body to the upper body and brain.

As a warm-up, you may wish to first teach modified cobra as it is easier, and then alternate between modified and full cobra, resting periodically and giving students an option to continue with modified cobra or proceed with full cobra.

Position: Lie on the stomach. Place palms flat on the floor under the shoulders with fingers spread apart. Heels are together.

Eye Focus: Eyes are open.

Full Cobra

1. Inhale into cobra pose, pressing the abdomen into the ground. Rotate your armpits in as you fully extend your arms and rise up vertebra by vertebra, starting from the neck to the base of the spine.

2. Stay in position with long deep breathing for 1 to 3 minutes.

Modified Cobra

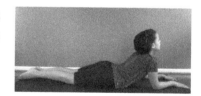

Begin by teaching modified cobra, an easier position that puts less stress on the back. People with back issues may prefer to stay with modified cobra.

1. Lying on your stomach, hands near your head, keep your forearms on the ground, and arch your back up, as with full cobra. However, forearms remain on the ground.

In either modified or full cobra, you can do long deep breathing or Breath of Fire (described in the next section). Continue for 1 to 3 minutes.

To End:

Exhale and relax down, turning your head on one cheek and totally relaxing your body.

Bent Knee Cobra

Another modification is bent-knee cobra. It can be done from either a full or a modified cobra position.

See also the yoga warm-up for letting go of anger, which is presented later in this chapter after a discussion of anger.

BREATH WORK

Breath work is essential to balancing and regulating one's emotional state of mind, health, and well-being.

Long Deep Breathing

Essentially, the long deep breath uses the body the way it is designed to work. It is complete and efficient. Present-day society's inability to relax and maintain peace of mind inhibits proper breathing. One of the body's responses to stress, both psychological and physical, is to increase the breath rate. Increased breath rate and/or shallow upper chest breathing leads to weak nerves, chronic tension, and stress-related illnesses. According to a nationwide survey conducted by the American Psychological Association (2015), 77% of adults experience stress that impacts our physical health. Though society is aware of the importance of exercise, a healthy diet, and a positive attitude, the value of breathing techniques is only now becoming recognized.

The following breath relies on a more formal approach to three-part breathing.

Position: This breath can be done in any posture.

1. Sit or lie down on the back. Place hands on the abdomen with fingertips touching. Fingers separate as the abdomen expands on the inhale. Fingertips rejoin on the exhale.

2. Inhale with a relaxed navel/abdomen area and allow abdomen/ribs to expand. At the end of the inhale, the upper chest lifts. On the exhale, the upper chest relaxes down, the rib cage releases back, and the abdomen relaxes back to normal, gently pulling the navel to completely empty the lungs.

THE MANY BENEFITS OF LONG DEEP BREATHING

- Relaxes and calms.
- Resets the brain for a clear mind in crisis situations.
- Assists proper decision making.
- Improves resistance to negativity, sickness, and accidents.
- Regulates the body's pH, increasing adaptability.
- Clears mucous linings of the alveoli of the lungs.
- Reduces and prevents toxic buildup by oxygenating the blood.
- Stimulates the production of endorphins in the brain.
- Decreases susceptibility to depression.

- Establishes positivity, coolheadedness, and clarity.

- Energizes, increasing awareness and alertness.

- Facilitates physical and emotional healing.

- Reduces fear and insecurity.

- Stimulates pituitary secretion, increasing intuition.

Heart Centered Breathing

This section presents an intimate view of key breathing strategies for connecting to ourselves and others to overcome trauma, fear, and a sense of failure. It incorporates breathing strategies from several mindfulness and yoga traditions.

Research demonstrates that taking deep breaths is not only one of the most effective tools to balance the brain and return the nervous system back to its ready state but also one of the easiest and quickest forms of relief. You take on more oxygen during intentional deep breathing, which results in better circulation, respiration, and toxin elimination. For our students, this means that there is more oxygen available to their brains and that chemicals are reduced to increase brain efficiency, elevate their mood, and reduce pain (Patel, 2018).

A simple heart centered breathing technique is to put your hands over your heart and breathe long and deep, breathing in love and peace to the heart center and exhaling love and peace to others. Continue this meditation for 5 to 8 minutes. For younger children, this can be as brief as 1 or 2 minutes.

*Introductory Comments About
Breath of Fire (for ages 14 and older)

Breath of Fire is complex, yet powerful, and unique to kundalini yoga. It may take several sessions or even months to feel comfortable with it. However, it is used in many of the yoga sets we teach. We often instruct our students to use Breath of Fire as they are comfortable and to return to regular breathing if they choose, but to continue to try it out over a period of time. Many of Christine Mason's regular students love this breath and in fact will request it if they do not practice it regularly.

This breath is for individuals who are 14 years old or older. In ancient yogic traditions, Breath of Fire is not practiced until puberty. Girls and women who are menstruating should avoid or only use a light Breath of Fire—regular long deep breathing can be substituted. As a teacher, we typically instruct our classes:

This is a powerful breath that creates a lot of energy. If you are pregnant or menstruating, substitute a regular long deep breath.

You can learn more about Breath of Fire (Nunez, 2020), including research supporting how it reduces stress; strengthens your diaphragm, nervous system, digestion, and abdominal muscles; and improves concentration, at www.healthline.com/health/breath-of-fire-yoga [online resources] (*also available on the Corwin Resources page at* **https://resources.corwin.com/ CultivatingHappiness**).

Breath of Fire is rapid, rhythmic, and continuous, with an equal inhale and exhale.

Caution: *Breath of Fire increases energy and circulation, which causes a detoxification reaction in the body that is immediate. Toxins, such as deposits from smoking, bad nutrition, and drugs, release from the cells and dump into the blood and lymph system. If a person has a lot of toxins, use caution with Breath of Fire and master it slowly and methodically.*

When students are first learning Breath of Fire, they may prefer an option to "return to a regular breath" if that increases their level of comfort.

*Breath of Fire

Position: This breath may be used in almost any posture.

Part I. To learn Breath of Fire.

Position: Seated.

Eye Focus: Close your eyes and focus on the space between the eyebrows.

1. Open your mouth and begin panting like a dog through your mouth (with the tongue sticking out).

2. When you feel comfortable, you can shift the breath to nostril breathing in a similar fashion, keeping the inhale and exhale equal in length, with no pause between them.

3. Practice for 2 to 3 minutes.

Note: *Beginners may feel some discomfort—this is easily resolved by the instruction to return to panting with the mouth open for a few seconds to "get back to the rhythm," and then return to nostril breathing.*

When students are first learning Breath of Fire, they may be more comfortable if only a few minutes of a class session include this breath.

After you have learned Breath of Fire, it can be practiced from almost any position.

Source: Khalsa, G. R. (Ed.), Kundalini Research Institute. (2020). *The Aquarian teacher level one instructor yoga manual.* Kundalini Research Institute.

Breath to Increase Energy

Once the basics have been learned, here is a breath that can be used on a regular basis. When teaching students ages 14 and up, many yoga teachers typically include 1 or 2 minutes of this version of Breath of Fire in every class.

This breath can be used for longer periods of time—even up to 5–22 minutes or longer. When practicing for a longer period of time, instruct students to lower their arms, if needed, but then immediately raise their arms back up. As we indicated in Chapter 3, as teachers we want to help students learn to challenge themselves. Learning about our individual capabilities is one of the ways we increase our consciousness.

Part II. Breath of Fire to Increase Energy (also known as "ego buster" or "ego eradicator").

Position: From a seated position, pull the chin back slightly so the back of the head is even with the spine. Raise your arms up 60 degrees—arms are straight, with thumbs up, and fingertips are on the mounds at the base of the fingers.

Eye Focus: Close your eyes, focusing on the space between the brows.

Begin Breath of Fire and continue for 1 to 2 minutes.

After 1 or 2 minutes, inhale and with straight arms touch your thumbs together above your head, exhale and open your fingers, and then lower the arms to your side.

Note: From a standing position, the angle is 30 degrees from the horizontal (for balance).

THE MANY BENEFITS OF BREATH OF FIRE

- Focuses the mind.
- Produces physical and mental energy.
- Releases toxins from blood vessels, mucus lining, cells, and lungs.
- Increases lung capacity for better health.
- Helps overcome addictions while cleansing the body of negative effects of tobacco, alcohol, drugs, caffeine, and sugar.
- Increases physical endurance.
- When practiced correctly, produces a global alpha rhythm in the brain.

Alternatives

Bunny breath (see Chapter 2) is a similar breath that can be taught to preschool and kindergarten students. With bunny breath, simply take short rapid breaths, twitching your nose like a bunny.

Elevator breath. For students in Grades 1–3, an elevator breath may be a good alternative. It can also be taught to any age group.

1. From a seated position, close your eyes, focusing on the space between the brows or brow point.
2. Place your hands in a horizontal position, left hand on top of right, palms down, elbows bent, hands in front of your abdomen.
3. Inhale through the nose, in short inhales, moving the hands upward at the same time.
   - Inhale into the abdomen.
   - Inhale into the lungs.
   - Inhale into the throat.
4. Exhale one long exhale, moving the breath and hands downward to the abdomen.
5. Repeat for 1 to 3 minutes.

A variation of elevator breath. This version of elevator breath can be used for students in Grades 4–12.

Position: Seated. Hands are in your lap, palms facing upward.

Eye Focus: Eyes are closed.

1. Inhale through the nose, in short inhales.
   - Inhale into the abdomen.
   - Inhale into the lungs.
   - Inhale into the throat.
2. Exhale one long exhale, moving the breath downward to the abdomen.
3. Repeat for 1 to 3 minutes.

More Breaths for Everyone

Body Position: Easy pose.

*Left Nostril Breathing

Time: 3 minutes.

This breath is soothing and calming. It initiates rest and relaxation. It's a perfect tool to quiet a group that needs to settle down. The left hand is in gyan mudra.

Position: Block the right nostril with the right thumb, fingers extended.

Breath: Initiate long deep breathing through the left nostril.

To End: Inhale and hold for 10 seconds.

*Right Nostril Breathing

Time: 3 minutes.

This breath is energizing. It stimulates one's active nature. It functions to increase alertness and mental focus. The right hand is in gyan mudra.

Position: Block the left nostril with the left thumb, fingers extended.

Breath: Initiate long deep breathing through the right nostril.

To End: Inhale and hold for 10 seconds.

*U Breath

Time: 3 minutes or longer.

This breath gives a quick lift and clears the mind. It can rebalance the emotions whenever one is feeling "off."

Position: The right thumb blocks the right nostril; the fingers of the right hand are raised.

Movement: Release the thumb and use the little (or index) finger to block the left nostril. Continue to alternate nostrils.

Breath: Initiate long deep breathing. Inhale through the left nostril, suspend the breath, and exhale through the right nostril. Then reverse, inhaling through the right, suspending the breath, and exhaling through the left.

There is a rhythm to the breath, inhaling for a count of 1, suspending for a count of 4, and exhaling for a count of 2.

*Sitali Breath

Time: 3 minutes.

This breath gives power, strength, and vitality. It can have a cooling, cleansing effect. The tongue initially tastes bitter and eventually becomes sweet.

Breath: Roll the tongue into a *U*, with the tip just outside of the lips. Inhale deeply through the rolled tongue, then exhale through the nose.

Alternatively, you can practice this 26 times in the morning and 26 times in the evening. Doing 108 repetitions provides a deep meditation and a powerful healer for the body and digestive system. Note that 108 has mathematical significance and can found in many references to astronomy, astrology, and nature; ancient yogis believed that by practicing chants, breath work, and yogic exercises in rounds of 108, people could "align ourselves with the rhythm of the creation" (Avery, n.d.). In kundalini yoga, there are often directions indicating that if you cannot do 108 repetitions, you should aim for 26.

*Basic Breath Series

Several of these breaths can be combined for a meditative experience that will help to balance your body and brain. It is a great breath meditation to practice before a more physical, strenuous kriya, or whenever you need a clear mind.

Position: Seated in easy pose.

Eye Focus: Eyes are closed, with eyes focused on the space between the brows or brow point.

Try combining the following, keeping the length of time consistent for each part of this breath.

1. For 1 to 3 minutes, engage in long deep breathing through the left nostril. Inhale and suspend the breath and exhale.

2. For another 1 to 3 minutes, engage in long deep breathing through the right nostril. Inhale and suspend the breath and exhale.

3. Next engage in 1 to 3 minutes of alternate nostril breathing—inhaling through the left and exhaling through the right nostril. Inhale and suspend the breath and exhale.

4. Engage in another 1 to 3 minutes of alternate nostril breathing—this time inhaling through the right and exhaling through the left nostril. Inhale and suspend the breath and exhale.

5. Then relax the arms down, hands in gyan mudra, wrists resting on knees, with 2.5 to 7 minutes of Breath of Fire.

6. **To End:** Inhale, suspend the breath for 10–60 seconds, circulate the energy, and relax or meditate. Relax the breath and concentrate on the natural flow of energy throughout your body for 1 to 3 minutes. Notice any changes in your thoughts or emotions. Then, inhale and meditate silently or ideally chant long *Sat Nams* for 3 to 15 minutes.

Alternatives

Giant Yawn

Eye Focus: Eyes are open.

1. Stand up straight and tall.
2. Raise your arms over your head, stretching up.
3. Open your mouth as if to yawn, and say "ahhhhhhh."

Repeat 3–4 times.

Clams

Eye Focus: Eyes are open.

1. Sit in easy pose with your arms out in front of you.
2. Close your shell: Bend over, exhaling as you bring your nose to your knees, and hang onto your toes.
3. Open your shell: Continue to hold onto your toes, as you inhale and raise your chin up.
4. Then release your fingers from your toes as you continue to inhale and raise your arms over your head.
5. Relax your hands down as you exhale, reaching for your toes.

Continue opening and closing your shell several times.

Eagle Breath

Students are standing. Suggest that students close their eyes and imagine an eagle flying.

Eye Focus: Tell students they can then keep their eyes closed or open them.

1. Now raise your arms slightly so they are out to your sides (and parallel to the ground).
2. Inhale as you raise arms like a bird flapping its wings.
3. Hold briefly.
4. Exhale as you lower your arms down.

Continue for 1–2 minutes. Younger children may want to move around the room (eyes open), flying like an eagle.

Source: Adapted from Purperhart, H. (2008). The yoga zoo adventure: Animal poses and games for little kids. Hunter House Publishers, Inc.

YOGA SET: POSTURE AND MOVEMENT

Yoga, combined with breath work, reduces stress, increases focus, and improves the capacity to learn. However, practice is required. Continuous benefits only come with practice.

In today's society, our bodies become so accustomed to daily anxiety and stress that eventually an imprint, or "body memory," is created that is extremely difficult and arduous to reprogram. When stress is inevitably presented, our bodies literally go on "autopilot," acting out their learned method of survival. This is why physical movement and specific exercises are utilized in Heart Centered Learning—to break the toxic cycle of the sympathetic nervous system's dominance over the body and return it to proper glandular equilibrium. Additionally, physical changes in adolescence can be quite difficult for students to navigate gracefully, which is another reason that Heart Centered Learning employs physical exercise. Carefully chosen physical exercises and postures that enhance circulation, promote energy flow, and unlock physical manifestations of stress are utilized to drastically lessen the negative effects of body memory and increase confidence. Posture and movement consist of all of the following:

- Physical exercises and postures that systematically work with the body, breath, and sound, enabling students to personally induce relaxation and mental tranquility.

- The cultivation of increased self-esteem and self-awareness through the achievement of specific stress-relieving exercises that help young people develop dynamic strategies for resolving internal/external conflicts before they escalate into inappropriate behaviors or reactions.

- Demonstrating alternative responses to psychological pressures and physical challenges with empowered self-control and peaceful creativity.

....

Breath, yoga postures and movement, and meditation may be combined in a set or "kriya." When times are provided for a kriya, the rule is to never practice for longer than the suggested time.

....

*Surya Kriya: "Sun Kriya" (ages 6 to adult)

The surya kriya is named after the energy of the sun. *It builds the ability to focus on many tasks and helps the mind become alert and ready for action.* This kriya will help build strength, improve digestion, and hold your weight down. The accompanying images show a youth approximating the correct postures.

This kriya has seven parts.

1. *Breathing. This gives you a clear focused mind.*

Position: Easy pose. The right hand is in gyan mudra.

Eye Focus: Eyes are closed, focused on the space between the brows or brow point.

Breath: Begin right nostril breathing. Block the left nostril with the thumb of the left hand. The other fingers point straight up like an antenna. Begin long, deep, powerful breaths in and out of the right nostril.

Continue for 3 to 5 minutes. Inhale and relax.

2. *Sat kriya. This brings energy from the lower body to the brain.*

Position: Sit on the heels in rock pose with the arms overhead, hugging your ears, and the palms together. Interlock the fingers except for the index fingers, which point straight up. As comfortable, cross one thumb over the other. (To strengthen masculine qualities put the right thumb over the left, and to increase feminine qualities put the left thumb over the right.)

Eye Focus: Eyes are closed, focused on the space between the brows or brow point.

Rhythmically chant *Sat Nam* (translated as "Truth is my/our identity").

As you chant, draw the navel point to the spine on *Sat* (pronounced "sut") and relax the navel on *Nam* (pronounced "nam"). The pace is moderately fast—at almost one *Sat Nam* every 1.5 seconds.

Continue for 3 minutes.

To End: Then inhale deeply. Apply root lock by squeezing the muscles tightly from the buttocks, imagining energy going up your spine and out of the top of your skull. Exhale. Inhale deeply. Hold the breath out and once again apply root lock, pulling energy.

3. *Spinal flex (see Chapter 2). This warms up the spine and increases flexibility.*

Position: Sit in easy pose. Grasp the shins with both hands.

Eye Focus: Eyes can be open or closed.

Alternate positions as you flex your spine. Begin by inhaling as you lean forward, drawing your shoulder blades together in back, keeping your chin up and out with your head parallel to the horizon. On the exhale, bring your navel point to your spine and let the spine flex backward, squeezing the buttocks and pulling upward from the buttocks.

Mentally vibrate *Sat* on the inhale and *Nam* on the exhale. Repeat 108 times (or for at least 2 to 3 minutes).

To End: Inhale, suspend your breath, and stretch the spine perfectly straight.

4. *Frog pose. This position brings energy from the lower body to the navel point, heart center, and mind.*

Position: Squat, toes on the ground, and keep the heels together and up off the ground. Fingertips are on the ground between the knees, arms are straight, and head is up (like a frog sitting on a lily pad).

Eye Focus: Eyes are open.

Inhale and raise the buttocks high and lower the forehead toward the knees. Exhale and return to the initial squat position.

Continue 26 times.

5. *Neck turns. This activity opens the throat, stimulates circulation to the head, works on the thyroid and parathyroid glands, and helps relieve tension in the neck and shoulders.*

Position: Rock pose, spine straight, sitting on the heels, with hands on the thighs.

Eye Focus: Eyes are closed, focused on the space between the brows or brow point.

Inhale, turning the head to the left, as you mentally chant *Sat.*

Exhale, turning the head to the right, as you mentally chant *Nam.*

Continue for 3 minutes.

6. *Spinal bend. This activity distributes the energy over the whole body, balances the magnetic field, and improves spinal flexibility.*

Position: Sit in easy pose with your hands on your shoulders, fingers in front and thumbs in back. Elbows and upper arms are parallel to the ground.

Eye Focus: Eyes can be open or closed.

Inhale as you bend to the left, then exhale as you bend to the right. This is a gentle swaying motion.

Continue for 3 minutes.

7. *Meditate. This will bring deep self-healing.*

Position: Sit in a good yogic position with the spine straight.

Eye Focus: Eyes are closed with a focus on the space between the brows or brow point.

Pull the navel point to the spine—hold it and apply root lock.

Observe your breath. On the inhale, listen silently to *Sat,* and on the exhale, listen silently to *Nam.*

Continue 3 to 6 minutes or longer.

This will take you into a deep self-healing meditation.

Gaining Clarity

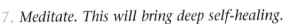

To become more conscious or aware of self and others, it helps to have a sense of clarity. The following set was designed to "become crystal clear." It impacts the heart, the breath, the navel point, and the flow of energy between the navel point and heart. The version presented here is most appropriate for students in Grades 4–12.

*Yoga Movement Lesson: Becoming Crystal Clear

This set has five basic steps.

Position: Sit in good yogic posture (see Chapter 5) in easy pose, legs crossed at the ankles.

Eye Focus: Eyes are closed, focused on the space between the brows or brow point. *For this set, remember, if you reduce the time, to reduce it proportionately across each part of the kriya.*

1. Arms are out at the side, parallel to the ground, with palms facing forward. Alternate bringing one palm to your chest and then the other—but do not touch the chest. Do this rapidly, and Breath of Fire will automatically develop from the motion. Imagine that you are pulling energy in with each movement of your arms. Continue for 1 to 6.5 minutes.

2. Bring your hands to the center of your chest as if to clap them in front of your face, but do not touch the hands together. Bring force and control to this movement. Continue for 2.5 minutes.

3. Hands are out at your side, elbows bent, facing forward. Move both hands up and down at the same time as if you are bouncing a ball with each hand. Imagine that you are bouncing energy against the ground. Continue for 30 seconds.

4. Lie down on your back and place both hands on your navel point. Press hard. Raise your heels about 6 inches off the ground and keep them up, lowering them as you need to, but striving to keep them up. Continue for 2 to 6.5 minutes.

5. Lie down and relax deeply. You might even go to sleep. Imagine that your body is filled with light.

   - Focus on your navel point. (The recording "Naad" was originally played in class.) Continue for 3 to 7 minutes.

   - After 3 to 5 minutes, students begin powerfully moving the navel point; in the original class, students also sang along with "Naad." Continue for 3 to 7 minutes.

JULIET JONES EXPLAINS THE VALUE OF YOGA AND MEDITATION

Juliet Jones in Oakton, Virginia, has been a regular yoga student with Christine for the past five years.

Yoga has been essential to my survival. I just marked my 10-year anniversary of giving up my own life and moving back to the house I grew up in to care for my

(Continued)

(Continued)

parents, first through my mom's progressive supranuclear palsy and then through my dad's long, slow decline from Alzheimer's. Yoga is just about the only piece of my life that I have carved out just for myself, the only reliable oasis I have from the noise in my mind and the constant, unpredictable demands from both my job and my dad. I know it has been a big reason I stay sane and keep going. I use the breathing and mantras when I wake up in the morning and frogs when I go to bed at night. Many of my coworkers are on antidepressants, and many of my fellow Alzheimer's caregivers develop terrible physical and mental health problems from the stress and demands. I am so grateful that so far, I am doing okay. I think yoga, even the small amount I do, is a big part of it. Practicing for an hour seems out of reach, so I try to work in a few exercises here and there. I try to do a mantra every day, even if not for the full recommended 11 minutes. I will keep hanging onto this and trying to build my practice and strength in small ways until someday when I hope to have time and focus to do it in a bigger way.

The Kriya for Elevation is available on the Corwin Resources page at **https://resources.corwin.com/CultivatingHappiness.**

MEDITATIONS

Meditative practices are an essential "upload" of positive affirmations that lead to greater well-being, confidence, and emotional clarity.

Mindfulness Helps Students Understand More Deeply, Reframe, and Adapt

Developing a higher consciousness or awareness involves turning inward through reflection and mindful meditation. Developing the ability to reflect is the core and heart of mindfulness and Heart Centered Learning.

- Students and adults, certainly teachers, benefit from mutual practice and reflection.

- Teachers are better able to focus, building greater capacity to observe more closely and *tune in* so that the needs of their students are met and addressed prior to introducing any learning.

Similarly, when we take the time to help students through difficulties or crises, their brains become more at ease and open to learning. Students are better able to concentrate, calm their minds and bodies, and utilize the prefrontal cortex area of the brain needed for cognitive learning, decision making, and overall executive functioning (Mason et al., 2019). Intentionally mediating the learning environment for our students by creating consistent safe and supportive havens for learning provides rich learning opportunities for discovery and exploration of self and others around us and, in turn, helps our students let go of the daily stressors and pain associated with their lives as they begin to experience trust and security (Mason et al., 2019).

Through mindfulness practice and self-reflective activities, we can gain a more all-encompassing and holistic view of the world, our students, and ourselves.

When we intentionally provide opportunities for students to examine and reflect on their own insights, ideas, and experiences through consciousness exercise, we can help students reframe to better understand and further conceptualize real-life situations they are experiencing or witnessing. So many inequities, injustices, and disappointments have been experienced and exposed during COVID-19, leaving us in need of support to alleviate our pain and suffering. Mindfulness practices can help us all to channel our attention and sustain motivation even in the midst of unspeakable frustration, disappointment, loss, and pain. Mindfulness can help our brains reorganize thoughts and ideas and soothe our emotions, thereby reducing stress, increasing our ability to cope with our daily lives, and improving our overall physical and mental health (Mason et al., 2019).

During 2020, we not only experienced COVID-19; we also saw an increased consciousness of disparities and opportunities to support greater equity and justice. As Paulo Freire indicated in the *Pedagogy of the Oppressed* (1970/2018), educators have a role to play in increasing the conscious awareness of others regarding suffering and oppression. Whatever we can do to increase our consciousness can facilitate not only an understanding of ourselves but also our ability to deeply understand the concerns and needs of others. This understanding is critical for conscious problem solving and the development of solutions not only for individuals but for cultures and across cultures as well.

In *Mindfulness Practices*, we provide several examples of ways to help students become more aware as they "reframe" (Mason et al., 2019).

- One way to reframe events is to try to obtain a deeper understanding. Consider the idea of windows and mirrors. Windows allow us to see a glimpse of others, their environment, and their circumstances. Windows also provide light and air. On the other hand, mirrors provide a reflection of ourselves. Other people in our lives may also serve as mirrors. Consider someone with similar beliefs and how that person may have even shaped or influenced your beliefs. Building on these concepts, students can consider characters in literature or even modern-day leaders as windows or mirrors (adapted from Michie et al., 2014, as cited in Mason, Rivers Murphy, & Jackson, 2020, pp. 48–49).

- We can also reframe events by leading students through "what if" problem-solving scenarios, asking students to take on different roles and to put specific events within a larger context (adapted from Gasson & Donaldson, 2018).

If you are teaching a unit and using reframing or facilitating discussions to deepen understanding of racism, discrimination, equity, and justice, the yoga-mindfulness-meditations in this chapter may be particularly useful to help students process information and think more clearly.

Yoga-Mindfulness-Meditation for Emotions

There are many breaths, yoga sets, and meditations to help balance emotions. Heart centered breathing is one of the techniques for helping to center oneself with a sense of being grounded, steady, loving, and calm. There are guided meditations for increasing a sense of security and removing fears, and almost any of the breaths that focus on long deep breathing will help increase your sense of well-being.

One common meditative practice is to focus on the breath and as thoughts come to mind simply observe them and let them go. This practice can be a huge help in letting go of jealousy, envy, fear, or even sadness. However, when it comes to anger, sometimes some additional work is helpful.

Working With Anger

Anger is an emotion that has quite the list of close relatives: frustration, impatience, annoyance, rage, irritation, and crankiness. The endless variations of anger can cause us to lose ourselves in its embrace. Anger impairs our thinking and feels overwhelming; it causes us, quite literally, to lose our mind. Many times, when we are angry, we act impulsively in ways that ultimately hurt us and others around us. Shouting, threatening, fighting, rudeness, and disrespect are a few examples of this place we find ourselves. Often, anger can come out in less obvious ways, such as gossiping, excluding others, and making others feel less than ourselves. Most of all, anger hurts our physical and mental health, social relationships, and well-being, reducing our happiness to almost zero. We all intuitively know this is bad for us.

Why *Choose* Anger?

We can feel ourselves "ramping up" to anger. Try a conscious approach to difficult emotions. When you feel yourself getting angry:

- Stop and pay attention. *Notice with keen interest where you are feeling the anger in your body.*

- Rather than running and not paying attention, turn your focus toward these feelings. *What are your thoughts as you observe these feelings? Do they change as you observe them?*

- Experience the feelings as though you are observing them from a distance, like birds chirping outside your window. Watch carefully; where are they centered in your body? *Can you think of your anger as a sudden storm outside? Can you not act on these feelings as you watch the storm pass by and subside?*

- Tune into your heart centered breathing and see if you can "ride the wave" of your anger without acting on your impulses; specifically, initiate left nostril breathing or Sitali.

- If possible, complete the spinal exercise regimen from Chapter 2.

- Complete the *Meditation for a Calm Heart* (see Chapter 7) or *Tranquilize the Mind* (described later in this chapter).

You can use this approach to address any difficult feelings. Surf the wave of your anger, annoyance, sadness, boredom, disappointment, jealousy, and other such feelings, noticing how they come and go. This process is not fun, but it *is* the secret to self-mastery. Not acting on these impulses leaves you more empowered and in control of your relationships and reactions.

Anger is the most common adolescent response to stress, anxiety, depression, and fear. Skills to address and mitigate anger are introduced to support strong life choices.

What happens physically when you are angry? Your amygdala, the part of your brain responsible for the fight or flight response, kicks into overdrive, flooding your body with chemicals that are useful if you need to fight or flee (Ressler, 2010). Your breathing speeds up, heart rate accelerates, and adrenaline releases, which causes a state of hyperarousal. At the same time, the prefrontal cortex, the area that helps you to make good decisions, is essentially taken offline.

What happens next is the real problem when it comes to letting go of anger. The brain has a flagging system, like a memory bookmark, that saves the reference of the bad thing so that you can better avoid similar bad things in the future. Your brain is designed to hang on to those negatives for your safety (Hanson, 2020). Essentially, you become addicted to the anger response.

Many exercises, breathing techniques, and meditations are introduced within this text that specifically address anger, but they are most effective when practiced in quick succession:

- Tuning in to calm down.

- Breathing for optimum oxygenation.

- Exercising to maximize energy flow.
- Relaxing to integrate glandular changes in the mind–body system.
- Meditating to overcome negative thoughts.

Yoga Warm-Up for Letting Go of Anger

Sometimes we may not even realize we are angry. Yet, anger accumulates in our system. It is only natural, with the upsets that occur in our lives, that we will become angry. The following warm-up provides a way to get the anger out of our bodies and our minds. It can be done for 5–20 minutes as needed.

If we are to become fully conscious and open ourselves up to becoming compassionate, it helps to be rid of any anger that we may be holding inside.

Part I. Opening awareness.

Position: Sit in easy pose with arms up 60 degrees, palms to the ceiling.

Eye Focus: Eyes are closed, focused on the space between the brows or brow point.

1. Listen to some peaceful music.
2. Begin Breath of Fire (or the optional breath is long deep breathing).
3. Continue for 3 to 5 minutes.

As you continue, if needed, relax your arms down, then bring them back up and into position.

Part II. Physical release of anger.

Position: Continue to sit in easy pose.

Eye Focus: Eyes are closed.

1. It is helpful to play some energetic music: Punjabi drum music or other drumming is an excellent choice.
2. Inhale, hold your breath, and close your hands in fists and begin punching the air in front of you. Punch until you start to run out of breath.
3. Exhale, then immediately inhale again and begin punching. (Instructors can coach, "Now is your time—be vigorous, be forceful, and get the anger out.")
4. Continue for 3 to 8 minutes.

Part III. Letting go.

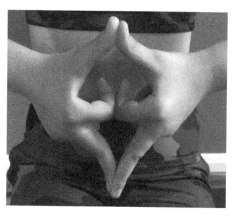

Position: Stretch your legs out in front for a couple of minutes, before returning to sitting in easy pose.

Eye Focus: Eyes are closed and focused on the space between your brows. Return to soft, soothing music.

1. Once you have returned to sitting, bring the arms back into position—arms up at a 60-degree angle, palms to the ceiling.

2. Begin Breath of Fire (or long deep breathing).

3. Imagine that there is a fire in your belly and that any anger you have is turning into smoke and being released to the edges of the universe. If you like, you may picture scraps of paper with words about your anger being burnt. (Teachers can guide the meditation and then coach, "Release any anger" or "Let it go.")

4. Continue for 3 to 5 minutes, lowering your arms as needed and then bringing them up into position.

To End: Lower your hands into your lap, keep your eyes closed, and focus on the space between your brows. Spend 2 to 3 minutes breathing deeply.

You can easily find yoga and meditation sets online for reducing anger.

*Tranquilize the Mind

This meditation tranquilizes (calms) the mind within 3 minutes. The hand position is called "the mudra which pleases the mind." Buddha gave it to his students for control of the mind.

Posture: Seated with a straight spine and relaxed shoulders.

Hand Position: With the elbows bent, bring the hands up to meet in front of the body at the level of the heart. The elbows are held up almost to the level of the hands. Bend the index fingers of each hand in toward the palms and press them together along the second joint. The middle fingers are extended and meet at the fingertips. The other fingers are curled into the hand. The thumb tips are joined and pointing toward the body. Hold the position about 4 inches from the body with the extended fingers pointing away from the body.

Eye Focus: Focus on the tip of your nose.

Breath: Inhale completely and hold the breath while repeating the affirmation of your choice 11–21 times. Exhale, hold the breath out, and repeat the affirmation an equal number of times.

Time: Continue for 3 minutes.

HOME PRACTICE

- Practice conscious, heart centered, or long deep breathing for at least 3 minutes at a time, twice per day.

- When you are ready, practice Breath of Fire or alternate nostril breathing each day.

- Practice the heart centered exercises several times a week.

- Practice the heart centered meditations at least once per day.

- For optimum results, do all three: first breathing, then exercise, then meditation.

Practice your own selected mindful activity. Note your observations and reflections in the following space.

_____

_____

_____

_____

CONSCIOUSNESS CURRICULUM INTEGRATION PLANNER

The Five Cs Curriculum Integration Planner is available on the Corwin Resources page. In Figure 6.1, we provide a few examples of how you can use this planner in making decisions about adaptations, or in logging in notes as you continue to use the warm-ups, breath work, yoga postures, meditations, and yoga sets or kriyas.

Figure 6.1 • Consciousness Curriculum Integration Planner

ACTIVITY	GRADE LEVEL	SUBJECT/CONTEXT	ADAPTATION/NOTES
Balance warm-up	Grades 5–12	Challenges—such as a literature story, a lesson from history, or the challenge a scientist or mathematician faced in making a discovery	During the week when a unit is taught, at appropriate times, some of the exercises from this chapter can be introduced and practiced. Challenge students with the ability to keep their legs up for a longer period of time in each position. In this case, the discussion will be concerning the "physical challenge."
Long deep breathing or heart centered breathing	Pre-K	Story time	Place a stuffed animal on each child's belly. The child gives the animal a "ride" so that the stuffed animal moves almost like a roller coaster as the child inhales and exhales. This is a useful activity before nap time; a good calming activity.
Breath of Fire	Ages 16+	A great breath to use when tiredness sets in or when additional alertness is needed	Remind students that they can shift to regular breathing if needed. Also, this breath can be used in different yoga postures such as cobra.

online resources 🔖 Available at https://resources.corwin.com/CultivatingHappiness

CONSCIOUSNESS OPENS US TO COMPASSION

As we become more conscious of ourselves and others, we open ourselves up to compassion, build confidence and courage, and create a more engaged and supportive community. With practice, we can become more conscious of what we are feeling, what is going on around us in the classroom and in the world, and what others are feeling and experiencing. We can learn to identify and regulate our breathing, emotions, and attitudes, while becoming more aware of and compassionate toward others.

Building our consciousness allows us to better understand ourselves and others. As we become more self-aware, we are more in tune with our feelings, preferences, skills, and experiences. Learning more about our strengths and interests allows us to focus on developing them and becoming our best selves.

Additionally, as we become more mindful and reflective, we can pause to contemplate situations and make more thoughtful decisions and responses.

For example, when students are acting out, we can stop and consider why they might be behaving this way. Perhaps something negative is going on at home, and they are desperately seeking attention and guidance. Or when teachers become irritated and impatient, they can slow down and ask themselves why they are feeling this way. Perhaps they are stressed and feeling overwhelmed, frustrated that their students seem disinterested and unengaged.

Author Tara Brach explains in the book *Radical Compassion* (2020), "If we want to become clear and nurturing mirrors to others, we need first to be conscious, present, and intentional" (p. 182). A huge part of this is related to introspection or reflecting on ourselves, which can be useful for a multitude of reasons, including becoming more aware of our feelings, emotions, and needs.

MINDFUL REFLECTION

1. What excites you most about incorporating consciousness into your lessons?

2. Which breathing techniques did you like the most? How will you use them with your classes?

3. Which breathing techniques were the most challenging? How can you introduce and scaffold them with your students?

ONLINE RESOURCES

Visit https://resources.corwin.com/CultivatingHappiness

Online Resource 6.1   Kriya for Elevation

Online Resource 6.2   Home Practice

Online Resource 6.3   Consciousness Curriculum Integration Planner

Online Resource 6.4   Mindful Reflection

CHAPTER SEVEN

Compassion

KEY PRINCIPLE

An open heart can bring healing and compassion to ourselves, each other, our communities, and our world.

TEACHER NOTES

To ensure that students have multiple experiences with compassion that help establish a foundation for compassionate action, teachers need to include a variety of yoga sets and meditations that address the various aspects of compassion.

- Compassion-based meditations that allow for practice of compassion for self, others, and our planet, as well as acceptance and nonjudgment, help students tune in and lean in toward others' suffering.

- First practicing self-compassion exercises such as "How Would You Treat a Friend?" (Neff, 2021) teaches us how to be kinder with ourselves so that we can, in turn, cultivate the capacity to be kinder and gentler with others.

- Practicing stillness, quietness, and "calming of the mind" meditations helps to open our hearts and minds to the mutual experience of hurting.

- Practicing breathing and heart beaming mindfulness activities helps us to focus on sending love and kindness to people we love, neutral people, and people who feel difficult to love at times, helping students to expand their heart centeredness and compassion capabilities.

- Compassionate meditation exercises aim to alleviate suffering while promoting empathy, health, and well-being through increasing our mutual understanding and awareness that we are not alone in our suffering.

- Practicing love and kindness meditations, such as wishing others well and being happy in our thoughts and feelings, continues to cultivate and activate the empathetic systems of our brains.

- Neuroscience supports compassion-based meditation practices that can rewire the brain circuitry, affecting the brain systems associated with empathy and compassion while also improving our moods and relationships and reducing stress.

Including yoga postures that activate the heart center, such as gentle back bends, cobra, upward dog, and bridge pose, encourages compassion. Discussing the mind–body connection can start with paying attention to how the heart feels physically and metaphorically before, during, and after yoga practice. Compassion can also be discussed as students and teachers challenge their bodies in novel ways and practice self-compassion when they do not "master" a pose the first time they attempt it.

INCREASING INDIVIDUAL COMPASSION FOR SELF AND OTHERS

Once conscious awareness is introduced and practiced, instructors increase individual compassion for self and others by embedding science-based exercises, breathing, and meditative work that leads to, and allows for, compassion as a primary value in classrooms. Instructors also address the common hurdles to compassion—anger and good decision making—that are daily challenges for modern adolescents. Teachers can focus on modeling compassion and helping students reframe situations, leading to reduced stress and increased kindness and caring.

In *Onward: Cultivating Emotional Resilience in Educators*, Elena Aguilar (2018) speaks of "listening with an open heart, with the knowledge that your heart will not break and that it can hold the pain and suffering of many" (p. 107). She instructs us to "be present with and understand the humanity of the person who speaks" (p. 107).

Yet, we know that not everyone is equally ready to be compassionately understanding of self or others. Some of us have been raised with a sense of shame or a fear of being "less than" others. Paul Gilbert (2005) is among those who caution us to remember that compassion does not come easily for all of us. When we have experienced trauma, violence, or abuse, we are less open to being compassionate.

Jeff Donald et al. (2019) explain compassion this way:

> Compassion means that we care about others, treat them with kindness, and feel a strong desire to help people in need. Compassion is empathy in action. It can look like reaching out to a peer who has been left out—or hearing about a community

need and wanting to do something to help others, even if we do not know them. (p. 88)

We can cultivate compassion (and happiness and well-being) through kindness—kind words go a long way. Listening without judgment of others is also important. However, we also know that we can learn from our breath, from our bodies, and from quieting our negative thoughts and emotions.

CURRICULAR CONTEXT

The materials in this chapter can be used to accentuate lessons on compassion, including lessons from literature as well as lessons related to metacognition and self-knowledge.

- Each of us should be taught to have self-compassion as well as compassion for others at a very young age. This can happen informally through being raised in nurturing environments with adults who both show and model compassion in their interactions with us. However, this can also be taught in a more formal sense. An ultimate aim of our work is to create a cultural shift toward compassion within schools and society.

- Academic lessons that might be particularly relevant to this chapter include lessons on community workers such as firefighters and police, as well as medical providers who are looking after the welfare of others.

- When lessons are taught about alleviating stress, the material in this chapter can be a valuable addition to the curriculum.

Setting the stage for creating a compassionate learning environment is essential to meeting the needs of the whole child. When compassionate interactions, lessons, protocols, and policies are reflective and evident in a school community, there is a greater sense of health and well-being, and there are protective factors that blanket and strengthen the school community with stronger social connections and concrete support to families. One compassionate adult is all it takes to help a child build resilience and recover from difficult experiences (Mason, Rivers Murphy, & Jackson, 2020).

MODELING THROUGH EXAMPLE HELPS CREATE A GENTLE SHIFT

Teachers and other school staff can build their own capacity for compassion as they model compassionate behaviors:

- Take a deep breath, pausing to cultivate a more heightened awareness/consciousness of what is really happening. This helps us to respond rather than react, increasing our ability to demonstrate greater compassionate caring and understanding (Mason, Rivers Murphy, & Jackson, 2020).

- Set a positive and loving tone when teaching and in informal interactions with students, families, and each other.

- Incorporate role playing with instances where students are given opportunities to resolve problems in ways that demonstrate compassionate understanding and caring.

MINDFUL COMPASSION EXERCISES: GRADES 6-12

The following two suggestions are appropriate for Grades 6–12.

- Students first generate a list of ways they may be able to show compassion during the week. Then they take 3–5 ideas from their lists and write down a reminder on a sticky note (provided by the teacher), in their agenda book, in their binder, or on a whiteboard.

- The teacher discusses the importance of self-compassion and how it is often easier to be compassionate to others rather than oneself, as well as how when we are more compassionate toward ourselves, we often are more compassionate toward others. The teacher then asks students to keep a parallel list during the week. In column 1 are examples of when the student was compassionate to self, and in column 2 are times when the student was compassionate to others.

Weaving Compassion Seamlessly Throughout the Day

Teaching compassion is not like teaching math or science. While it can be advanced with structured lessons, it can also be woven seamlessly so that it permeates every aspect of the environment and touches our hearts. As you are learning and practicing yoga-mindfulness-meditation, remember that these practices can help create a sense of calmness and well-being, opening gateways to compassion and self-healing.

To reach the hearts of others with compassion, we first need to connect with our own hearts. Many people who have trouble expressing compassion for others also struggle with self-compassion. Researcher Kristen Neff (2011) explains the wisdom of nurturing self-compassion:

Over the past decade, research that my colleagues and I have conducted shows that self-compassion is a powerful way to achieve emotional well-being and contentment in our lives, helping us avoid destructive patterns of fear, negativity, and isolation. More so than self-esteem, the nurturing quality of self-compassion allows us to flourish, to appreciate the beauty and richness of life, even in hard times. When we soothe our agitated minds with self-compassion, we're better able to notice what's right as well as what's wrong, so that we can orient ourselves toward that which gives us joy.

When we nurture our students' capacity to think about the inherent goodness and caring that are part of who we are, as well as the potential within each of us, we help students develop a growth mindset (Dweck, 2015). Over time, with practice and conscious awareness, we increase their understanding of the brain's remarkable malleability. Over time, this also leads to nonjudgment of self and others, a foundation for acceptance, empathy, and healing.

GENTLE REMINDERS

- Keep cool under fire.

- Maintain a positive and warm attitude and approach.

- Provide the space needed for students to grow and learn from each other, helping further growth mindset and a sense of well-being and security.

COMPASSION WARM-UPS

So far in this text we have introduced spinal flexes, cobra, and conscious balance exercises to use as warm-ups. Other yoga poses that can be effective warm-ups that children and adults alike tend to love are cat-cow, downward dog, and front plank.

Cat-Cow

Cat-cow is a simple movement that warms up the spine—increasing the flexibility of the spine. It is often used to introduce other yogic postures such as downward dog or front plank.

Position: Begin on your hands and knees; your wrists are directly underneath your shoulders, and your knees are underneath your hips. Your head is up, and your shoulder blades are pulled together in back.

Eye Focus: Eyes are open or closed.

1. Inhale into cow pose, with your back sagging like a cow's, by bringing your head up while at the same time pushing your stomach down.

2. Exhale into cat position as you bring your head down and chin toward your chest, rounding your back to arch like a cat getting ready to "hiss."

3. Alternate the position back and forth.

You can start at a slow pace, and as you warm up, begin moving faster. Continue for 2 to 3 minutes.

Downward Dog

Downward dog pose helps to stretch tight hamstrings, strengthens the nervous system and the spine, and increases blood flow to the brain.

Position: Start with cat-cow, alternating between the cat and cow positions for 1 to 2 minutes.

Eye Focus: Eyes are open.

1. After 1 to 2 minutes of cat-cow, inhale with your head up.

2. On the next exhale, rotate your armpits in. As you keep both hands and feet on the floor, lift your body off the ground, pulling your navel point to your spine, bringing your chest toward your thighs, and bringing your shoulder blades together. Your arms and legs remain straight or slightly bent, so your body looks like an inverted *V*. Continue a gentle breath.

3. Your heels may lift off the floor as you do this. If this happens, work toward gently moving the heels to the ground. You may wish to alternate putting one heel to the ground and then the other.

4. Stay in position and breathe for 1 to 3 minutes.

Front Plank

Front plank is an arm- and spine-strengthening pose that also tones abdominal muscles.

Position: Begin in downward dog.

Eye Focus: Eyes are open.

1. Inhale, step your feet back, and shift your weight forward until your shoulders stack directly above your wrists (arms remain straight, or have a slight bend in the elbows). Your body will be in a diagonal plane from your feet to your head.

2. Tuck your chin slightly so your neck is a continuation of your spine. Stay in position for 1 to 3 minutes. Your legs are now straight. Keep your thighs lifted. This should feel and look like the top of a push-up.

You are in proper alignment when you can shift back and forth between plank and down dog without having to move your arms or legs.

To End: Exhale as you move onto your knees and sit back on your heels, then bring your forehead to the ground in child's pose.

BREATH WORK

Cannon Breath

Cannon breath is a powerful breath for getting rid of toxins, strengthening the nervous system, and improving digestion.

It can be done in different positions—seated, standing, side lying, and cobra, for example.

It is done on the exhale. Form an *O* mouth, keeping the cheeks firm, and powerfully exhale through the mouth, pulling the navel point to the spine as you exhale.

Continue for 1 to 3 minutes.

Throwing Water Over Your Shoulders

This is used to release tension and ease burdens.

Position: Sit in easy pose. With elbows bent, your arms are straight out in front of you, shoulder-width apart, palms up.

Breath: Through the nostrils.

1. Inhale as you move your arms up and forward.
2. Exhale as you move your palms back in a circular motion as if you are throwing water over your shoulders.
3. You'll find that naturally the exhale will be stronger.

Continue for 1 to 3 minutes.

YOGA SET: POSTURE AND MOVEMENT

*Yoga for Tolerance and Compassion

As Jenni Sells (2020) says in her introduction to using this kriya,

> if you find yourself unable to connect with the tolerant, compassionate, loving part of your heart and want to open that space within yourself, "Kriya for Tolerance" from Sadhana Guidelines is a great place to start. To gain the strength needed for tolerance and humility, the navel center needs to be developed. This kriya works on the abdomen, stimulating the navel energy to rise to the higher centers and then integrates it with the aura. It is a great preparation for meditation.

*Yoga for Tolerance and Compassion

Position: Sit in easy pose with the spine straight.

Eye Focus: Eyes are closed.

1. *Bear grip at navel point.*

   - Form bear grip, locking the fingers together with the right palm facing down and the left hand facing up, with the side of the hands on the navel point.

   - Exhale completely through your nostrils as you press the side of the hands into the navel point.

   - Hold the breath out briefly.

   - Inhale through your nostrils, holding the breath for 7 to 8 seconds.

Continue this cycle for 3 minutes.

2. *Sat kriya with palms flat.*

Position: Sit on the heels and raise the arms overhead with the palms flat together.

Eye Focus: Eyes are closed.

- Pull in the navel point as you say, "Sat."

- Relax your navel point and say, "Nam."

Continue for 3 minutes.

3. *Raise legs with Breath of Fire and belly laugh.*

- Sit with your legs stretched out straight in front of you.

- Put your palms on the ground behind you.

- Inhale through the nostrils and raise both legs to 60 degrees.

- Hold and begin Breath of Fire.

Continue for 2 minutes.

To End: Inhale, exhale, and apply root lock. Then relax into easy pose and belly laugh loudly for 1 minute.

4. *Punching with breath held.*

Position: Easy pose.

- Bring your hands into fists at the shoulders.

- Inhale and then suspend the breath.

- Begin punching forward (as in boxing) with alternate hands. When you must, exhale and inhale deeply to continue.

Continue for 3 minutes.

5. *Alternate between camel ride and shoulder shrugs.* Camel ride is similar to spinal flex. You can imagine riding a camel and perhaps feeling a rolling motion as you flex your spine.

Position: Easy pose.

- Place your hands on your shins.

- Inhale through your nostrils as you flex the spine forward.

- Exhale through your nostrils as you extend the spine back.

- Inhale and lift the shoulders up to the ears.

- Exhale and drop the shoulders down.

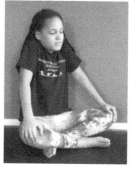

Continue the cycle at a moderate pace with deep breaths for 3 minutes.

To End: Inhale, exhale and apply root lock, squeezing your buttocks. Relax.

*Kriya for Balancing Head and Heart

This kriya helps to balance thoughts and emotions.

  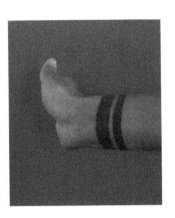

1. *Arm twists.* This activity works on the glandular reactions in the brain and strengthens the wrists.

Position: Sit in easy pose. Your arms are straight out to your sides with your hands bent up at the wrists to a 90-degree angle as if your arms are pressing against a wall. Palms face outward. Fingers are together. There is pressure on the wrists.

- Inhale in starting position, with palms facing out away from your body and fingers pointing upward.

- Exhale, rotating your wrists and arms so that the fingers point straight forward. Palms remain facing outward.

- Inhale back to starting position.

- Exhale, rotating your wrists so that the fingers are pointing straight back. Palms remain facing outward.

Continue this four-part movement for 3 to 7 minutes, moving about 1 part per second. Make sure to keep your arms and elbows straight.

2. *Arc over head.* This activity brings energy to the brain, the heart, and the magnetic field.

Position: Sit in easy pose.

Eye Focus: Eyes are closed.

- Arms are out at the sides, palms facing outward as in the arm twist activity.
- Inhale as you bring your arms up to form an arc over your head, slightly in front of the top of your head—place one hand in front of the other, but hands do not touch. Palms are up.
- Exhale and return your arms to the first position (palms facing outward).
- Inhale and bring your arms up to form an arc, this time slightly in back of the center of your head, with one hand in front of the other, palms up, and hands not touching.
- Exhale and return your arms to the first position (palms facing outward).

Make the motion powerful. Continue for 1 to 2 minutes.

3. *Crow squats.*

Position: Standing.

Eye Focus: Eyes are open or closed.

- Add crow squats to the movement in arc over head.
- Exhale and squat in crow pose, with your feet about shoulder-width apart and flat on the ground and your arms out to the side.
- Inhale and come into standing, bringing your arms up to form an arc above the head, in front of the center of the head, palms facing outward. In the inhale standing position, alternate the arc in front and then in back of the center of the head.

Continue at the rate of 1 second per movement for about 2 to 4 minutes.

To End: Take a long, deep breath. Come to standing, arms overhead, and shake your body for 30 seconds.

MEDITATIONS

*Meditation for a Calm Heart

This soothing meditation relieves anxiety, strengthens the lungs, opens the heart center, and creates a sense of calmness.

Position: Sit in easy pose, with a straight spine.

- Place the left hand on the center of the chest at the heart center. The palm is flat against the chest, and the fingers are parallel to the ground, pointing to the right.

- With the right hand, touch the tip of the index finger with the tip of the thumb. Raise the right hand up to the right side as if giving a pledge. The palm faces forward, and the three fingers not in the mudra point up.

- The elbow is relaxed near the side with the forearm perpendicular to the ground.

Eyes: Either close the eyes or look straight ahead with the eyes one-tenth open.

Breath: Inhale slowly and deeply. Then suspend the breath in and raise the chest. Retain it as long as possible. Then exhale smoothly, gradually, and completely. When the breath is totally out, lock the breath out for as long as possible.

Concentrate on the flow of the breath. Regulate each bit of the breath consciously.

To End: Inhale and exhale strongly three times. Relax.

The home of the subtle force of *prana* is in the lungs and heart. The left palm is placed at the natural home of *prana* and creates a deep stillness at that point. The right hand, which brings you to action and analysis, is placed in a receptive, relaxed mudra in the position of peace.

This posture induces the feeling of calmness. It creates a still point for the *prana* at the heart center.

Emotionally, this meditation adds clear perception to your relationships with yourself and others. If you are upset at work or in a personal relationship, sit in this meditation for 3 to 15 minutes before deciding how to act. Then act with your full heart.

Physically, this meditation strengthens the lungs and heart.

This meditation is perfect for beginners. It opens awareness of the breath, and it conditions the lungs. When you hold the breath in or out for "as long as possible," you should not gasp or be under strain when you let the breath move again.

In a class, try it for 3 minutes. If you have more time, try it for three periods of 3 minutes each, with 1 minute of rest between them, for a total of 11 minutes. For an advanced practice of concentration and rejuvenation, build the meditation up to 31 minutes.

Self-Animosity and Self-Defeating Activity

In life there are no enemies, only challenges to our creativity. The greatest challenges—self-animosity and self-defeating activity—occur when we do not accept ourselves. We often instinctively reject ourselves, opposing our own success and accomplishment just to break with the boredom of steadiness. Self-animosity distracts us from the real gift of human life:

the adventure of our capacity to experience and confront ourselves. This mindfulness exercise is used to conquer that state of self-loathing by allowing you to establish constant consciousness and develop self-compassion.

*Kriya to Conquer Self-Animosity

Position: Seated, keeping the spine straight. Relax arms at the sides.

Movement: Keep an alert attitude and straight upper torso, with no rocking back and forth. The eyes are one-tenth open and fixed at the end of the nose.

Hand Position: With the upper arms relaxed against the body, bend the elbows, and bring the forearms up so that the hands meet at the heart level in front of the chest. Make fists and bring the fists together, palms facing each other, and extend the thumbs straight up and touching along the side.

Breath: Inhale through the nose and exhale completely through the mouth. Then inhale smoothly and deeply through the mouth and exhale through the nose. Continue this breath sequence.

Time: 3–11 minutes.

To End: Inhale and stretch the arms straight up over the head. Exhale and stay in this position as you take three more deep inhales and exhales. Then relax.

*Meditation for Inner Conflict

We are often confused and held in deadlock when inner conflict blocks our ability to think and act clearly. In these moments, the mind's energy is scattered and distributed in a disturbed manner. This breath pattern holds the breath out three times as long as it is held in. So, the body senses a lack of breath energy in vital areas of functioning and asks how it can quickly and optimally reorganize itself to respond to this survival threat. The mind rechannels the energy to form a new pattern filled with clarity and action potential. Your built-in computer can calculate your total resources and the level of challenge, then design a strategy to prepare and use the mind and body effectively. This meditation resolves many conflicts and is an automatic reflex for survival. Inner conflict is the result of excess or disturbed energy. The effect is certain, gradual, and simple. *Be honest with the breath timing, and the meditation will be honest with you.* Use this exercise to reflect and act more patiently and compassionately toward yourself and others.

Posture: Easy pose, with a straight spine and the chin pulled back slightly.

Eyes: Close the eyes nine-tenths of the way.

Mudra: Place the hands over the chest, with the palms on the torso at the level of the breasts. The fingers point toward each other across the chest.

Breath: The key to this meditation is attention to the breath. Inhale deeply and completely for 5 seconds. Exhale completely for 5 seconds. Hold the breath out for 15 seconds, by suspending the chest motion as you pull in the navel point and abdomen.

Time: 11 minutes.

To End: Inhale deeply and stretch the arms up over the head. Relax the breath, keep the arms up, and shake the arms and hands for 15 to 30 seconds.

YOUR REGULAR PRACTICE

Review the yoga-mindfulness-meditation practices that you have encountered so far in this book—with a focus on Chapters 1–6. Identify ones that you want to focus on—either because you love them and want to do more with them or because you believe practice will be beneficial.

- Which yoga-mindfulness-meditation practices from previous chapters did you select for your focus?
- Review the yoga-mindfulness-meditation sequences in this chapter and practice each of them.
- Now examine this chapter and choose one breath, one yoga posture or set, and one meditation to practice for at least 7 to 10 days.
- Set up a time for practice. Begin your practice and keep a log, noting changes in your body, breathing, emotions, and mindset.

Observations and Reflections

_____

_____

_____

_____

_____

_____

_____

_____

COMPASSION CURRICULUM INTEGRATION PLANNER

Compassion can be furthered through a combination of classroom instruction that is inclusive of academic instruction, social-emotional learning, and the breath work, yoga, and mindfulness activities in this chapter. In Figure 7.1, we have included some ideas for how you might infuse yoga-mindfulness-meditation into your classes.

Figure 7.1 • Compassion Curriculum Integration Planner

LESSON	GRADE LEVEL	SUBJECT/CONTEXT	ADAPTATION/NOTES
Compassion/ Introduction Story Time	Pre-K	Story Time	Use puppets to role play situations that demonstrate compassion.
Compassion/ Community Circle	1–3	Morning Meeting	Have a question that everyone answers, such as "When did a friend help you when you were sad?" to start a conversation about compassion.
Compassion/Heart Centered Breathing/ Long Deep Breathing	Pre-K	Morning Meeting, After Lunch or Recess, End of the Day	Give each student a pebble and ask them to place it on their belly. Have them watch it rise up as they breathe in and come down as they breathe out.
Compassion/ Community Circle	1–3	Morning Meeting	Have students form a circle and hold hands. Tell the students that you have love in your left hand. When you squeeze the hand of the person next to you, it passes the love on. Practice passing the love around the circle. Then, introduce the kindness you have in your right hand and pass that along in the opposite direction. Combine the two, passing love in one direction and kindness in the other.

online resources Available at https://resources.corwin.com/CultivatingHappiness

MINDFUL REFLECTION

1. How will you integrate compassion into your classroom? Which exercises are you most excited about?

2. How might you use yoga and meditation to increase students' compassion for themselves as well as others?

3. What benefits have you seen from encouraging compassion in the classroom previously?

ONLINE RESOURCES

Visit https://resources.corwin.com/CultivatingHappiness

Online Resource 7.1   Your Regular Practice

Online Resource 7.2   Compassion Curriculum Integration Planner

Online Resource 7.3   Mindful Reflection

CHAPTER EIGHT

Confidence

KEY PRINCIPLE

Confidence is the key to sustainable success.

TEACHER NOTES

- Confidence spills over from one area of our lives to other areas.

- When we have inner self-confidence, we are on our way to happiness and developing a sense of purpose in our lives.

- Our confidence also affects our availability to be there for, respond to, and help others who most need our support.

- The breath work, yoga postures, and meditations in this chapter, including the affirmations, all work in tandem to develop a sense of mental, physical, and emotional well-being.

- Confidence often is developed with practice; as we master certain parts of our lives, our lessons, or even our movements and our breaths, we are creating pathways for future success.

- Leadership, mentoring, and attitude are all critical to helping teachers, staff, and students feel and develop confidence.

CONFIDENCE FOSTERS MENTAL HEALTH, WELL-BEING, AND HAPPINESS

After understanding and building our consciousness and compassion, we can focus on developing greater confidence within ourselves. Once we feel calm, reflective, and supported, we are more confident in our abilities both inside and outside the classroom. As we understand our emotions, reactions, and strengths better and are full of empathy and kindness, we allow ourselves to release constrictive feelings of hesitation, doubt, and worry. We rely more on ourselves and trust more in our abilities. We are more self-assured, and we trust others to work with us to achieve our collective goals.

Confidence is an important component for fostering our own personal mental health, sense of well-being, and happiness. When we lack confidence, we are more likely to be fearful, anxious, or even depressed. We are also less likely to approach new or challenging tasks; hence our ability to adapt is also reduced. Living with a reduced sense of confidence can be compared to living life in a space of two, rather than three, dimensions. Without confidence, we are less likely to fully live life—we are less likely to be truly available for ourselves or others, and we are more likely to be dissatisfied and to wonder about why we are caught up in what may be a vicious cycle of disappointment. As we explain in our book *Compassionate School Practices* (Mason et al., 2021), "it's easy to fall into anxiety or depression if you haven't built the confidence that you can get through any situation" (p. 48).

There are many factors that impede developing a sense of confidence. In 2020, the impact of long-standing inequities, racism, discrimination, implicit bias, and co-occurring fears came to the forefront as people around the globe stood in unity to lift up people of color and to demand change. We are starting to see some shifts in policies in schools and other institutions, yet much work remains. The damage runs deep and wide (Kendi, 2019).

Whether feelings of unworthiness stem from societal attitudes and practices, the hateful presence of those wishing us harm, or our own personal real or imagined failures, we can help each other by being kind, lifting each other up, and intentionally moving to eradicate injustice. All of this will increase a sense of health and well-being for individuals and for communities.

Whether feelings of unworthiness are a result of being raised in an abusive environment or with parents who lacked effective parenting skills, or result from our own mindset and not truly accepting ourselves for who we really are, these feelings are barriers that can be removed with intentional effort and practice.

STREAMING NEGATIVE THOUGHTS REDUCES SELF-CONFIDENCE

In a recent article in *HeartMind e-News*, the monthly newsletter of the Center for Educational Improvement, Kahlil Kuykendall, a gender economist and mindfulness instructor, describes the relationship between a stream of negative thoughts and lack of self-confidence:

> While lack of confidence can be related to simply not knowing, lack of confidence is often caused by a constant stream of negative thoughts, and behind that stream, one's identification with these thoughts.

- For instance, many will hear an inner voice that suggests personal unworthiness and assume this is true.

- It might even be feared that if the voice fell silent, personal existence would cease.

- Many fear it is better to perpetually criticize oneself because of feelings of personal inadequacy.

- For some, confidence development can seem like an overwhelming task. (Kuykendall, 2021)

It may take a while to overcome a sense of failure—we may even develop a fear of success, asking ourselves whether we could even adjust to success. These are times when leadership, mentoring, and guidance are invaluable. Confidence is easier to build when leaders at the top express optimism and confidence, rather than negativity and distrust. It is easier to build our own sense of confidence when we understand that mistakes are a part of a cycle of life, that with our efforts we will make gains, and that we need not be stuck in a circle of defeat.

Leadership for Success

Leaders have a significant role to play in developing confidence, celebrating successes, recognizing leadership in others, and taking a positive approach to problem solve through focusing not on the problems but rather on the potential solutions (B. Brown, 2015; Bunting, 2016; Mason et al., 2021; Mason, Liabenow, & Patschke, 2020; Wells, 2015). A leader's positive mindset is crucial to developing confident staff and students.

Developing a Pathway to Confidence

Whether you are a leader or on ground zero, cultivating self-practice is essential. To develop confidence requires being consciously aware and accepting of ourselves, our emotions, our strengths, and the areas where improvement is needed. We can create our own pathways to confidence:

- Examine your mindset (Dweck, 2015). When we have a fixed mindset, if we believe we can't improve, then it will be more difficult to change our perception of our value or worth.

- As we practice our yoga-mindfulness-meditations with discipline and intention, perhaps during our daily practice (*sadhana*), we can learn valuable skills in the safety of our sessions. For some of life's lessons, it will certainly be easier to strive to improve and see growth in a somewhat controlled environment without all of the variability and hardships that may occur in a larger societal context.

- Realize that success sometimes takes time. Typically, we will need to set time aside for practice and look for opportunities where we can continue to grow and learn.

As we learn, and as we increase our confidence, we step into a positive reinforcing cycle. With one success, we build a ramp to our next step. In the best of all possible worlds, we will take our own mindful steps and exude a more positive attitude, reduce our feelings of fear and anxiety, gain energy and motivation to take action, and perform better, inspiring others to join in.

- As we continue, we learn strategies to become more effective and assertive, sometimes surprising even ourselves with what we can achieve.

- As we develop confidence, we also develop trust in ourselves as students to be able to understand and master the material, and we trust in ourselves as teachers to be able to effectively support and cultivate our students in their growth.

- Over time, confidence leads to retaining knowledge and skills and establishing a reservoir of success.

In this chapter, we will explore activities and exercises to increase our inner resilience, communicate in a positive and affirmative way, and help students develop their own confidence and self-assuredness.

CURRICULAR CONTEXT

1. Developing confident learners at all grade levels is essential to curricular mastery and success.

2. Building student metacognition helps them to develop a keener awareness of their own thinking, their personal strengths, and therefore their confidence in how they learn.

3. Meeting students *where they* are as opposed to *where we think they should be*, using the KWL chart (what they think they *know*, what they *want* to know, and what they have *learned*), helps build confidence in the learning process.

4. Mutual learning theory of eminent cognitive psychology affirms that people learn best when they are engaged. Developing highly interactive and engaged student-led lessons increases student efficacy.

5. Overcoming learning challenges through problem-solving opportunities can be a positive way to build stronger self-confidence while nurturing one's self-determination. Students can better move past what is most difficult to learn and move through to the other side, finding success when challenges are met with love, care, and support.

6. Developing perseverance to succeed or the power of *yet* (TEDx Talks, 2014) helps students understand that there is a learning curve and process to finding success. The underlying messaging of *yet* naturally embedded in the learning process can help students develop a growth mindset of "I *can*" as opposed to a fixed, self-defeating mindset.

INSTILLING COMPETENCE INCREASES CONFIDENCE

I must not fear. Fear is the mind-killer.

—Frank Herbert, *Dune*

I learned early on that the number-one deterrent to becoming a confident and competent math student—no matter your age—is fear. Unfortunately, mathematics has always been shrouded in a cloud of mystery and intrigue. Too many youth and adults have said they lack the "compute" power to learn math. My personal experience helped me understand the crucial role that teachers can play in instilling mathematics confidence and competence in their students. For example, each class period, I help students recognize their own "weeds" of fear and negativity so that they can remove them, then replace the weeds with seeds of confidence and positivity. Then, when they begin to realize that they *can* learn and *do* math, this further propels them to work harder for greater academic success.

(Continued)

(Continued)

Additionally, I strive to instill in my students that they should never feel too proud to ask questions, and they should gradually adopt a consciousness that is not limiting but plays continuously in the mind: "I *can*, I *understand*, and I am *fearless*."

To overcome fear and math anxiety, I believe and communicate to each student that anyone can learn math, that every student brings something to the table, and that learning can be automatic. The first step in automating math learning is to ask students to change their language within my classroom by substituting the three forbidden mantras (mental thoughts):

1. I can't.
2. I don't understand.
3. I'm stupid.

with the three empowering mantras:

1. I can.
2. I will.
3. I'm intelligent.

By doing so, I am encouraging students to shift their mental vibration from a place of hopelessness and helplessness to a position of strength and empowerment. Throughout the course, I continually communicate to my math students that, "yes, you *can* learn math."

There are also some simple stress-relieving techniques that do not involve having your students try to position their body into complex, yogic postures. Stand and roll your shoulders or do simple, easy, and gentle neck rolls to help relieve stress. I also emphasize the importance of breathing from your abdomen with comfortable inhale-exhale combinations. Sitting in the *L* position slows down one's brain processes after only 15 minutes. Outside the classroom, students should be aware of the adverse effects diet, exercise, and lifestyle might have on academic performance.

Another key neuroscience-based learning tool in mastering not only mathematics but any subject is making use of the power of repetition. The brain is an amazing tool when learning a new subject. Even if you do not think you are learning when you are reading a new chapter in your math book, for example, your brain is still being imprinted or "marinated" with the new knowledge.

Dr. Kevin K. Green has over 26 years of research and development experience as an engineer. He is currently a scientist with NGA Research. Previously he taught high school math and served as an instructor for the University of Phoenix teaching adult learners' math and computer science programming.

CONFIDENCE WARM-UPS

Any combination of warm-ups can be used, including isolating parts of kriyas or sets. If you are in a standing position, it is often helpful to do hip rotations (see Chapter 4) and/or frogs (see Chapter 6). Feel free to use some or all of these.

Cobra Modification: Bent Knee

This warm-up exercise helps to strengthen your back and open up your hips.

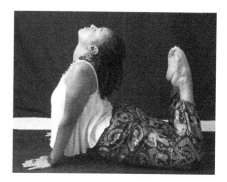

Position: Lie down on your belly, hands beside your head.

Eye Focus: Eyes are open or closed.

- Practice coming in and out of modified and then full cobra a few times, always inhaling up and exhaling down (for more on cobra, see Chapter 6).

- Lie down, and this time bend your knees so the soles of the feet are facing upward. Then, gradually arch your chest and upper body up into a modified cobra.

- In this modified, bent-knee position, begin moving your feet out to the side and then back to center (a *W* movement).

- Repeat a few times, then relax down onto your belly, turn your head to the side, and rest your head on one of your cheeks. Totally let go of any tension in your body.

Diagonal Stretch

Position: Resting on your belly, ease yourself into position so that your head is slightly off the ground and your left arm is extended forward and your right leg is straight and raised off the ground. This will provide a diagonal stretch.

Reverse sides.

Go back and forth a couple of times, then relax down onto your belly.

Scorpion

Position: Remaining on your belly, make your hands into fists and insert them at the fold where your legs attach to your torso.

- Lift your head off the ground in a straight line with your back.

- Legs are together and straight. Raise them a few inches off the ground and hold.

Breath: Long deep breathing or Breath of Fire.

Continue for 1 to 2 minutes.

Rocket Squats

This warm-up exercise is good for your knees and bringing energy from your lower body to your upper body. This a fun modification to squats used in many yoga and fitness classes.

Position: Stand with your feet shoulder-width apart; arms are straight and out in front of you, parallel to the ground, palms down.

Eye Focus: Eyes are open or closed.

- Exhale as you bend your knees and come into a squatting position, as shown.

- After three or four regular squats, switch to a "rocket squat." Exhale down, bending your knees, then move your hands close to your thighs and, on the inhale, bounce back up so that you are upright.

- Continue three or four of these with an energetic movement and breath.

- Then prepare for "rocket squat 2." For this version, exhale down, bending your knees, and inhale as you move your hands to hang by your thighs. Then, as you come up, lift your arms up (elbows straight) so that your arms are over your head.

- Continue three or four times.

To End: Come into mountain pose—a standing relaxation. For mountain pose, the navel is pulled back to the spine, the heart and chest are elevated, and the chin is pulled back so the back of the head is even with the spine. Arms are hanging loosely by your thighs, and knees are straight but not locked. Breathe long and deep.

Eye Focus: Eyes are closed; focus on the space between your brows.

Continue for 2 to 3 minutes.

Squats With Punching

This warm-up exercise is good for the knees, chest, lungs, and rib cage, as well as for toning your arms and torso.

Continue squatting up and down (regular squats); however, alternate forceful punches as you go from standing to squatting and back to standing. Continue for 2 to 3 minutes.

Table Back

This warm-up exercise is for your lower back, opening the chest, and getting oxygen to your brain.

Position: Begin in standing position by inhaling your head and arms up and back.

Eye Focus: Eyes are open or closed.

- Bend forward from your waist to the table back position with a flat back, parallel to the ground, and the arms back in a *V* position with palms up.

- Then inhale up, rotating your arms and stretching back with palms to the ceiling.

- After three or four of these, switch so that upon your next transition from table back to exhaling your arms are down in a "hanging" forward bend position.

Tripod

This is a fun and challenging modification to a standing forward bend.

Position: Begin standing, feet shoulder-width apart, and on an inhale, move your arms up and back (arms straight). On the exhale, bend over to touch the ground. Note the picture shows a student approximating tripod; if possible, try to move your head closer to the ground.

Eye Focus: Eyes are open.

- After three or four forward bends, increase your stance so your legs are wider apart.

- On an exhale, move down to table back (flat back, parallel to the ground) with arms behind you in a *V*, palms up.

- Inhale, then exhale as you continue to move your head toward the ground, swinging your arms around in front as you attempt to bring your head to the ground. You can "tip" forward slightly and walk your hands forward a few inches so that your head and hands are about 3–4 feet from your body.

- Hold and breathe for a count of 3 to 5 seconds.

- Inhale up into table back, palms up.

- Exhale, then inhale up, rotating your palms forward.

To End: Come into mountain pose.

Camel

Camel is good for your thyroid and metabolism.

Position: On your knees, shoulder-width apart.

Eye Focus: Eyes are wide open; try not to blink.

- From a kneeling position, arch your head backward, leaning back so that your hands are resting on or near your ankles.
- With eyes open, begin Breath of Fire, trying not to blink.

Continue for 2 to 4 minutes.

BREATH WORK

Cannon Breath

Use this breath for getting rid of toxins and disease resistance.

Position: Cannon breath can be done from almost any position.

Eye Focus: Eyes can be open or closed.

- Cannon breath involves a forceful (explosive) exhale through an *O* mouth.
- Start cannon breath and continue for 1 to 2 minutes.

Polishing Our Energy Field

This is an invigorating, uplifting breath with movement.

Position: Sit in easy pose.

Eye Focus: Eyes are wide open.

- Arms are bent at the elbow, with elbows out at your side, hands at the heart center, fingers spread wide apart and tight, and palms facing outward.
- Begin a circular movement, almost as if you are polishing a mirror, inhaling as your hands go up and exhaling as they circle back down. Movement is from the shoulders in a vertical plane, parallel to your body.

Continue for 3 to 4 minutes.

YOGA SET: POSTURE AND MOVEMENT

*Kriya for Prana Apana Balance (ages 12–adult)

Note: Prana is the universal life force that we receive in what we ingest, such as our in-breath we inhale, and *apana* is breath associated with elimination, with the out-breath that gives motion within, and with letting go.

1. *Rising up on knees.*

Position: Sit on your knees. Open the legs from the knees to the feet so that the body rests on the floor. Hands are relaxed on thighs.

Eye Focus: Eyes are closed, focused on the third eye point.

- Breathe naturally for 2 minutes.

- After 2 minutes, stretch the arms out to the sides parallel to the ground with the palms up.

- Slowly inhale for 6 counts, while you rise to a kneeling position.

- Suspend the breath and position for 12 counts.

- Slowly exhale for 6 counts, while lowering to starting position.

- Repeat 7 times, and on the 8th time, clap hands overhead.

2. *Push–pull legs.*

Position: Lie on the back with hands at sides, palms down, and raise the legs 1.5 feet off the ground.

- Begin alternating legs in a push–pull position, with elongated strokes and keeping legs parallel to the ground, for 2.5 minutes.

Note: Exercises 1 and 2 stimulate the internal organs, digestive system, and navel points. They mix the *prana* and *apana* at the navel point.

3. *Leg lifts.*

Position: Remain on back.

- Immediately inhale as you raise your legs to 90 degrees.

- Hold for 30 seconds.

- Slowly exhale and lower the legs.

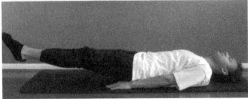

4. *Modified stretch pose.*

Position: Remain on back.

1. Lift the legs 6 inches off the ground and hold with Breath of Fire for 1 minute.

    - Inhale, hold, and then relax, lowering your legs down to the ground.

5. *Arching spine up.*

Position: On the stomach, clasp hands in Venus lock in back (see Chapter 5).

- Inhale as you arch the spine up from the waist, with your eyes closed. Hold for 30 seconds.

- Exhale powerfully, and open your eyes as you lower your torso to the ground.

Repeat this cycle 10 times. (If you keep your eyes open on the inhale, it can cause temporary dizziness as you rebalance.)

This exercise opens your heart and releases pent-up muscle tension.

6. *Heart center pull.*

Position: On your back, raise your arms straight up to 90 degrees, palms facing each other.

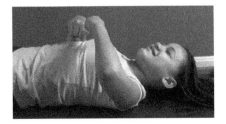

- Hold the position with Breath of Fire for 1 minute.

- Then inhale, and with great tension make fists, clench your teeth, and slowly pull your energy and fists down to the chest almost as if you were pulling 100-pound weights toward your chest. Exhale and repeat once more.

7. *Relax*. Move the mind to the navel point and listen to the heartbeat there. You may focus on *Ong, Ong, Ong* (*Ong* = "One").

Feel that you are at home, resting at the center of yourself. The heart rhythm is powered by the cosmic, creative sound of *Ong, Ong, Ong*. This will elevate you and give you mental relaxation and sensitivity.

 The kriya for new lungs and circulation is available on the Corwin Resources page at **https://resources.corwin.com/ CultivatingHappiness**.

MEDITATIONS

*"I Am Happy" Meditation for Children (ages pre-K and up)

Meditations with movements tend to work well with children.

Position: Sit in easy pose. Elbows are bent, and hands are in fists with index fingers extended up.

Eye Focus: Eyes are open or closed.

Mantra:

I Am Happy, I Am Good, I Am Happy, I Am Good

Sat Nam, Sat Nam, Sat Nam Jee

Wha-Hay Guroo, Wha-Hay Guroo, Wha-Hay Guroo Jee

Note: Sat Nam = "Truth is my/our identity"; *Wha-Hay Guroo* = "The ecstasy/ the wonder of universal knowledge and guiding truths"; and *Jee* is a sign of respect.

Hand Movement:

Children shake their index fingers up and in rhythm with the mantra.

Comments:

Children, especially under the age of 6, have shorter attention spans than adults. All meditations with movement and variation usually work well.

This meditation is very relaxing. With this meditation, your breath will automatically move toward a meditative pace to renew, relaxing your heart and mind. To heal the emotional wounds of the heart, we need to calm our nerves. This meditation creates balance as the hand position produces a subtle pressure that adjusts the heart and brings energy to the brain.

Position: Sit in easy pose with a straight spine and a light neck lock. Palms are together, lightly touching with the middle finger at the level of the brow point. Forearms are horizontal to the ground with elbows held high.

Eye Focus: Eyes are closed, focused on the space between the brows or brow point. Look within.

(*Note:* No mantra or breath is specified.)

Time: Continue for 3 to 62 minutes.

To End: Inhale, exhale, relax the breath, and with clasped hands stretch the arms up for 2 minutes.

Connect Your Finite Personality With the Infinite or the Universal

Ask students to consider who they really are—the finite "I am": their physical appearance, where they live, what they do, how they spend their time—and the infinite "I am," which represents your feelings about who you really are, what you are meant to achieve or to do with your life, your sense of purpose, and your connection to the larger reality of the planet and the universe.

*I Am, I Am: Meditation Into Being

Position: Sit in easy pose, with the left hand placed in front of your chest,

palm toward your chest, lower arm parallel to the ground, fingers pointing to the right. The right hand is in gyan mudra, resting on your right knee.

Eye Focus: Eyes are one-tenth open, looking straight ahead through the closed lids.

- Start with the left hand 6 inches in front of your chest, fingers pointing to the right, forearm parallel to the ground.
- As you chant "I am," move your hand closer to you (about 4 inches from your chest).
- The first time you chant "I am," emphasize the *I*.
- Chant "I am" as you bring your left hand approximately 12 inches away from your chest. Emphasize the *am*.
- Take a short breath through the nose as you move your hand back to the original position.
- Then continue in a steady rhythm and motion.

Continue for 3 to 31 minutes.

To End: Inhale deeply, exhale, and relax.

Positive Manner and Tone Contribute to Confidence Building

Learning can be a tricky and complicated matter. The manner and tone in which we teach and lead influences whether a learner becomes confident or defeated. Words and the tone that we use to communicate and interact matter. Often, 10 positive comments of encouragement or praise cannot override a single unintentional negative comment made, so carefully choosing positive, supportive language is essential. Paying attention and using a positive and affirming approach is most conducive to cultivating confidence in others.

Instilling confidence can be done in simple, natural ways:

- Encouraging curiosity
- Helping others learn from mistakes and errors in a gentle, compassionate way
- Celebrating success (Smith, 2016)

Positive Affirmation and Visualization Boost Confidence

Practicing positive affirmations regularly helps us to reinforce confidence in our abilities and self. Strong, positive statements repeated often like "I can," "I will," or "I am" can lead to a self-fulfilling prophecy just as negative statements have the propensity to do the same. When we have a strong belief that something will come true, often it does because of the spoken expectation that it will come true. "We cannot dismiss the power of positive thought" (Mason et al., 2019, p. 123). In the most challenging and grueling circumstances, we have the capacity to strengthen our confidence and positivity through specific affirmations or "positive talk." When a negative thought comes into play, simply notice, "delete," take a breath, and replace it with a strong affirmation. The practice of countering negative thoughts with positive thoughts and affirmations naturally increases our confidence and ability to control engrained "negative self-thought" patterns so that they don't spiral out of control or become self-destructing.

In *Mindfulness Practices* (Mason et al., 2019, pp. 123–125), we shared many naturally woven ideas of positive affirmation to be infused into a community:

- *Begin and end the day* with a strong group verse: "I am Somebody. If my mind can conceive it and my heart can believe it, then I can achieve it . . . because I am SOMEBODY!"

- *Use half-minute confidence boosts* before tests, a new lesson, or activity: "I am smart; I am important; I can do anything if I try."

- *Create a "live life large" jar:* Students fill this jar with positive quotes, words of encouragement, or original affirmations that they pull out of to read with morning announcements.

- *Weave magically:* Take an inspirational quote, hang it in plain sight as a visual reminder for the day or week, plan lessons around its meaning, and naturally infuse the goodness of its inspiration within the classroom so that behaviors, interactions, and learning center on it.

Visualization or "mental rehearsal" is also an important step toward helping you achieve a goal or intention. In the meditative sense, when we take deep breaths, gently close our eyes, and imagine *what we wish something to be*, in vivid detail and imagery, it becomes the first brain-imaging step of creating how we believe something will unfold.

- When we purposely visualize an act such as an athletic event or an important test we are to take, "the brain generates an impulse that tells our neurons to perform the movement or task. This creates a new neural pathway—clusters of cells in our brain that work together to create memories or learned behaviors" (Niles, 2011), helping our bodies to automatically respond because of the regular and consistent manner of visualization practice of the event or task.

- When your mind goes through its mental rehearsal/visualization, it helps prepare both the mind and the body for the challenge and outcome ahead, increasing your ability to focus, concentrate, and feel confident toward the imagined, favorable outcome.

CONFIDENCE CURRICULUM INTEGRATION PLANNER

Our self-confidence can be advanced by improving our self-care, by observing the growth that we make as we are able to hold our breath for a longer period of time, as we move more smoothly into and out of yoga positions, and as we still our mind. Figure 8.1 presents some ideas for making some of the activities in this chapter into games. Also included are a few ideas for using our confidence-building activities in academic lessons.

Figure 8.1 • Confidence Curriculum Integration Planner

LESSON	GRADE LEVEL	SUBJECT/CONTEXT	ADAPTATION/NOTES
Confidence building (in our breath)	Any	Use during transition times or as "mind breaks" during the day.	Ask students to choose a breath (long deep breathing, heart centered breathing, Breath of Fire, or cannon breath) that they will individually practice each day during a "choose your breath" time. Older students can discuss or journal about the breath afterward.
Confidence movements	Grades 4–12	Students form circles of 8–10 students. Use a "talking stick" to pass the leadership from one student to the next. The leader chooses a yogic posture, and demonstrates it. Others repeat. Leaders can lead for one to three movements before passing the stick on to the next leader.	Consider how to group students. Random sometimes works very well; however, sometimes it is good to consider abilities or preferences. Students can be clustered, for example, according to their preferred activities.
Meditation to Heal a Broken (or Sad) Heart	Any	Use after traumatic events or when sadness is a concern.	Play soft, gentle music in the background.

 Available at https://resources.corwin.com/CultivatingHappiness

MINDFUL REFLECTION

1. Consider how you can use this chapter to develop your own confidence in teaching yoga-mindfulness-meditation. Which postures, breaths, kriyas, or meditations will be the focus for your own practice?

2. Identify two or three students who seem to have the greatest need to develop their own self-confidence. Which postures, breaths, kriyas, or meditations in this chapter might be most helpful for each of these targeted students?

3. Developing student leadership is one way to develop self-confidence. Are there students in your class who might be good candidates for becoming yoga-mindfulness-meditation leaders? (*Note:* Sometimes this is a perfect avenue for developing leadership for students who may lack self-confidence; it isn't always the most competent students who become the best leaders.)

ONLINE RESOURCES

Visit https://resources.corwin.com/CultivatingHappiness

Online Resource 8.1   Kriya for New Lungs and Circulation

Online Resource 8.2   Confidence Curriculum Integration Planner

Online Resource 8.3   Mindful Reflection

CHAPTER NINE

Courage

KEY PRINCIPLE

True courage comes from grit that is integrated into our psyches in a healthy way. It is found in a willingness to embrace challenges, face our own vulnerabilities, and accept the vulnerabilities of others.

TEACHER NOTES

To ensure that students have multiple experiences with courage, teachers need to include yoga sets and meditations that address the various aspects of courage.

- Practicing self-awareness allows us to be open to learning new ideas and perspectives. Having students participate in meditations that heighten their awareness of the five senses provides opportunities to connect with sensations in the body. This focused stillness helps to create awareness in the body of any fears or worries that may arise when learning something new. From this awareness comes the ability to tap into the courage needed to immerse in the unknown.

- Breathing exercises that develop awareness of the entire path of the breath can activate the deepest places to take in as much oxygen as possible. Feeling the capacity to breathe completely and fully awakens a sense of inner strength. Following the path of the breath can inspire the courage to transcend any externally imposed barriers.

- Courage-based meditations can create spaces where intellectual analysis is open and nonjudgmental. Guided meditations with affirmations of trusting one's own inner voice can develop moral, emotional, and intellectual courage.

When you hear of courage, what images come to mind? Do you see a fire-fighter rushing into a burning building? A soldier in battle? A mountain climber? Or perhaps a teen admitting she needs help? As Brené Brown (2010) describes it, having courage means allowing ourselves to be vulnerable. Courage is multifaceted and very personal. We each have our own parameters. What might take a considerable amount of courage for one person may be a relatively easy undertaking for another.

FINDING OUR VOICE, LIVING IN THE PRESENT, AND CO-CREATING

Courage typically involves risks. It may be the courage to make a difficult moral or ethical decision, an act of physical courage, or the emotional risks we take when we reveal our true feelings to another person. It can also be a process. In *The Four Agreements*, Don Miguel Ruiz (2018) talks of "finding your voice for asking for what you want" (p. 72) rather than assuming others know of your needs or desires.

Consider for a moment the courage it takes to live mindfully in the present—not rushing toward a future goal or dwelling on a past victory or sorrow. In *Inner Engineering: A Yogi's Guide to Joy*, Sadhguru (2016) describes how we suffer by focusing on the past as well as how we suffer by concerning ourselves with what might happen the day after tomorrow: "What most people forget is that the past exists within each one of us only as memory," and if "you are in a compulsive cycle of reactivity, memory distorts your perception of the present, and your thoughts, emotions, and actions become disproportionate to the stimulus" (p. 56).

If we are caught in a vicious cycle, it will take courage to change. However, as Sadhguru (2016) says, we are often limited by our perceptions. Our perceptions of our potential, or what we can influence, are often intertwined with our mindset. As Carol Dweck (2015) indicates, with a growth mindset we believe in our potential; with a fixed mindset we seem to be doomed to our present limitations.

Sadhguru (2016) suggests,

> If you sustain this awareness of your limitless nature for just one
> full minute, you will achieve a tremendous transformation. . . .
> Just one minute can elevate you to a different dimension of
> experience and function. (p. 70)

It takes courage to lead and courage to follow. With time, as we build our courage, we might uncover the co-creative courage to problem solve at the community level. Hari Charn Kaur Khalsa (2020) explains the collective power of courage:

It is important to have the courage to let go of what we think the solution may be and to embark on a co-creative inclusive process of discovering answers and new questions together . . . whether this is in support of an individual or a community. Each person brings unique wisdom and challenges to the process. This paradigm is circular rather than top-down and invites questioning what is.

YOUR PERCEPTIONS AND COURAGE

- Look for a moment at your own life. Have you held yourself back, or been afraid of failure?

- Consider what you might choose to do if you truly had an ounce more of courage.

ADVANCING OUR COURAGE WITH MOVEMENT, MEDITATION, AND BREATH

Courage can be advanced in many ways. Dialogue and problem solving can be useful. However, as we implement self-care practices, we sometimes become more in tune with ourselves and gain strength and courage to act on our beliefs. For example, strengthening our core can help give us a grounded sense of who we are and what we are seeking to achieve. Including yoga postures that activate the throat such as cat-cow stretches can encourage expressing ideas with confidence and courage. Gentle shoulder openers like cobra and gentle upper body twists in lunges can attune students to their energy flow. This awareness opens the channels to access courage. Students need time to pause and to check in on how they feel before, during, and after the exercises targeted to tap into their courage. The class can weave the experiences felt in the body into the flow of the learning in the class community.

CURRICULAR CONTEXT

Teaching about courage can be integrated into learning in many ways. Courage is a consistent theme found in literature and is often a character trait used to analyze heroes in novels and plays. When studying Shakespeare, for example, students can look at the actions of Hamlet through the lens of courage. Did Hamlet display courage by refraining from taking revenge on his underhanded uncle, or would he have been courageous for avenging his father's death?

Courage can be displayed in so many ways.

- Whether it is taking your first steps as a toddler, preparing for a marathon, or stepping in front of your screen to present findings from a recent science experiment, there are many moments each day that take courage.

- With conscious awareness of our students, we can find ways to help build their courage and resilience (or ability to bounce back).

- We need to acknowledge that setbacks will happen—success is not always inevitable. However, by taking risks, we bring ourselves to opportunities for growth and fulfillment.

- There are also "degrees of courage"—courage for the monumental firsts, courage that may have tremendous consequences, and courage that allows us to face each new day, to simply get out of bed and attend to everyday tasks.

- Teachers can help students understand more about their own courage and resilience by discussing courage, providing scaffolds, modeling courage, and celebrating achievements. With a focus on the positive, teachers can uplift students and add to their reservoir of success.

- *Practicing your words* through role playing age-level scenarios is also an effective way to learn how courage can be developed, especially under peer pressure situations. When we practice, we can more easily find the courage needed in a real-life situation or circumstance.

SUPPORTING A BEST GUESS

Karin Tulchinsky-Cohen is a vice principal at Beall Elementary School in Maryland.

A talented instructional assistant in my school works with small groups of students who have learning difficulties. Each of the students has an individualized education program (IEP) that guides the specialized instruction provided by the instructional assistant. These are students who have struggled to learn, and they are often uncomfortable with taking intellectual risks during class. One of the key components of success that this assistant has developed with her students is an understanding that they just need to "take their best guess." Her focus is on getting students to feel safe to take a risk, which requires courage.

There was one student who had struggled with reading and had taken on the self-image of being a nonreader. He would not write answers down on his whiteboard or offer to participate before he saw what his peers had written. He was completely unwilling to take a risk because of all the other times in school when he had experienced being wrong. The assistant was invested in boosting this child's confidence so he could manifest the courage needed to independently write an answer on his whiteboard. Every time that the assistant met with this small group of students, she focused on developing courage by saying, "Give it your best guess. We learn from our mistakes. It doesn't matter if it's right or wrong. What matters is that you try."

Still, the one student would always wait to see what the other students in the group had written before he would answer any questions. The assistant continued to repeat the messages about trying one's best. One day she asked the reticent student to write his answer first, and for the others to wait. Everyone was quiet. He wrote his answer. The assistant celebrated his courage to take a risk and to give it his best guess. The word he had written was not spelled correctly. But that really didn't matter. This student had entered the realm of learning—where it is truly *nothing ventured, nothing gained.*

Evidence of learning requires that students take an array of steps to show their understanding and skills. For some, and particularly for those who have struggled or failed in the past, courage is needed.

Having the courage to take action as a learner is distinctively important for many key pedagogical reasons.

- It is essential for the teacher to see students' progress, to know if they have mastered the skills taught.

- It is even more significant that students are willing to take risks when they could be wrong or, even worse, lose face in the presence of their peers.

- Wrestling with ideas requires entering the murky waters of ambiguity.

- Developing awareness of our reaction to new or confusing ideas increases our understanding of ourselves.

- Stress is inherent in many situations, and some degree of courage may be required—even very positive situations can sometimes create distress.

- Courage undergirds actualizing and applying learning through action.

COURAGE WARM-UPS

Stretch Pose

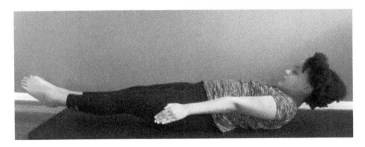

Stretch pose helps to strengthen the abdominal muscles, giving us courage to act and speak from our center. (Don't do this pose if you are pregnant.)

Position: Lie on your back and raise your head and heels 6 inches off the ground.

- Focus your eyes on your toes and stretch your toes so they point away from you.

- Place your arms above your thighs with your palms facing down but not touching your legs, or alongside your legs with your palms facing but not touching your body.

- Begin Breath of Fire. Continue for 1 to 3 minutes.

Note: You may use your hands under your buttocks to support your lower back, or you may lift one leg at a time, but keep the Breath of Fire powerful.

Leg Lifts

Position: Lie on your back. Legs are straight. The navel point is pulled back to the spine.

- You may put your hands under your hips to help regulate the movement as you inhale up and exhale down.

- Keep your lower back pressed into the floor to engage your abdominals and protect your spine.

- Leg lifts can be done at a slow, moderate, or fast pace.

- At a slow pace, carefully exhale down, slowing the pace as you near the ground. This creates greater resistance against gravity, giving your abdominals more of a workout.

Knees to Chest

This is a good counter position to stretch pose and leg lifts as it reduces any pressure that has been placed on the lower back. The knees-to-chest position is also the best way to begin stretch pose, as it keeps the lower back anchored to the floor and reduces strain on the back as the legs are extended forward to complete the position.

Position: Lie on your back, pull your knees into your chest, and wrap your arms around your knees.

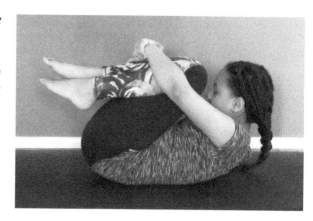

- Tuck your chin into your chest, elongating the back of your neck.

- Breathe deeply.

Continue for 1 to 2 minutes.

Tree Pose

With tree pose, you can gain confidence and courage as you are able to stay in position for longer and longer periods of time.

Position: Stand with your feet together.

- Look at a spot in the distance with an unfocused gaze.

- Bring your hands to the center of your chest, palms pressed together and fingertips up.

- Inhale and bring one leg off the ground, placing your foot above or below the opposite knee.

- Breathe as you maintain your balance for 1 to 2 minutes.

Mini-Rotation at the Spine

This exercise is good for digestion and strengthening your navel point.

Position: Easy pose.

Eye Focus: Eyes can be open or closed.

- Take three sipping breaths through your mouth.

- Hold your breath and with your navel point pulled to your spine begin a grinding motion, with a small circular rotation at the base of the spine.

- When you can no longer comfortably hold your breath, exhale through your nose.

- Inhale, hold your breath, and continue, exhaling when you need to.

- Repeat one final time.

- Reverse directions, and repeat the entire exercise going three times in the reverse direction.

*Archer Pose

This position is good for the spine, the quadriceps, muscle tone, physical stamina, developing your core, and alignment.

Position: Stand with one foot forward, your feet 2–3 feet apart.

- Start with your right foot forward, toes pointing straight ahead, and your left foot at a distance of 2–3 feet, with the foot positioned at a 45-degree angle (heels back and toes forward).

- Pull your navel point to your spine.

- Bend your right knee so that the knee is almost parallel to the ground, ensuring that it does not end up beyond your toes. The body faces to the left.

- Lift your right arm up, parallel to the ground and over the right knee, with your hand in a fist as if holding a bow; your thumb is up and pulled back.

- Turn your head to face your right hand, and focus your eyes beyond your right thumb. Your chin is pulled in, and your chest is out.

- Start with your left hand near the center of your chest, and keeping your left arm parallel to the ground, pull your arm back as if pulling back a bow and arrow.

- Feel the expansion across your chest, as your shoulder blades come together in back. Keep your elbows up and parallel to the ground.

- Hold for 1 to 3 minutes.

Repeat on the opposite side.

Children's Warm-Ups for Courage

Children assume various animal postures, moving like animals and sometimes even adding a vocal component, such as roaring like a lion or hissing like a snake as they slither on the ground.

Possible Animals to Consider

- Jump like a kangaroo.

- Hop like a bunny.

- From a standing position, lean forward, hands interlocked in front. Move like an elephant, swinging your arms like a trunk.

- Move like a bear—leaning over from a standing position, with your hands and feet on the ground, make heavy, bearlike movements.

BREATH WORK

The following meditation involves long deep breathing.

*Meditation on Change

Change is constant—we must accept it and adapt accordingly. To adjust, we must regularly reflect and check in with ourselves, which takes courage.

Position: Sit in easy pose with a straight spine and lifted chest.

Eye Focus: Eyes are closed.

Breath: Begin long deep breathing. Follow the flow of the breath.

- Curl the fingers in as though you are making a fist, placing the fingertips on the pads of the hands, just below the fingers.

- Bring the two hands together at the center of the chest. The hands will touch lightly at the knuckles of the middle fingers and the pads of the thumbs. The thumbs are pressed together and extended toward the heart center.

- Hold this position, feeling the energy across the thumbs and knuckles. Continue for 3 to 31 minutes.

To End: Inhale deeply, exhale, and relax for 2 to 5 minutes.

*One-Minute Breath

Try to breathe one time per minute. You may need to work up to this.

Position: Easy pose.

Eye Focus: Eyes are closed, focused on the space between the brows or brow point, unless you are timing yourself by watching a clock.

- To begin, inhale slowly to a count of 20.
- Hold for a count of 20.
- Exhale for a count of 20, pulling your navel point to your spine and holding.

Continue for 3 to 5 minutes.

YOGA SET: POSTURE AND MOVEMENT

Kriyas for Courage

*Yoga for Complete Workout for the Elementary Being

This entire series of movements is considered one exercise. Move rhythmically and continuously, without stopping, from one position to the next. Chant the mantra *Har* once per count.

Position: Begin standing.

Eye Focus: Eyes are open or closed. Open eyes for balance.

Extend your arms straight over your head, hugging your ears. Clap your hands *8 times*, firmly striking the entire surface of your palms. (1a)

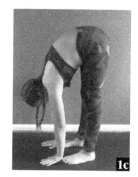

- Immediately bend forward and strike the ground with your palms *8 times*, striking hard enough to make a noise. (1b and 1c)

- Straighten your body and extend your arms to the sides parallel to the ground, palms facing down. Pump your arms 30 degrees up and 30 degrees down as though you are trying to fly. Repeat the 2-part motion *8 times*. (2)

- Stand with your feet shoulder-width apart and extend your arms to your sides parallel to the floor, palms facing down (3a). Jump up and land with your arms and legs crossed (3b). Jump up again and land in the original position, arms extended and feet spread apart. Keep the arms straight and parallel to the ground and alternate the top arm and front leg. Chant *Har* with each jump. Continue for 4 complete cycles or 8 counts.

- Turn diagonally and come into archer pose. Using the strength of the thighs, bend your front knee deeply over your toes *8 times*. (4)

- Turn to the opposite diagonal and come into archer pose with the opposite leg forward and again bend the front knee deeply *8 times*.

- Repeat the crisscross jumps. (3a and 3b)

- Keep your feet apart and extend your arms over your head, hugging your ears, and stretch backward 8 times. (5)

- Repeat the crisscross jumps. (3a and 3b)

- Stand with your feet shoulder-width apart, arms extended above the head. Bending from the waist, stretch *8 times* back. (5)

- Repeat the crisscross jumps. (3a and 3b)

- Stand with your feet shoulder-width apart, arms extended above the head. Bending from the waist, stretch *4 times* to the right and *4 times* to the left. (5)

- Repeat the crisscross jumps. (3a and 3b)

After doing this exercise for an extended period of time, you may wish to relax.

- If you practice it on consecutive days, alternate between the following positions for relaxation: One day rest on your back with your knees pulled into your chest and your arms wrapped around your bent legs. The next day rest in baby pose by sitting on your heels with your forehead on the ground and your arms by your sides.

- Relax in these postures while listening to uplifting music. Rest deeply.

MEDITATIONS

Guided Meditation for Courage: You Are Capable

We all question our strength and ability to accomplish something at one time or another. Courage is often a big barrier, as we feel we are incapable. This guided meditation, adapted from Archer's (2020) "Guided Meditation for Courage," focuses on courage and reminds you that you are capable, and you have everything you need to move forward and achieve your goals.

Position: Sit or lie down in a comfortable position.

Eye Focus: Eyes are closed.

Begin

- As you breathe, notice your breath—the way it flows in, the way it flows out. Let the rhythm of it settle you, the way rain settles the dust of a blustery day. Breathe in, breathe out.

- Perhaps you are having a bit of blustery day, a blustery month, or maybe even a blustery decade.

- That is okay. The wind will blow, the clouds will form, the rain will fall, and the dust will settle.

- You, my friend, will settle as well as you breathe. Breathe in, breathe out. Settle.

- Along your dusty, blustery path, there have also been moments of sun—times when life had a silver lining, a sigh of relief, a moment of triumph. Find a moment in your life when you felt the joy of triumph.

- Do not worry about it being big or small, impressive or overshadowed. Think triumph. Victory. A moment when you knew in your very core that you had succeeded in doing something worthwhile.

- A moment when you knew that your rain would come and your dust would settle.

Deepen

- Once you find your moment, think about it for a little time. Think of the way you hoped and dreamed. The way you *worked*.

- Your moment might have lasted for a day or for a second. But for at least that second, you tasted victory.

- Feel again how that victory felt. Did your heart rush? Did your stomach flip? Did you feel so elated that you could have burst?

- Or was it a soft sort of euphoria? A weight off your shoulders, an ease in your breath and your step?

- Feel it again, that happy, serene, wonderful moment. Embrace the way it changes the way you feel both physically and emotionally. You know how it feels now as confidently as you knew how it felt then.

- This triumph, this victory, this celebration of achievement is part of you forever.

End

- Focus on your triumph for a little longer. When you are ready, return your attention to your breath—to the settling of your mind, to the settling of your heart.

- Whatever winds arise to stir the dust in your world, you have felt the rain. That rain is part of you now, and so is the sun that comes after.

- Your path is not easy, with all its wind and clouds. But it is *your* path, and the rain is yours too.

- As you breathe, remember your goals and the reasons behind them. While you cannot always control your storms, you can always create goals to guide you forward.

- Think on this for a moment. What direction do you want to go? What goals will bring you there? That will bring the rain.

- You have felt the rain before. You will feel the rain again. It is part of you.

To End: Breathe, breathe, settle, and awake.

Meditating on the Good

As you practice, feel yourself being showered with health, wealth, happiness, success—whatever you long for. This is a very restful posture. The pressure against the rib cage meridian points causes relaxation. When you are given a gift, accept it as it is given. Don't try to change it to your liking. Accept it gracefully so it can open doors for you.

Position: Sit in easy pose with a straight spine and your upper arms close to your sides, pressed against your rib cage. Bring your hands to heart level side by side and cupped. Silently ask for what you need or want.

Eye Focus: Eyes are one-tenth open.

- Allow gifts to come to you; ask for whatever you need; know yourself to be receiving gifts; feel the boundless flow of energy. Just let it happen.

- Fill your heart and soul with all the bounties of nature.

- Continue for 3 to 12 minutes at first, working your way up to 31 minutes or longer.

To End: Simply meditate on the boundless flow of universal energy and consciousness and feel a deep sense of peace and gratitude.

*Overcoming One's Sense of Limitation

Position: Sit in easy pose.

Eye Focus: Eyes are open or closed.

1. *Wrist circles.*

This exercise can bring great healing to the body.

Position: Sit in easy pose.

- Bend your elbows so that your upper arms are near your rib cage and your forearms point upward. Your hands start in front of your shoulders, with your fingers spread apart. Your palms face outward, and your thumbs point at each other.

- Twist your wrists inward with your thumb leading the way until your palms face your body and your thumbs point out to the side.

- As your wrists twist inward, your fingers close into a fist. Your fingers reopen as your wrists twist outward to return to the starting position.

- Make your mouth into an *O* shape and do a panting dog breath through your open mouth. Your wrists twist in time with your breath.

- Move quickly. Look at the tip of your nose. Continue for 3 minutes.

- Inhale, hold your breath for 15–20 seconds, tighten your fingers into fists, and tense every muscle in your body. Exhale. Repeat this sequence two more times.

2. *Arm pushes.*

This exercise will work out your blocks.

Position: Sit in easy pose.

- Begin alternately pushing your arms and hands forward as if pushing something away from you. Push one hand out as you pull the other back along your side.

- Keep your hands and fingers open, letting the heel of your palm lead the movement.

- Make an *O* with your mouth and do a panting dog breath through the open mouth. Continue for 3 minutes.

- Inhale. Keep one arm extended while you hold the breath for 15–20 seconds and squeeze all the muscles in your body. Exhale.

- Inhale. Extend the other arm while you hold the breath for 15–20 seconds and tighten all your muscles so your body shakes from tension. Exhale.

- Inhale. Change arms again while you hold the breath for 15–20 seconds and tighten all your muscles. Exhale and relax.

3. *Arm circles.*

This exercise benefits the heart.

Position: Sit in easy pose.

- Open your arms wide with your elbows slightly bent, your fingers spread open, and your hands slightly cupped.

- Move your arms in backward circles as you do a panting dog breath through an *O*-shaped mouth.

- Move vigorously. Continue for 3 minutes.

To End:

- Inhale. Stick out your tongue and hold your breath for 15–20 seconds. Tense the entire body so much that it shakes from tension. Exhale. Repeat this sequence two more times.

*Meditation for Mind to Follow Consciousness (also known as Amarti Mudra Kriya)

This meditation was taught in China. It was brought from Ceylon in the 14th or 15th century. It is used so that the mind follows our consciousness, and we act more consciously.

Position: Sit in easy pose.

Eye Focus: Eyes are open to start.

- Raise your hands near your shoulders, palms facing forward.

- With your right hand, touch the thumb and little finger. Other fingers are straight.

- With your left hand, touch the thumb and ring finger. Other fingers are straight.

- To begin the meditation, concentrate on your hands and keep the fingers straight. See what happens.

- Close your eyes and, between the eyebrows and the root of the nose, beam out like a light; beam of light, beam out. Just concentrate.

To End:

- When the position and the light beam are correct, chant *Ong Kar* ("The oneness of everything—everything we see, hear, and the unknown") mentally from the heart center. Continue for 5 to 30 minutes. *Alternative:* Chant another mantra of your choosing such as *One* or *We are one.*

HOME PRACTICE

- Select one breath, one warm-up, one kriya, and one meditation.
- Over the next month, practice these several times per week.
- Observe changes in your body, thoughts, or emotions. Perhaps even keep a log.
- Reflect on resilience. Did you note any changes in your resilience during this past month?

*Remember you can build up to a full practice; perhaps beginning with only a few steps of one of the longer kriyas.

COURAGE CURRICULUM INTEGRATION PLANNER

Courage building can easily be supported in academics by referring to the courage of many leaders, the courage of characters in books, and through discussions of how we have overcome personal challenges and fears (see Figure 9.1).

Figure 9.1 • Courage Curriculum Integration Planner

CHAPTER/LESSON	GRADE LEVEL	SUBJECT/CONTEXT	ADAPTATION/NOTES
Community helpers	Grades 1–3	Community helpers talk about courage.	Could include visits to community settings, background research, role plays, or art.
Civil rights	Grades 4–12	Discussion of courage, equity, and justice in terms of civil rights leaders. As appropriate, during the academic unit, practice the "Meditation on Change."	Could also consider courage to leave one's home and migrate to another country.
Discussion of true courage	Grades 4–12	Discussion of bravado or false courage—dares, being reckless or uncaring. During the academic unit, perhaps in relation to a specific novel or short story, talk about why people are sometimes reckless and work on developing an underlying sense of courage. Incorporate some of the yoga warm-ups, such as tree pose, and sets, such as "Overcoming One's Sense of Limitation."	Could also relate to discussion of adolescent behaviors, and how sometimes we feel peer pressure to go along with others.

online resources Available at https://resources.corwin.com/CultivatingHappiness

MINDFUL REFLECTION

1. How have your students fared this past year in terms of their courage, grit, and resilience?

2. Are there ideas from this chapter that you might be able to implement to improve their courage?

3. Examine the Courage Curriculum Integration Planner (Figure 9.1). Are there similar ways you could integrate courage into your classroom discussions?

ONLINE RESOURCES

Visit https://resources.corwin.com/CultivatingHappiness

Online Resource 9.1   Your Perceptions and Courage

Online Resource 9.2   Home Practice

Online Resource 9.3   Courage Curriculum Integration Planner

Online Resource 9.4   Mindful Reflection

CHAPTER TEN

Community

KEY PRINCIPLE

We are a part of many communities—our school community, our neighborhood, our nation, and our global community. Individual and collective self-care is essential for our well-being, for our sense of purpose, and for a sustainable future.

TEACHER NOTES

- Our individual consciousness and self-care affect our collective self-care and community. We build our community by building our own practice and increasing our awareness, our compassion, our confidence, and our courage.

- As our strength and resilience builds, we are better positioned to support others and strengthen our collective good.

- The yoga-mindfulness-meditation exercises in this chapter can be repeated frequently and may be particularly important in times when we are challenged globally, such as during a pandemic, a natural disaster, or an act of communal violence or suffering.

- The sustainability of our planet is affected by our collective consciousness, our awareness of what we can do to support others, and the knowledge that our individual attitudes, actions, and well-being can create better lives for ourselves and others.

WARM, SUPPORTIVE ENVIRONMENTS FOR LEARNING

Vicki Zakrzewski (2020) reiterates the importance of mindfulness in creating "a kinder, more compassionate, and equitable world through education," stating that although this may seem like a daunting task—and it is . . . we must start somewhere.

Even choosing just one thing, like starting a class with a mindful moment or ending a staff meeting with a gratitude circle or offering a warm welcome to families on the first day of school, can have a ripple effect greater than we can imagine.

See Greater Good in Education (2019a, 2019b, 2019c).

 Resources from Greater Good in Education are also available on the Corwin Resources page at **https://resources.corwin.com/ CultivatingHappiness**.

The ripple effect that Zakrzewski (2020) describes begins with warm, supportive learning environments. In their book *The Triple Focus: A New Approach to Education*, Daniel Goleman and Peter Senge (2014) remind us that

> learning in general happens best in a warm, supportive atmosphere, in which there exists a feeling of safety, of being supported and cared about, of closeness and connection. In such a space children's brains more readily reach the state of optimal cognitive efficiency—and of caring about others. (p. 28)

Feeling safe, supported, and connected sets the stage for happiness, for transcending our circumstances—even our traumas—and for freeing ourselves to consider what we most want to do with the precious time we have. As we wrote in *Compassionate School Practices*, "we must feel as though we belong to some community. We must feel that we are wanted and our ideas are valuable to those in our circle" (Mason et al., 2021, p. 149).

As we build courage, vulnerability, and resilience, we strengthen our communities. We are more willing to speak out to support others, further our own growth, and make difficult decisions. Being aware of and compassionate toward others, building trust in each other, and being courageous enough to speak out and help others are all key components of a supportive, kind, and inclusive community.

When educators consciously create positive and compassionate school environments, we increase the opportunities for staff, students, and families to feel valued, appreciated, and important.

As students feel more secure and respected, they are better able to leave their trauma behind and to focus on learning. They build deeper relationships, feel more connected, and become more committed to their community and understanding what is being taught at deeper levels.

- Strong communities see increased engagement, attendance, and academic achievement.

- Strong communities foster empathy and address the whole child, considering social and emotional well-being in addition to academic goals.

As school communities, we can come together to foster meaningful connection and develop empowered and successful lifelong learners.

Community, Inclusiveness, Healing, and Justice

The ground beneath your feet may be shifting, but mindfulness can help you find your way forward with skill and passion. Let your practice be your guide.

—Jeremy Hunter (2021)

During this particularly challenging time of global pandemic, racial injustice, and lack of acceptance for those different from us, we have learned that no one person is immune to suffering. With suffering, there is a need for healing. Otherwise, happiness and well-being seem to be beyond our reach. When our health, including our mental health, is compromised, every part of our life, from relationships to school, work, and fun, is compromised.

One healthy way to help our own suffering is to extend our heart to others in need of comfort. When we use our pain to help others also in pain, healing can help triumph the deepest hurt and suffering. Whether you extend a hand, a smile, or a hug to help someone get through the day, or whether you champion an environmental cause or become active in advocating with people in your community who need support, a compassionate heart helps heal both you and the other person. When we establish a network of pockets of collective healing, we form the basis for larger-scale collective healing. Mindfulness has a role to play in all of this.

In *The Inner Work of Racial Justice*, law professor and mindfulness instructor Rhonda Magee (2019) describes the need for collective healing:

> Personal healing must precede the transformation of our communities. We already have every potential, every capacity that we need to do more to actually overthrow the racism that has plagued our nation for so long. If we have the will to commit, to learn together, and to work on ourselves to help us remain awake and willing to grow, we can do this. (p. 91)

Magee (2019) continues, "Our formal practices of mindfulness and compassion can increase our ability to have not merely difficult, but increasingly complex, conversations" (p. 194).

As you deepen your mindfulness practice, we urge you to see how you can bring it to every aspect of your life and to each of your contacts, whether they be colleagues, peers, friends, or family that you see online or in person. Connection is such an important part of community. As Magee (2019) goes on to say,

> at the heart of compassionate engagement with other people is the openness and desire to connect. We must make the decision each day to engage with one another, especially when racism has made it difficult . . . when we view humanity as one family whose members have forgotten who we are, we see ourselves in different ways in relation to one another. (p. 293)

We have inner circles of families; we have peripheral circles of extended families, friends, and coworkers; and we have the wider community as well as the worldwide global community. Just as smaller communities have codependent needs, we depend on the larger community to help meet our needs. Although the world is full of many different people and cultures, there are certain universal characteristics that bind us as humans who share the world stage. Global communities teach us the power of numbers as members who share collective thoughts and actions. This allows us to work collectively toward impactful and sustaining change.

A GLOBAL COMMUNITY

From Krishna Kaur

I have been traveling, training, and teaching yoga and meditation to people around the world for over 20 years. I love exploring different cultures, traditions, kinds of food, and ways of dealing with issues that plague us all no matter where we were born. It validates for me again and again that the teachings of kundalini yoga and mindful meditations work on everyone regardless of language, dress, gender, or beliefs. We laugh the same; we cry the same; we battle stress and worry about the future of our children and our communities in the same way whether we are in Ghana, Mexico, Beijing, or Los Angeles. There is a language that has no words and speaks louder than any voice on the planet. It is the language of the heart. It is a frequency that travels faster than the speed of light and uplifts all who are able to tune into it.

When I look into the eyes of a stranger, I see my family. I see seeds of the same joys, the same sorrows, the same longing for answers to the same questions. No matter where I go or with whom I share these teachings, I'm at home. I see me in them and them in me. Our different cultures provide exciting textures to the external, but everything else is pretty much the same. So, we can cross these artificial lines that try to make us feel separate whenever we are ready. I like that!

EXPANDING OUR COMMUNITY CONSCIOUSNESS AND CREATING TRANSFORMATIVE CHANGE, WITH MINDFULNESS

Ivan Sellers, an activist in mindfulness and one of the organizing committee members for the Soul Initiative, explains how mindful leadership is influencing a global initiative to transform education:

> To implement mindfulness in schools, we used Theory U. Developed at MIT, the Theory U process involves sensing a system and then listening intuitively for the wisdom that emerges on how to bring care and flourishing. There are introductory courses offered on a regular basis through the Presencing Institute at www.presencing.org. The Theory U process includes these five steps: co-initiating, co-sensing, presencing (a mindful approach that involves connecting with inner knowledge), co-creating, and co-evolving.

> We began by identifying the many stakeholders in the school system, and then used various "sensing" techniques to feel the system, to understand the perspective of each of the different groups comprising the system. Mindfulness helped our team get centered and find a common intention. Mindfulness helped us to engage in active listening. We learned to sense with an open heart, an open mind, and an open will.

> As Otto Scharmer, one of the Presencing Institute founders, states, "you cannot understand a system unless you change it. You cannot change a system unless you transform consciousness. You cannot transform consciousness unless you can make a system see and sense itself" (Borges, 2020).

> Mindfulness helped each of us learn to listen to ourselves at every moment: while sensing the system and while seeking clarity on a way forward to bring flourishing to the system. This is a fundamental aspect of Theory U; Scharmer explains how this is at the basis of generative dialogue and collective intelligence. Once our team was in this mode it was beautiful to sense that we chose not to take any steps without first discussing and finding a solution that came out of a collective process.

> Theory U helped our team to enter the school system, to engage with its stakeholders, to sense deeply by listening actively, and to find clear indicators of where and how we could help the schools to effect change. All the while mindfulness underpinned our listening, our quiet as we sensed, and the way we allowed solutions to emerge.

Where mindfulness proved challenging throughout the process is that, at a collective level, it requires time and patience to sow its seeds. In schools, time is often in short supply, so one needs to find a group that is really committed behind the idea of finding new ways to address issues that are causing discomfort. It also helps to have diverse groups so many opinions can be heard and integrated.

One of the things that helped us to bond as a group also comes from mindfulness: the ability to sit with discomfort. Theory U trains you to listen to people's challenges and pain without offering solutions—simply holding space, providing empathy, and sharing in our common human experience. This was often just what was needed to help us feel we were connected and not alone. (Ivan Sellers, personal communication, April 2021)

CURRICULAR CONTEXT

We help teach community by providing a *wraparound hug* that serves the "whole child" intellectually, physically, socially, emotionally, and academically:

- Offering students opportunities to speak out and be heard
- Building strong healthy relationships and a sense of belonging
- Encouraging positive, respectful relationships
- Using restorative justice
- Considering students' and families' needs
- Fostering effective communication
- Practicing meditation, breath work, and mindfulness

We foster communication and community in schools by intentionally establishing community-building activities, such as the following:

- *Class meetings*, where students set goals and expectations, identify problems, and problem solve together
- *Buddy programs*, where older students mentor their younger peers, perhaps even completing joint art or service projects
- *Homeside activities* with resources for parents such as conversation starters and finding other ways to connect students' learning to their home lives
- *Schoolwide community-building activities*, such as family film nights, that are naturally embedded in the school community culture (Mason, Rivers Murphy, & Jackson, 2020, pp. 140–141)

Creating Compassionate Classrooms

Heather Malin, director of research at the Stanford University Center on Adolescence, in her book *Teaching for Purpose* (2018), describes conditions for creating a compassionate classroom:

> A compassionate classroom requires that students are seen and heard . . . Teachers can go further in creating a compassionate classroom by "checking in" with students. Checking in is a daily activity that starts with the class, either formally in a class meeting, or finally as the teacher assesses the emotional energy of students as they arrive and ask check-in questions to make sure students are ready to learn. (p. 107)

Malin (2018) goes on to discuss the value of checking in at specific times when students aren't working at their usual level, urging teachers to "listen deeply and probe gently to find out what might be causing the student to act out or fall behind" (p. 107).

Lisa Flook and Laura Pinger (n.d.) have provided additional insights into creating compassionate school communities:

> If you had visited one of our classrooms during the 12-week program, you might have seen a poster on the wall called "Kindness Garden." When kids performed an act of kindness or benefitted from one, they added a sticker to the poster. The idea is that friendship is like a seed—it needs to be nurtured and taken care of in order to grow. Through that exercise, we got students talking about how kindness feels good and how we might grow more friendship in the classroom.

> Another day, you might have found students in pairs holding Peace Wands, one with a heart and one with a star. The child with the heart wand speaks ("from the heart"); the other child (the "star listener") listens and then repeats back what was said. When there was a conflict between students, they used the wands to support their communication.

COMMUNITY INCLUDES FAMILIES

It is often said that parents are their child's first teachers. Family becomes our first introduction to community, helping us develop a sense of safety, belonging, social relationships, education, and values. For some, the family unit is clearly intact, loving, and supportive. For others, there is an inherent struggle on many fronts, sometimes with food and economic insecurities, drug and alcohol misuse, physical and mental health challenges, and even violence. Nevertheless, it is the first sense of community one has. There is much schools can do to help elevate a sense of belonging and community. For children raised in dysfunctional families, this can be a critical support to achieving well-being.

HOW ARE YOU CREATING A SENSE OF COMMUNITY AND BELONGING?

As you read about Michele's family, reflect on the families of your students, and what else your school could be doing to create a sense of community and belonging.

FAMILIES AS OUR MAIN ORBITS IN 2020

Michele Rivers Murphy reflects on family during the year 2020.

Over the past year, our most inner community, called "family," most certainly became the main orbit of our world as our busy lives suddenly were forced into a hard stop. It was a time in our lives when we all faced our own mortality as we were bombarded with physical and mental health challenges. The importance of family became a stark reminder that our inner circle of community was the new normal of school, work, and play, all under the same roof, with invisible boundaries that often spilled over to the other.

As a parent, I looked for cues from both our girls that perhaps they had additional needs. On the days that our girls were faring all right, we needed to be all right as well. On the days that they were challenged, we listened, stayed in their presence, hugged, or cried together. We practiced mindfulness, and continued our gratitude reflections, family dinners, conversations, and long walks or hikes outside as we healed together. We learned that children, youth, and young adults have a built-in flexibility and a mechanism called resilience, when surrounded by a loving family community. This gave us all hope.

We can do no great things, only small things with great love.

—Mother Teresa

Being a part of a larger community and, more importantly, wanting to *make a difference,* is a common desire we share as human beings. The world needs much right now, on so many levels.

As Elaine Smookler (2021) has indicated, to live freely and "mindfully is an invitation to stand up for social justice and environmental stewardship." *Right now, with so many planetary needs, conscious awareness and conscious consideration of our global community must result in conscious activism.* Michele's family has intergenerational activism in their blood. Learning from her parents, her own personal activism includes volunteering in a community kitchen serving people who are homeless, as well as spearheading several initiatives to protect local natural resources and combat industrial encroachment in western Massachusetts. Her oldest daughter, Julia, who is involved with environmental justice, recently completed a senior honor's thesis on how targets of environmental racism process their victimization at Providence College.

Michele's 17-year-old daughter, Abigail, has also been busy. If you ever wonder how you can make an impactful difference, here is Abigail Murphy's story:

BAGS OF LOVE: "YOU ARE LOVED. YOU ARE IMPORTANT. YOU MATTER."

This past winter, I was in a rut. I did much thinking and reflecting as one day rolled into another. There was not a lot to do during the winter months, so I was thankful for my nightly dance classes to keep me busy. Before long, as I drove through town, I noticed a saddening increase of people begging for money out on the streets in the middle of frigid winter. Reflecting on their needs, I became inspired to create *Bags of love—I got your back.* I put together backpacks filled with winter essentials like hats, neck warmers, and hand warmers, as well as vital toiletries such as toothbrushes, toothpaste, and deodorant, along with a message: "Know that you are loved. You are important. You matter."

I delivered the first 24 bags to the local emergency shelter. My next round of 24 bags were distributed through a Christian center that had added warming shelters for people to rest on cold days. I have been touched by the incredibly kind notes from those who received my bags. We have also seen many people who, even as they continue to ask for money, have both backpacks and hats on their head. (A. Murphy, personal communication, March 2021)

As we support students, there are also many ways that schools can support families. Often it is not so much a matter of big, glorious events, but a matter of quiet, consistent, mindful awareness and determination to be active in support of families.

TEACHING PARENTS TO STOP AND BREATHE

Francine Ronis, LPC (personal communication, January 2021), a child and family therapist and mindfulness coach, shares some of her mindfulness work with parents:

Working with parents and mindfulness directly affects children. When I teach parents to stop, breathe, and work with a situation, instead of just react, everything changes. Interactions become manageable and thoughtful. Being mindfully aware of parent–child interactions can be challenging. So many of them are riddled with unexpressed desires, expectations, worries, and triggers that parents can be completely unaware of.

My classes are designed to not only teach mindfulness, but to go under the layer of thought, which is where most of us spend much of our time.

- If our child doesn't do their homework, that is not usually what makes us yell, punish, threaten, or worse. It's what is under the trigger that has us react.

- Our fears are what usually get the best of us.

- We project what might happen in the future, and we are often struck by an emotion we have felt in childhood.

- So, our underlying worry might be that our children won't be successful in life, and we may feel disrespected. Neither of those things are true; they are stories we make up. In actuality, we just have a child that didn't do their homework.

As we work with mindfulness, we unpack and explore the triggers, and then can often proactively face a situation with exactly what is, instead of what we make up about it. Our relationships get better, and our children learn they can slow down and do the same.

COMMUNITY WARM-UPS

Standing-Up Sequence

The sequence can vary; however, the components will help get you up and moving, increase flexibility, and aid digestion.

- *Hip Rotations.* Begin with your feet shoulder-width apart. Stay in an upright position, inhaling as you rotate your hips back and exhale forward. Continue for 30 seconds to 1 minute and reverse directions for another 30 seconds to 1 minute.

- *Hip Rotations—Wider Stance.* Move your feet so they are further apart, and repeat hip rotations. Notice the difference in how you feel.

- *Squats.* Proceed with a regular squat or the rocket squats (see Chapter 8), inhaling up and exhaling down, for 1 to 2 minutes.

- *Windmills.* Stand with your feet shoulder-width apart. As you exhale down to the left, twist so that your right hand crosses over the midline toward your left foot. Your left arm is up behind you. Then alternate to the right. Continue alternating sides for 1 to 2 minutes.

- *Side Bends.* Stand with your feet shoulder-width apart. Inhale up to center, and exhale as you gently bend to the left. Inhale up to center, and exhale as you gently bend to the right. Continue for 1 to 2 minutes, gradually deepening the stretch. *To End:* Inhale up, stretch further to the left, and hold for 20 seconds; inhale up, exhale to the right, and hold for 20 seconds.

- *Twisting.* Stand with your feet together, angled out to the side. Your arms are stretched out, parallel to the ground. As you inhale left, twist, bend your right elbow, and bring your right hand in front of your chest. On the exhale, twist right. Continue alternating positions.

- *Variations.* Include one or more of these: kicking out side to side as if you are in a chorus line, marching in place, or standing and shaking, arms above your head.

Continue for 12 to 15 minutes.

To End: Stand in mountain pose. Inhale deeply and relax.

BREATH WORK

Whistling Breath

Whistling impacts the vagus nerve (see Chapter 1) and parasympathetic nervous system, creating a sense of calmness and well-being. However, it is also energizing. With whistling, the nerves in the tongue are stimulated; they in turn activate the thyroid and parathyroid glands, and lung capacity is increased.

- Whistling may be continuous, or it may be practiced only when you inhale or only when you exhale.

- On the inhale, pucker your lips as you whistle a high-pitched whistle, then exhale through your nose.

- Notice the difference in what you hear and feel—a vibration with the inhale and a soft relaxation with the exhale.

- For the exhale, reverse so that you inhale through the nose and whistle on the exhale. Again, notice the difference in how you feel and what you hear.

*Self-Care Breath Kriya

This self-care breath exercise increases inner energy and strength, boosts the immune system, and cleanses the body.

Position: Sit comfortably in a meditation posture.

Eye Focus: Eyes are closed.

- Open your mouth and form a circle that is tight and precise—a boar's mouth.

- Cross your hands over the heart center, right over left.

- Sense the area under your palms.

- Breathe a steady, powerful cannon breath through the mouth. Let your mind focus on the mouth ring and shape the breath into a ring. Continue for 5 minutes.

To End:

- Inhale and hold your breath. Relax your mouth. Mentally repeat: "I am beautiful, I am kind, I am kind, I am beautiful." Exhale through the nose. Do this a total of five times. Then relax.

YOGA SET: POSTURE AND MOVEMENT

Radiant energy moves through the world and flows in each and every one of us. This energy, known in the yogic tradition as *prana*, is carried throughout our bodies through *vayu*, which translates to "wind." Our *vayus* transfer this energy throughout our bodies. Although *vayus* are subtle, they have a huge impact on how our bodies feel, so learning to move with their natural rhythms and find balance is vital for our health.

*Achieving Equilibrium: Balancing Energy

Eye Focus: Eyes can be open or closed.

1. *Mini-rotations at the spine.*

Position: Sit in easy pose.

- Put your hands on your knees, keeping your spine straight and stretched upright. Keep your arms straight.

- Create a small circular motion at the base of your spine. The circular movement of the upper body should not be broader than that at the base of the spine. Don't let the spine bend, so that the movement of the entire spine is governed by the circling movement at your base. Continue for 1 minute.

2. *Bending to knee.*

Position: Sit in easy pose. Keep your hands on your knees.

- Bend to the left, touching your forehead to your left knee.

- Rise up and then bend to the right, touching your forehead to your right knee. Continue for 1 minute.

3. *Twisting.*

Position: Sit in easy pose.

- Place both hands, one on top of the other, on your chest at your heart center.

- Twist your body left and right, moving from your navel, using your shoulders as a fulcrum. Continue for 1 minute.

4. *Rising up.*

Position: Sit in easy pose.

- Lock your hands behind your neck, keep your spine straight, bend forward toward the ground, and rise up. Continue for 1 minute.

5. *Cat-cow.*

Position: Cat-cow position.

- Begin flexing your spine up and down as rapidly as you can for 15 seconds.

- Then, as your head comes up in cow, lift your hands from the ground and clap.

- As your head bows down in cat, return your hands to the ground. Continue for 1 minute.

6. *Frog pose.*

Position: Frog pose.

- Squat down in frog pose with your heels together off the ground and your fingertips on the floor between your knees. Balance on the balls of your feet.

- Inhale and straighten your legs, exhale, and return to the squatting position. Repeat 21 times.

7. *Kangaroo jump.*

Position: Standing up.

- Stand like a kangaroo with your knees bent and your arms close to your sides, bent at the elbows and wrists so that your arms look like a kangaroo's forepaws.

- Jump up and down. Repeat 21 times.

8. *Cobra.*

Position: Lie on your stomach with your heels together and your hands on the ground under your shoulders.

- Rise up into cobra pose.

- From cobra pose, quickly roll your body to the left so that you end up lying on your back on the ground.

- Roll back onto your stomach and rise back up into cobra pose.

- Next, roll your body to the right, rolling over quickly so that you again end up on your back on the ground.

- Roll back onto your stomach, rise up into cobra pose, and continue for 1.5 minutes.

9. *Bow pose.*

Position: Lie on your stomach and grab your ankles.

- Press your legs away and raise your chest up, coming up into bow pose.

- Begin a strong Breath of Fire so that your belly button moves. Continue for 1 minute.

10. *Leaning back.*

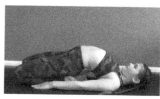

Position: Sit on your heels and spread your knees, placing your buttocks on the ground between your heels.

- Then lie back so that (if possible) your upper back is on the ground. With your fists, begin drumming your upper chest (the lymph area) for 20 seconds, then gently drum on your belly for 15 seconds, then heavily drum your thighs for 15 seconds, then gently drum your navel point for 10 seconds, and then drum both sides of your neck for 15 seconds.

11. *Seated rotations.*

Position: Sit in easy pose.

- Sit once more in easy pose with your hands on your knees. Rotate your upper body 51 times counterclockwise, squeezing the digestive area.

12. *Diagonal stretch.*

Position: Lie down flat on your back.

- Extend your left hip and shoulder downward while you stretch your right hip and shoulder upward. Then extend your right hip and shoulder downward toward your feet while stretching your left hip and shoulder upward. Move diagonally and move powerfully. Continue for 2 minutes.

13. *Leg lifts.*

Position: Lie down flat on your back.

- Straighten your knees and keep your heels together.

- Lift your legs up to 90 degrees and lower them back down with Breath of Fire. Move quickly. Continue for 1.25 minutes.

14. *Extended sit-ups.*

Position: Lie down flat on your back.

- Lock your hands behind your neck and rise up straight (as shown).

- Bend forward, bringing your upper body down to your thighs, and then lie back down flat. Move quickly and continue this movement for 1.5 minutes.

To End: *Relaxation.*

Position: Lie down flat on your back.

- Completely relax your body for up to 10 minutes, listening to the music of your choice. If possible, find music that has a subtle drive or repeated rhythm that occurs at a moderate pace.

- Feel the energy moving in your spine from your tailbone to the top of your head.

- If available and appropriate, Jai Te Gang can be used (see Spirit Voyage, n.d.), with a gong played to further activate the energy.

MEDITATIONS

*Healing Hands

Here's a simple routine to increase the kindness and effectiveness of your healing touch.

Position: Sit in easy pose.

Eye Focus: Eyes are open or closed.

- Rub the palms of your hands together briskly for 3 to 5 minutes. Feel the heat in your hands.

- Stretch your arms out to the side, parallel to the floor, palms up, thumbs pointing back. Do Breath of Fire for 3 minutes.

- Inhale and hold your breath in. With your arms still out to the sides, bend your wrists so your palms face out as if you are pushing on the walls on either side of you. Feel the energy in the center of your palms flowing to your entire body. Exhale and relax the breath.

- Rub your hands together again for 2 minutes.

To End:

- Hold your arms in front of you and bend both elbows, keeping your forearms parallel to the floor. With your left hand in front of your diaphragm, palm facing up, place your right palm facing down about 8 inches above your left palm. Meditate on the exchange of energy between the palms of the hands for a few minutes. Practice this full routine for 11 minutes every day.

*Finding Happiness and Peace Within

Position: Sit in easy pose with your spine straight, chin in, and chest out.

Eye Focus: Eyes are closed.

Warm up by chanting *Ong* in the long form, taking approximately 10 seconds to chant *Ong* one time. Chant through the conch, with the mouth slightly open and the breath only coming out of the nostrils.

To End:

- Chant in this manner five times, and then gradually begin to chant *Ong* faster, chanting one *Ong* every 3 to 5 seconds. Start with 1 minute of rapid *Ong* and gradually work up to 2 minutes.

*Saa Taa Naa Maa Meditation

This is a very powerful meditation that will help activate pathways in your brain, increasing alertness and blood flow to the brain, improving memory, and supporting healing. It may take some practice to feel successful with this, as it involves several simultaneous components (breathing, chanting, visualizing light energy, and finger movements). The benefits are supported by several scientific studies (D. S. Khalsa et al., 2009; S. B. S. Khalsa, 2004).

Position: Sit in easy pose.

Eye Focus: Meditate at the brow point.

- The following sounds will be chanted:
  - *Saa:* Infinity, cosmos, beginning
  - *Taa:* Life, existence
  - *Naa:* Death, change, transformation
  - *Maa:* Renewal of life

- Each repetition of the entire mantra takes 3 to 4 seconds. From the Infinite comes life and individual existence. From life comes death or change. From death comes the rebirth of consciousness to the joy of the Infinite through which compassion leads back to life.

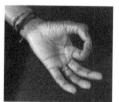

- As you chant *Saa Taa Naa Maa*, alternate through four mudras:
  - On *Saa*, touch the first (index) finger; gyan mudra (knowledge)

  - On *Taa*, touch the second (middle) finger; shuni mudra (wisdom, intelligence, patience)
  - On *Naa*, touch the third (ring) finger; surya mudra (vitality, energy of life)

  - On *Maa*, touch the fourth (little) finger; buddhi mudra (ability to communicate)

- Chant in three voices of consciousness:

  - Normal or loud voice (the world)
  - Strong whisper (longing to belong)
  - Mentally; silent (infinity)

- As you chant, imagine the energy of each sound moving down through the top of the skull and then out through the brow point. Project the sounds to Infinity.

- Begin the kriya in a normal voice for 5 minutes; then whisper for 5 minutes; then go deep into the sound, vibrating silently for 10 minutes. Then come back to a whisper for 5 minutes, then chant aloud for 5 minutes. The duration of the meditation may vary, as long as the proportion of loud, whisper, silent, whisper, loud is maintained.

To End:

- Inhale, then exhale, followed by 1 minute of silence.

- Stretch the spine. With your hands up as high as possible, spread your fingers wide, taking several deep breaths. Relax.

*Mantra for Healing: *Ra Ma Da Sa*

This mantra provides a conscious focus on healing for self, others, and the universe (Ramdesh, n.d.).

Position: Sit in easy pose, arms out to your sides, elbows pressed against your rib cage. Your arms are halfway forward and out to the sides (about 45 degrees), with the forearms up. The palms are flat, fingers together and thumbs stretched away. Consciously keep the palms flat throughout the meditation.

Eye Focus: Eyes can be open or closed.

The words to this mantra are *Ra Ma Da Sa Sa Say So Hung.*

- *Ra* means the sun, and connecting with this frequency gives you energy.

- *Ma* means the moon, and it aligns you with receptivity.

- *Da* is the energy of the Earth, grounding you in your roots.

- *Sa* is Infinity, and as you chant this, your energy rises upward and outward, drawing in the healing of the Universe. Pause briefly.

- When you chant *Sa* a second time, you pull the energy of Infinity into you.

- *Say* is a way of honoring the all-encompassing Thou. It is personal.

- *So* is a vibration of merger.

- *Hung* is the Infinite, the vibrating real. It is the essence of creation. Vibrate *Hung* as a nasal sound and again pull the navel point to your spine as you chant *Hung.*

Chant for 11 to 31 minutes.

To End: Stay in position, palms up. Imagine an arc of healing energy over your head.

- Inhale deeply, hold your breath, and visualize a white light, sending healing love and energy to yourself. Exhale.

- Inhale again and expand your circle to include family and friends, particularly anyone who is sick or suffering, again visualizing healing energy. Exhale.

- Inhale a third time and expand your circle to include the entire planet, visualizing healing energy. Exhale and relax.

- Stretch your arms up and vigorously shake your hands and arms.

COMMUNITY CURRICULUM INTEGRATION PLANNER

The yoga-mindfulness-meditation exercises in this chapter can enhance academic learning and your classroom environment. Refer to Figure 10.1 for a few examples of what you can do.

Figure 10.1 • Community Curriculum Integration Planner

LESSON	GRADE LEVEL	SUBJECT/CONTEXT	ADAPTATION/NOTES
Developing community/ class rules	Any	During a time when it is appropriate, incorporate exercises, breaths, or meditations so that students have opportunities to strengthen their sense of collective purpose. The "Saa Taa Naa Maa Meditation" is particularly good for decision making as it activates the hypothalamus and pituitary glands. Using it prior to developing or discussing class rules may be beneficial.	Use with whistle breath to bring calmness, and with one of the meditations from this chapter—for example, "Finding Happiness and Peace Within."
Discussion of race and discrimination	Grades 4–12	Discussion of race, discrimination, justice, and the importance of community.	Could use with the "Mantra for Healing: Ra Ma Da Sa."
Sustainability	Grades 6–12	Discussion of sustainability and our planet, ethics, and caring for others.	Any of the meditations. Could do Healing Hands, and then envision that you are holding a globe. Could journal afterward.
Test prep	Any	Preparation for a difficult assignment/perhaps studying for exams.	Practice the "Saa Taa Naa Maa Meditation" for several weeks in advance—perhaps even for 5 to 10 minutes, 3 to 5 times a week.

online resources Available at https://resources.corwin.com/CultivatingHappiness

MINDFUL REFLECTION

1. Consider community building, welcoming newcomers to your classroom or school, infusing kindness and compassion in your community, or lessons regarding racism and injustice. How could mindfulness, breath work, or meditations be used to further understanding?

2. Which breaths, kriyas, or meditations were most appealing to you? To your students?

3. How inclusive is your classroom community? Are improvements needed? Doing breath work, kriyas, and meditations together can help foster a sense of community. Consider student leaders, peers from other grades, and others. Could they help you build a more inclusive community?

ONLINE RESOURCES

Visit https://resources.corwin.com/CultivatingHappiness

Online Resource 10.1   SOBER Breathing Space for Teens

Online Resource 10.2   Gratitude Circle for Staff Members

Online Resource 10.3   Making Families Feel Welcome

Online Resource 10.4   Community Curriculum Integration Planner

Online Resource 10.5   Mindful Reflection

Leadership

Kirsten Richert, Jeffrey Ikler, and Margaret Zacchei (2020) describe how school leaders can create cultures of change by beginning with greater self-awareness and contemplation: "Using those contemplative practices, we train ourselves to become ever more mindful. We gradually carve out a quiet, safe, emotional space that allows us to more fully exercise our sense to bring what's around and inside us into greater clarity" (p. 94), which in turn leads to greater emotional intelligence. With that greater emotional intelligence, we are more aware and better communicators, naturally preparing us to be better leaders.

In *Cultivating Happiness, Resilience, and Well-Being*, we have repeated a similar mantra: "Start with yourself," establishing your own practice first. This value is reiterated by many. As you read the following, consider the consistency in the advice from these different sources:

- Monica Sharma (2017), trained as a physician and epidemiologist, has worked at the United Nations for over 20 years. As she discusses radical transformational leadership, she urges us to consider new ways of learning and leading with a focus on inner wisdom:

  My inner wisdom capacity . . . leads me to compassionate action in the world, giving me inner guidance, insight, and light that clarifies universal, life-giving principles. My wisdom and inner capacity resolve and release fear, anger, separation, and anxiety. I know what I care for deeply and I am anchored in my universal values in a way that sets me free. I engage in compassionate action in the world. (p. 64)

Monica also reminds us of the value of listening deeply, a critical tool for leaders:

  Listening deeply also creates new openings for action. Everyone can make a difference. It is not about expertise or opinions. Listening deeply helps to unfold the full potential of another human BEING. (Sharma, 2017, p. 191)

- As education professor and author Dennis Shirley (2016) states, "in an ideal world students and teachers would thrive in classes full of purposeful learning" (p. 9). Referencing the high numbers of students facing depression and anxiety, Shirley asks us to plan for "opportunities for students to get to know themselves," stating that "education can awaken the conscience, teach compassion, and spark a lifelong dedication to contribution to a better world" (p. 126).

- Dan Domenech, executive director of AASA—The School Superintendents Association, implores educators to become consciously aware of students' personal interests not only to personalize classrooms and teaching, but also to personalize leadership and governance. He advises leaders to ensure that "every student is engaged in education as a lifelong pursuit. Every student should become a critical thinker and creator, exploring interests and avenues of personal aspiration and engagement" (Domenech et al., 2016, p. 23). As leaders, we need to understand not only more about ourselves and our coworkers, but also more about our students—about their passions—to help them explore alternatives for their futures.

- Brad Gustafson, an elementary principal and author, spells out some of the things that students most need—to have their voices amplified, to be involved in directing their own education, and to have opportunities for connectedness. However, Gustafson (2017) also describes what leaders must do to personalize learning, facilitate team building, advance innovation, and transform learning spaces, asking, "What feeling or vibe do you want to create for students in your classroom?" (p. 125).

- Consider for a moment the "vibe" you may be aiming for in your classroom or school. In this book, we have explained the energy that is created with the yoga-mindfulness-meditation techniques we recommend. We also have described the value of shifting energy from the lower body to the upper body (heart center and throat) and the brain.

Best-selling author and longtime meditation teacher Sharon Salzberg (2002), in her book *Lovingkindness: The Revolutionary Art of Happiness*, describes the energy and vibrational patterns of a universe in a state of constant flux:

> Outside ourselves we see alternating rhythms of photosynthesis and the respiration of plants. Within ourselves we see the biorhythms of our own biochemistry. Everything is moving, vibrating, pulsating in rhythm. These alternations are also found within the rhythms of the planet, in the ebb and flow of the tides, the cycle of night and day, and of the seasons, and all the cycles of the natural world. When we look at our own lives, we see extraordinary patterns of flow and movement. (p. 139)

We believe it will be helpful for leaders to consider the changes they are making not only from a linear perspective (e.g., Steps 1, 2, and 3), but also from an awareness of the energy that coexists among all beings and things on the planet. This means that we are interested in creating a positive flow of energy, removing blocks—including blocks within our bodies and our minds—and developing communal spaces that support positive networking and growth.

LEADING AND BEING A STEWARD OF MINDFULNESS

Dr. Renee Owen (personal communication, February 2020) offers mindful advice for school leaders:

"Listen to the bowl, and when you can no longer hear it, let's take three breaths together. One big breath in . . . and out . . ." Five-year-old Taisha leads morning mindfulness with confidence and clarity. She has been practicing mindfulness at school since she was three. It's completely natural to her.

For over a decade, I was the leader of Rainbow Community School, a holistic school where each child and adult engaged in a practice we called centering for the first 20 to 30 minutes of each day. We would sit on the floor in a circle and begin centering by lighting a candle (as a visual focus), ringing a bowl or chime (as an auditory focus), and taking three breaths together. After this mindful opening, each class would engage in centering activities designed for many purposes: to bring the class together as a community, to learn about inner and outer lives, and much more. No matter what the centering activity was, it always began and ended with mindfulness.

- Throughout our days at Rainbow Community School, it was a natural part of the culture to pause and breathe or to put our hands on our hearts when strong feelings were expressed.

- Adults were as much a part of the mindful culture as children. Every meeting—faculty meetings, board meetings, administrative meetings—began with centering.

Mindfulness wasn't something students did; it was central to who they were. A culture of mindfulness creates a sense of well-being that extends to everyone around us.

(Continued)

(Continued)

Today, I am an assistant professor of education leadership at Southern Oregon University's Holistic Teaching and Learning Center, training the region's next generation of public school administrators. I find that today's school leaders find themselves desperate to transform their school culture from one narrowly focused on academic achievement to a more holistic and authentically inclusive atmosphere.

Thanks to my experience at Rainbow Community School, I am able to draw for them a vision of what is possible. I offer three major steps leaders can take to create mindful schools.

Foster a shared vision of mindfulness. When visioning, pair achievement data with meaningful, personal stories from students and families. Use available forums (newsletters, speaking engagements, meetings, trainings, social media) to provide stories and information to demonstrate the positive effects of mindfulness in schools.

Once a healthy tension has been created that demonstrates the gap between current reality and what is possible, utilize visioning tools (see Mason, Liabenow, & Patschke, 2020) so that each group of stakeholders writes their own vision statement for what a culture of mindfulness might look like, feel like, and sound like for them. Each classroom should write their own mindfulness vision to guide their class behavior.

These vision statements can be crafted into an overall mindful vision for the school. For example:

- "We envision a school where mindfulness is an integral part of every day. Each child and adult uses mindful techniques to soothe stress and regulate emotions. Mindfulness brings us together."

Redesign structures. Rather than expecting teachers to squeeze mindful moments into overstuffed schedules, school leaders must have the courage to restructure school days to include explicitly scheduled time for communal mindfulness.

- Teachers also commented on how centering didn't just help children as individuals, but it brought the class together into a cohesive whole, greatly diminishing behavioral issues and increasing compassion (Owen, 2019). Bullying was nonexistent.

- There are many models for morning circles teachers can use with younger students: restorative circles (Pranis, 2015), Positive Discipline meetings (Nelsen et al., 2013), Conscious Discipline's Smart Start (Bailey, 2015), or the Responsive Classrooms morning meeting format (Center for Responsive Schools, 2015).

At the middle school and secondary level, more research is demonstrating the necessity for advisory rooms or homerooms, where youth gather every morning with a teacher or caring adult for mindfulness, social-emotional learning, mentoring, physical exercise, or other communal activities. Mindful homerooms become an emotional resource that is critically necessary for developing a sense of safety, support, and belonging at school.

Become a steward of mindfulness. It is impossible for teachers and other leaders to effectively lead mindfulness if they don't have their own practice. Leaders who are mindful demonstrate daily compassion and nonreactivity in times of crisis, making the presence of a mindful leader a salve for stress.

Anytime leaders are facilitating a meeting or training, they can lead a mindful moment for three breaths, a body scan, or any act of mindfulness so that groups can make decisions and learn in a state of focus and compassion. Put mindfulness on the agenda for the beginning and ending of every meeting.

Highly developed mindful leaders know when to ask for moments of silence when people need to think deeply or to process difficult news or emotions. Any moment taken for mindfulness saves time, as it frees hearts and minds to think clearly and receive inspired solutions to problems. As Parker J. Palmer has said, "Don't speak unless you can improve upon the silence" (see Kaufman, 2011, p. 85).

As leaders in today's public schools, we must see ourselves as change agents, transforming our schools from places of stress and isolation to islands of peace and belonging. It's a lofty vision that is only possible when we believe it.

In Part III, Valerie Brown and Jeffrey Donald share their recommendations for mindful leadership. While each time a teacher picks up yoga-mindfulness-meditation practices the number of students who learn to listen to their inner voices—to calm themselves—increases, there is much power in our collective capacity. To achieve the global transformational change in thinking that is called for in this era of climate change, insurrection, and viral pandemics, shifts in our mindset are needed. We have research-based tools at our disposal, and as they are implemented, we not only help our students; we also increase the most meaningful supports for ourselves, our communities, and future generations.

MINDFUL REFLECTION

1. Do you know any mindful leaders? What do you know of their individual mindfulness practices?

2. What did you learn by reading about Dr. Owen's mindful leadership?

3. What is your leadership role? What are you hoping to learn by reading more about mindfulness leadership?

ONLINE RESOURCES

Visit https://resources.corwin.com/CultivatingHappiness

Online Resource PIII.1   Mindful Reflection

CHAPTER ELEVEN

Mindful Educational Leadership

Practices to Transform You and Your Leadership

By Valerie Brown, JD, MA, PCC

KEY PRINCIPLE

Mindfulness supports development of the "inner faculty" of leadership. Leadership is more about emotional intelligence skills of self-awareness, self-regulation, motivation, empathy, and social skills, such as fostering trustworthiness, and less about positional authority. As leaders face growing complexity, mindfulness supports greater calm, stability, and responsive decision making.

JADA'S STORY: "YOU HAVE TO KNOW HOW TO MANAGE PEOPLE"

Jada has been a teacher for more than 20 years and loved her job teaching reading in a large urban public school, serving largely Black and Brown students. However, lately, her new role of teacher-leader and coach has brought with it many sleepless nights. She describes herself as a reluctant leader and says she wants to "build people up"—to see them succeed, do well, support students, and move test scores in the right direction. And this isn't happening.

In our virtual interview, Jada sits on the edge of her chair, wringing her hands, shifting her weight back and forth in her chair, glancing from left to right, and even on the virtual platform of Zoom, I sense she's anxious, uneasy. I ask Jada to describe a typical workday.

It's 5:00 a.m. when Jada gets a jump on her day with her phone and begins scrolling her news feed for the latest, then rolls out of bed to check emails while skimming the district accountability report on her phone. She lets the dog out, starts the automatic coffeemaker, and turns back to her phone only to find herself sidetracked reading through backlogged emails and text messages, her shoulders tightly hunched to her ears. Briefly, she looks up from her phone and thinks to herself, "I've got to get back to the gym when it's safe to do so after I'm vaccinated against COVID-19." She takes a shallow breath and turns back to the glow of the phone in the darkened room. As she scrolls through the feed, she comes across an image of a gorgeous white sand beach and recalls the promise to herself to take that dream vacation with her daughter. Her attention lands on an article on healthy eating, and she momentarily vows to give up diet soda and regular runs for a bacon, egg, and cheese biscuit to go, and to instead begin the day with instant oatmeal to fuel up her body.

It's 5:25 a.m. when the sun begins to rise through draped windows. Outside, very early spring red-breasted nuthatches and tree swallows fill the air with song, yet this is lost on Jada. She is unaware of the warm glow of the rising sun and morning light, unaware of the birdsong, and she barely tastes the coffee. Uneasily, she straightens her shoulders and wonders about the pain in her lower back. "Tomorrow," she says, "I'll make an appointment with the doctor."

It's now 6:45 a.m., and Jada pulls her car into the school parking lot, barely aware of how she got there, lost in thought about the latest instructional calendar, teacher observations, and the district's rollout of the new literacy plan. Jada's day moves swiftly, from observation to observation, meeting to meeting, with no time even for lunch. It's 2:45 p.m. when Jada realizes that she left her snack sitting on the kitchen counter as she grabbed her cell phone and ran out the door in the morning.

Feeling overwhelmed and hungry, she gets a bag of chips from the vending machine to hold her over until she can pick up something quick for dinner at the local drive-through. When Jada finally gets back home, it's 5:45 p.m. She falls into the couch and grabs the remote, surfing through channels, but she's fast asleep within minutes, only awakened again by the pain in her lower back.

In stepping into her new teacher-leader and coach position, Jada wants to know how to build people up, and has long believed that "you have to know how to manage people." However, Jada has not yet understood that "managing" others begins with managing herself.

MY JOURNEY INTO MINDFULNESS

I cowrote *The Mindful School Leader: Practices to Transform Your Leadership and School* (2015) along with my friend and colleague Dr. Kirsten Olson after meeting with hundreds of educational leaders like Jada. Nearly all of them said the same thing in different ways. They all felt stressed, overwhelmed, and on the edge of burnout. They all wanted mindfulness practices in their schools for their students to help them focus attention and as a behavioral management system for some students. When I asked about mindfulness practices to support them as leaders, they all offered similar responses: "Work and life is overwhelming." "There is no time in my already crammed, packed day." I could understand these sentiments, because in many ways this was my life.

My journey into mindfulness began in 1995 when I attended a talk by Vietnamese Zen master Thich Nhat Hanh at Riverside Church in New York City. He spoke about how to embrace painful emotions, to take care of them, and to hold them tenderly. This was revolutionary for me. As an Afro-Cuban woman, my habit was the opposite: to push painful emotions away and numb myself through work. I was combative with my feelings of grief, hurt, and sadness, and I held myself to punishingly high standards in fear of failure.

I know now that this habit stemmed from my childhood. Growing up amidst poverty and violence, I carried the weight of my mother's sacrifice as a single parent and a maid at the Hotel Manhattan. I wanted to do good, to make her proud of me, and I wanted her sacrifice to amount to something. In my confusion, I ran from my home to college, from college to grad school, from grad school to law school, and from law school to a "Big and Important Job" as a lawyer-lobbyist. I momentarily felt safe and secure in my status as a lawyer and believed it would insulate me from oppression. I was wrong.

I absorbed middle-class values and status symbols of success, and I spent years trying to "measure up," assimilate, and "fit in." I straightened my hair, wore neutral-colored business suits, and made sure my jewelry was nonoffensive. I did my best to fit into white culture and silenced myself so others could feel comfortable. After years living this way, I was exhausted from constantly trying to prove myself, constantly monitoring every aspect of my behavior. I felt numb and isolated as a Black woman in a white world. I didn't know what to do. My journey to healing began, in part, when I found Thich Nhat Hanh and the mindfulness practice. When I began practicing mindfulness, I was a closet meditator, fearing that this was another part of myself that I could not share with work colleagues.

A crucial moment in healing was visiting a local sangha (Plum Village community) and attending retreats at Thich Nhat Hanh's practice centers. I joined the Plum Village Order

(Continued)

(Continued)

of Interbeing, founded by Nhat Hanh, in 2003. More often than not, I was one of very few people of color at these gatherings. A turning point came in 2004 when I attended the Colors of Compassion Retreat at Deer Park Monastery. Among hundreds of other people of color, I found my "true home," a safe place to begin to accept myself, to feel compassion for myself, and to cultivate compassion for others. I also began to rethink the notion of "status" as a lawyer.

During that retreat, I wrote this teaching of Thay's (which means *teacher* in Vietnamese and is another name for Thich Nhat Hanh) in my journal in big letters:

> In the teachings of the Buddha, it is very clear that what determines the value of a person is not her race or caste, but her thought, speech, and action. We are not noble because of our race, but because of our way of thinking, our way of speaking, and our way of acting.

In community, I recognized the universality of suffering and saw that healing was possible. After years in the practice, I began to notice (as did others) changes within me. I felt softer and less reactive. I was able to notice and take good care of strong emotions. I was able to connect on a "heart" level instead of a "head" level with others, and it changed the quality of my relationships and my life. Practicing mindfulness in the Plum Village tradition allowed me to heal and transform strong feelings of separation and isolation, and it allowed me to offer this healing to others.

Several years ago, I joined ARISE (Awakening through Race, Intersectionality, and Social Equity) in order to help heal the wounds of discrimination in the sangha and in our world. The work of ARISE is a reflection of my deepest aspiration: to transform inequity into compassion, understanding, love, and peace. Additionally, as a consultant, a writer, and a co-director of Georgetown's Institute for Transformational Leadership, I am deeply interested in working with leaders to embody greater compassion and develop trustworthy relationships. Our society is in great need of healing on many levels, and this healing is the foundation for love.

THE INNER LIFE OF LEADERS LINKED TO OUTER LIFE OF LEADERSHIP

Teaching, like any truly human activity, emerges from one's inwardness, for better or worse. As I teach, I project the condition of my soul onto my students, my subject, and our way of being together.

—Parker J. Palmer, *The Courage to Teach* (2007, p. 102)

The effectiveness of mindfulness practices on students and teachers has been demonstrated over decades by hundreds of empirical studies and supported by many organizations that specialize in helping teachers and students bring mindfulness practices to the classroom and other learning environments. However, for school leaders and their leadership, mindfulness is largely absent, and they are hugely underserved.

Far too often, I hear statements from school leaders like "It's selfish and self-indulgent to think about myself" or "So many people depend on me. I can't ask for or receive support." I understand why they feel this way. But after years of habitual and toxic stress and poor coping skills, their leadership decisions often suffer. Even high-performers find themselves slipping into simply maintaining the status quo, or coping day to day and hoping that external events will bring a change.

STRESS: AN INVITATION TO GROW

Ironically, stress and even crisis are invitations to grow, to expand our ways of understanding ourselves and our habitual reactions. Through mindful body attunement practices and reflective exercises outlined in this chapter, leaders can learn some of the fundamental building blocks of sustainable and coherent mindful leadership and use these tools to reboot themselves on the job, enjoy their leadership lives more, and lead more boldly and with more support from others around them and within themselves.

John Dewey, the American scholar, famously said, "We don't learn from experience . . . we learn from reflecting on experience." Many school leaders we interviewed for *The Mindful School Leader* (V. Brown & Olson, 2015) spoke of very little time dedicated to reflection and integration. As with Jada, their days were spent "putting out fires" with little meaningful reflection. In studying at the Center for Courage & Renewal and with my mentor, the Quaker educator and writer Parker J. Palmer, I've relearned the importance of alignment and congruence between the inner and outer life of leaders. There is a connection and relationship between our inner values, perceptions, and beliefs and our daily actions. Reflecting on this movement between inner—what we believe—and outer—how we act—is a key part of leadership discernment that makes for authentic and grounded leadership.

During my high-pressure career as a lawyer-lobbyist, I believed that effective leadership was about a set of competencies that included technical skill and expertise, power, status, and control. I believed that leadership was largely about positional authority and superior technical skills. The person at the top of the organizational chart was the leader. I played by these rules for decades, believing that if I had the right educational degrees, the right skill set, and the right experience, I would be a successful leader.

A New Leadership Language

Today, working with leaders across professions, I've learned that a new language around leadership has emerged. Leadership requires self-awareness, emotional intelligence, integrity, and trustworthiness. In the face of complexity, ambiguity, and uncertainty, leaders are called to be adaptable, to embrace paradox and polarity, and to hold unsettled tensions. Time and time again when I teach leadership and ask about what makes for an outstanding leader, participants almost never point to technical skills. Instead, they refer to these skills of emotional intelligence, authenticity, kindness, good listening, honesty, and more.

Mindfulness supports development of the "inner faculty" of leadership as leaders engage skills and practices for the long haul of leadership. These practices include learning to slow down and to focus, without rushing to back-to-back meetings, to develop greater body literacy and emotional intelligence.

What Is Mindfulness?

Mindfulness is mainstream. Sometimes it seems impossible to open a newspaper, listen to a podcast, or read a blog or magazine without finding a reference to new mindfulness practices and the innovative ways in which they are being applied. Training in mindfulness—*the intentional cultivation of moment-by-moment nonjudgmental, focused attention and awareness*—seems to be everywhere.

With regular practice, mindfulness can alter the neural architectures and reaction patterns of our brains and shift the ways in which we regard ourselves, our lives, and the contexts in which we operate as leaders. With practice, mindfulness can allow educational leaders to disengage from habitual reactions and become more able to observe themselves in action and to act more effectively in the midst of chaos, overstimulation, and threat, a condition of the lives of many educational leaders.

The foundational elements of mindfulness are focused attention in a purposeful, intentional, and nonjudgmental way, with kindness. Just as important as it is to speak about what mindfulness is, it is equally important to say what mindfulness is not. It is not about having thoughts, or about always being in a state of calm, bliss, or lack of stress, and it is not a relaxation technique. It is not about the absence of afflictive emotions, like sadness, loneliness, or despair. It is not a religion though it has roots in Buddhism. It is not "mental hygiene" though it is often described in these terms and is likened to a daily habit, such as brushing your teeth. It's not a behavioral modification system designed for troubled students. Nor is it a personal self-help technique though it is enormously supportive.

Mindfulness can help us to become more aware of our emotions, our body and environment, and our habits and patterns, such as interrupting and automatic or autopilot reactions. Mindfulness invites us to pay attention without mental elaboration and reactivity, without the constant editorializing. Mindfulness is about showing up and occupying the space of your own awareness no matter what's happening. In this way, we bring the full dimension of our being to daily life. Too often we live pulled by the past or projected into the future, asleep to this moment. When we are mindful, we are entering a capacity to relate to ourselves and to our environment more deeply and with more meaning, knowing that this moment is impermanent, temporary, fleeting. With this realization, we recognize just how brief and vulnerable life is, and we can touch a sense of wonder and gratitude.

Focused Attention

Similarly, we live in an attention deficit economy in a state of cognitive overload by too much information coming in too fast to make meaning, sort, or filter. In this reality, attention is a powerful tool. A well-known study by Daniel Gilbert and Matthew Killingsworth revealed that we spend approximately 47% of our waking hours thinking about something other than what we're doing (Bradt, 2010).

A *Diagnostic and Statistical Manual of Mental Disorders* category, Attention Deficit Trait, refers to the inability to focus due to overuse of high-tech devices. The researcher, Linda Stone, cited the phrase "continuous partial attention" to describe the many ways in which our attention is fractured (American Psychiatric Association, 2013). Mindfulness addresses this attention crisis by building greater awareness to address mind wandering and to redirect the wandering mind for greater sustained focus and attention.

How Mindfulness Helps You Become a Better Educational Leader

A 2020 study conducted by the Harris Poll for the American Psychological Association (2020b) found that nearly 8 in 10 adults (78%) say the coronavirus pandemic is a significant source of stress in their lives, while 3 in 5 (60%) say the number of issues America faces is overwhelming to them. Among educators, burnout is real and alarmingly high. In the United States, nearly half a million teachers move or leave the profession of teaching each year, and this attrition rate disproportionately affects high-poverty schools (The Graide Network, 2019).

Many factors are driving these numbers, including lack of autonomy, demands of educational benchmarks, and unhealthy, out-of-control pressures. Mindfulness cannot remove stressful life circumstances and conditions. However, it can affect how you react to stress and how stress "weathers" the body and mind. Stress increases the risk of getting diseases that can make you sick, as well as the risk of the body's natural defenses being overwhelmed by disease. Stress stimulates the adrenals, releasing cortisol, activating the body's sympathetic nervous system. Some stress can be useful, especially to motivate action. However, long-term, chronic, unmitigated stress can be more damaging than the stressor itself, especially when the stress is psychological. Today's school leaders, especially in the virtual learning environment, are undergoing extraordinary levels of stress.

LEADERSHIP AND EMOTIONAL INTELLIGENCE

Leaders, across many sectors, including education, are facing an imperative today because of rapidly escalating complexity and uncertainty. For leaders to navigate the change is to go well beyond competency, expertise, strategic planning, and managing a competitive edge.

MINDFUL LEADERSHIP IN INCREASINGLY COMPLEX SCHOOLS

Leadership requires greater levels of emotional intelligence: self-awareness, self-management, motivation, empathy, and social skills. Our schools—and the larger world in which we and our students navigate—are growing increasingly complex and unpredictable. Buffeted by global happenings, and the speed and pace at which we operate in school as information and connection are increasingly available at every moment, our leadership selves can be sorely tested and profoundly challenged.

- Not only are our leadership selves asked to grow bigger by sometimes tragic external events like the global pandemic, but the complexity of our leadership environments and accountability systems, and the always-on, always-available reality in which we are expected to respond to this complexity almost immediately, challenges us intellectually and spiritually in ways that are unprecedented in human life.

- This complexity, immediacy, overabundance of information, and potential for distraction has consequences for everyone, but perhaps most particularly for school leaders because they must lead and show the way forward during a period in which the education sector is undergoing transformational and truly groundbreaking change.

All of this change means that educational leaders are increasingly leading during times of transition, and for leaders this requires cultivating the capacity to hold ambiguity, tension, conflict, and unresolvedness, perhaps over sustained periods.

ENACTING CHANGE

- What challenges are you currently facing?

- What complexities, ambiguities, and tensions are you dealing with?

- What factors are within your control? What factors are outside of your control?

- What partners, resources, and supports can you turn to for help?

- What are concrete steps you can take to begin to address these challenges?

During times of great societal stress and suffering, the demands on leaders are significant. Today's leaders are challenged in so many ways as we go about a process of righting wrongs and establishing equity and justice, even as we strive to do our day-to-day work as heads of school. Yet, today we do this in communities wrought with divisiveness, adding a layer of complexity that requires even greater leadership. The capacity to hold others' points of view without championing one and making the other invalid, holding competing ends of a conflict, is healthy, creative tension, and sets a foundation for outcomes where all sides win.

Focused attention and the capacity to hold tension creatively are powerful tools of the human spirit. Yet, time and time again, I encounter leaders who struggle to stay focused, who are overworked, over-booked, and overextended—like Jada. We are addicted to multitasking and distraction. Increased performance demands when coupled with fractured focus amount to a true crisis for many of the people I work with in schools. I know these demands too well.

Mindfulness improves the ability to notice, slow down, and stop automatic reactions; regroup; and reassess habitual patterns to notice what's really happening. Mindfulness supports our ability to respond to complex and conflicting situations. Mindfulness sharpens focus and attention, so we become skillful at making choices and less reactive. Mindfulness supports our ability to be more creative in designing solutions to complex problems. Mindfulness practices are reflective and help us to tap into not just the head—the wisdom of the mind, the seat of intellect—but the wisdom of the heart, the seat of compassion, and the gut, the seat of intuition. Mindfulness strengthens our ability to achieve greater balance and resilience. As educators, we can live with a sense of time deficit—not enough time for us, family, our life—which slowly compromises well-being. Through purposeful, mindful pause practices and the informal practice of mindfulness, we can build well-being into our day, helping us counter the effects of daily stress.

Finally, and perhaps most critically, mindfulness practices help educational leaders develop the most important attribute of all: the capacity to connect with others and themselves. As we know, leading other people is extraordinarily challenging. As Jada said, as a leader, "you have to know how to manage people."

What Happens When You Are Calmer, More Focused, and Less Driven?

If you were calmer, more focused, and less driven by a sense that there is never enough time in the day, would your demeanor have positive effects on your staff and school climate? Would this approach help support a trusting, cohesive school culture and, ultimately, higher student achievement and student efficacy? The purpose of these practices for a school leader is, of course, not only to develop greater clarity, personal poise, and a sense of enhanced well-being, but also to become a more skillful leader.

Let's return to Jada, the teacher-leader presented at the beginning of this chapter. How is Jada's noticeable uneasiness affecting others around her at school and at home? How does the way Jada begins her day influence her energy levels and state of mind throughout the day? How is Jada's fractured attention affecting her performance as a school leader? What modeling does this signal to those Jada is seeking to build up?

You cannot buy mindfulness training for schools or districts, hold a few trainings about it, monitor progress, and assume it is working. Mindfulness cannot be "implemented" in a school culture (or in an individual leader) in a conventional sense because implementation implies that the result is known and anticipatable. Mindfulness is rather a commitment to practice, to daily "attentive repetition," with an understanding that for many of us, the benefits of a daily mindfulness commitment are subtle and require a noticing of slight shifts in ourselves and our reactions.

Educational leaders ***must engage with these mindfulness practices themselves to legitimately bring mindfulness initiatives to their schools.*** They must set the example others will follow and begin the journey of alignment of the inner work of leadership with the outer work of action.

DEVELOPING A DAILY MINDFULNESS PRACTICE

- What do you hope to get out of a daily mindfulness practice?
- What are the next steps in committing to a daily mindfulness practice?
- Who else will you invite to participate in a daily mindfulness practice? How can you support and encourage each other?

MINDFULNESS PRACTICES FOR EDUCATIONAL LEADERS

Before you begin practicing, these are helpful and supportive guidelines.

- Regardless of what happens (falling asleep, losing concentration, being distracted by thoughts, emotions, or physical sensations), just do it. If you're sleepy, try keeping your eyes open.

- When you are distracted by wandering thoughts, emotions, or other physical sensations, simply notice them as passing events, and then gently redirect the mind back to the present moment.

- Notice if you have ideas about "success," "failure," or "doing it right." These are just thoughts. The mindfulness practices are not a competition, nor are they a skill to perfect. Practice being open and curious about whatever you experience.

- Notice if you have expectations about what mindfulness practices will do for you. Allow this to function as a seed that you are planting. In order to cultivate it, you only have to give it the proper conditions: a time that you set aside and an open mind and heart.

- Cultivate a view of open friendliness to whatever is there, with the attitude "Okay, that's just the way things are right now." If you worry about unpleasant thoughts, emotions, or sensations, try to accept things as they are as best you can.

TRANSFORMATIONAL LEADERSHIP BENEFITS OF THESE MINDFULNESS PRACTICES

- Enhanced capacity for shifting, directing, and redirecting attention from wide to narrow

- Strengthened concentration and focus

- Greater self-awareness and self-acceptance

- Better impulse control

- More accurate self-perception

- Enhanced reflection

- More grounded and conscious leadership

- Increased resilience

Formal Mindfulness

Mindful Breathing Time Required: 5 minutes or less.

- Come into a comfortable posture, either seated, standing, or lying down, where you will not be disturbed.

- Allow your spine to be comfortably straight, but not rigid.

- Loosen any tight clothing around your waist, and please allow your head, neck, and spine to be aligned.

- Allow your eyes to be closed, if that is comfortable for you.

- Place your dominant hand on your belly and your nondominant hand on your chest.

- Observe, without judgment, the rise and fall of your belly.

- Notice the movement of your dominant hand at the belly and the movement of your nondominant hand at your chest as you breathe in and out of your nose for 10 breath cycles. There is no need to force or control the breath. Just be with the breath as it is.

- When you are finished, stretch gently, and open your eyes if they are closed.

Informal Mindfulness: Ways to Bring Mindfulness Into Your Daily Life

Time Required: 1 minute or less for each practice.

- Practice mindful walking—walking slower than usual, feeling your feet on the floor, noticing sound and sensations as you move from one meeting to the next.

- Practice one minute of mindful breathing before a stressful meeting.

- In your next conversation, notice your impulse to interrupt or finish someone else's sentence, and practice pausing and being fully present.

- Practice noticing emotions and feelings without pushing them away.

- The next time you eat, take 30 seconds without mobile devices or reading materials to taste the food. Chew it slowly. Notice digestion. Notice how you feel.

Body Scan Practice

Time Required: 10 minutes or less.

The world is changing faster than we can adapt. Grounded leadership is more important than ever before. The body scan, a mindfulness exercise of awareness and progressive relaxation, is a way of recognizing body sensations, emotions, and how they might influence behavior and emotions. The body scan is like giving all the parts of your body and emotions a big hug.

The Process

- **Pause**
  - Take a few moments to pause, sitting in a chair or lying flat on the floor or on a cushion or folded blanket. Bring your awareness to your entire body, and to the places where your body touches the floor or the chair. Feel the air around you. Become aware of your entire body from the crown of your head to the bottom of your feet.

- **Notice**
  - Notice where you feel your breath and exaggerate the breath for a moment, feeling the sensation of the breath coming in and going out, feeling the rise and fall of your belly and your chest expand and contract.

- **Open**
  - Open your awareness to sensations *internally* in the body: heat or coolness, numbness, tiredness, whatever is present. Then open your awareness to sensations *externally* around you, to sound, silence, smells, and sensations where your body comes in contact with the chair or the floor.

- **Relax**
  - Release tension, gently accepting yourself with kindness and allowing your body to be alert and yet tranquil, not sleepy. Gently soften the body, without pushing anything away. Allow for everything to be as it is, like an ocean tide coming in and going out or a door opening and closing. Note that this is how it is now, acknowledging what is already here. Meet tension with kindness, softening.

- **Connect**
  - Connect with the stability of the ground underneath you. Connect with the space around your body. Connect with warmth and the sense of your body, your heart, and your belly.

- **Feel**
  - Feel the crown of your head; your face, eyes, ears, nose, mouth, tongue, teeth, and lips; and the front, sides, and back of your head.
  - Feel your neck, front, sides, and back. Feel your chest, lungs, heart, and torso, and feel the sides of your body.
  - Feel your arms, front and back, and each finger.

- Feel the back of your body from the back of the neck through the upper, middle, and lower spine.
- Feel your belly, navel center, stomach, and digestive organs. Feel your buttocks and the side, back, and front of your legs and knees.
- Feel your feet and toes.
- Feel your entire body: front, back, and sides.
- Breathe deeply and stretch.

Reflective Inquiry

Time Required: 25 minutes.

Find a quiet place to reflect on the following questions: What brought you into your current role in education? What were your aspirations then, and what are they now? Reconnect with the values that you held when you entered your professional career and your values now. What do you notice? Journal or jot a note for 10 minutes. Discuss your reflections in a triad with two trusted colleagues where you can be safely vulnerable and maintain confidentiality. Each person takes 5 minutes to share their reflections.

Mindful Eating

Time Required: 5–10 minutes.

Eating is one of the great pleasures of life, yet too often we eat in distraction, barely aware of the food: the taste, color, aroma, and sensation of eating, and the larger issues of where the food comes from, how it was grown and transported to our plate, and the environment and social justice for the workers who grew, harvested, and transported the food to us. Mindful eating is the gift of doing just one thing: to just eat, to put down the cell phone or reading material, to turn off the TV and focus on the food. Mindful eating cultivates awareness of what and how we eat to strengthen appreciation, gratitude, and joy. Invariably, when I offer this practice to groups, nearly everyone comments that this might be the first time they truly tasted the food they are eating. It is revelatory.

The classic approach is simply to eat a few raisins with a quality of mindful awareness.

The Process

- Notice the raisin in your hand.
- Feel the texture.
- Notice the shape, size, and smell.

- Slowly bring the raisin to your lips and notice anticipation.

- Place the raisin on your tongue and slowly begin to chew until the raisin is liquid.

- When your mind wanders, gently redirect your attention to act of eating.

- Pause and then practice with another raisin.

- Notice how you feel.

Mindful Walking

Time Required: 5–10 minutes.

Like mindful eating, mindful walking can be practiced throughout the day. In this practice, we have an opportunity to connect with the body and with the environment to be fully present one step at a time.

The Process

- Come to standing and take a few deep breaths in and out of your nose.

- Notice how you are standing and whether you are leaning to one side or another, and try to balance and align your head, neck, and spine.

- Notice your surroundings: light, sound, warmth, coolness, sensory awareness.

- Feel your feet on the ground and feel your breath.

- Take a step and feel your breath.

- Notice balance.

- Take another step.

- Move at a pace that is slower than normal and yet comfortable.

- When your mind wanders, gently redirect your attention to feeling your feet on the ground and the sensation of walking.

- Continue for a few minutes, and when you are ready, stop and notice the stopping.

- Stretch in any way that is comfortable.

Reflection

- Reflect on these exercises. How did you feel? What surprised you?

- What did you learn?

- What do you want to continue to work on?

MINDFUL REFLECTION

1. How do you create space in your life for reflection on the state of your body, mind, emotions, and spirit? What have you noticed? If you don't have this space, how might you start?

2. What support would allow you to begin a mindfulness practice? How do you hold yourself accountable to prioritize mindfulness in your life and your leadership?

3. As you reflect on your life and your leadership, how might mindfulness support your growth and development?

ONLINE RESOURCES

Visit https://resources.corwin.com/CultivatingHappiness

Online Resource 11.1   Enacting Change

Online Resource 11.2   Developing a Daily Mindfulness Practice

Online Resource 11.3   Mindful Reflection

CHAPTER TWELVE

Being a Mindfulness Coordinator

KEY PRINCIPLE

To effectively grow a mindfulness program, schools or districts must invest in mindful leadership.

MINDFUL LEADERSHIP

Chapter 11 provided broad parameters for mindful leadership. In this chapter, we zero in on the nuts and bolts of coordinating yoga-mindfulness-meditation programs at the district level. A mindfulness coordinator is an essential role that can sustainably grow an integrated mindfulness program by providing the resources, training, guidance, and ongoing support that schools need to keep their mindfulness programs thriving. Here are just a few of the many valuable things a mindfulness coordinator can accomplish:

- Locate, create, or refine mindfulness curriculum materials for schools to use.

- Share resources and provide training so that staff are better equipped to integrate mindfulness practices into their work with students.

- Collaborate with school leaders to ensure they have the resources and support they need to grow their mindfulness programs.

- Serve as a liaison to families and the community to expand mindfulness programming beyond classroom walls.

- Provide continued professional development opportunities for staff to introduce them to mindfulness as well as to keep them growing in their own practice.

- Facilitate a professional learning community of interested staff members who wish to exchange ideas, share experiences, and grow in their learning together.

There is a special responsibility in mindful leadership, where sharing the science of these meditative practices can be a challenge. The mindful leader must transform what has traditionally been viewed as a "tree-hugging, hippie activity" here in the West into a scientifically validated intervention that is tailor-made for usage in school settings. For some, these practices often carry a stigma of forbidden religious content in certain populations, so the focus is to present this science purely, while being practical, approachable, and attainable. This often requires the very purposeful usage of language, a bevy of studies and data, and the patience to change minds over time.

Jeff Donald's position as a mindfulness coordinator in Maryland truly began organically without any intention or plan. He spent 14 years in the high school classroom, where the prerequisite for any learning whatsoever (no matter the subject) was building relationships and trust with his students. As Jeff explains,

> I was quite efficient in becoming the trusted adult in these students' lives, and in doing so, I was privy to their suffering and pain. It was not unusual to come into contact with food insecurity, homelessness, abuse, neglect, and many other challenges my students faced. As my relationship with yoga-mindfulness-meditation grew, so did the realization of how much my students deserved the chance to experience this clarity and purpose in their lives—particularly my students who faced substantial challenges.
>
> There was a certain day where I had a very difficult morning; the students were obnoxious and argumentative, and pushed me to the edge of my composure. Normally I would keep my door open during lunch to allow students to use my room as a lunch space, but that day I needed to retreat and regain my objectivity. I closed my door, pulled out my yoga mat, and began the process. The only thing I had forgotten was to lock that closed door. . . .
>
> Two of my toughest students entered the room looking for something one of them had left there earlier in the morning and, upon seeing me there, asked me (expletives aside) what I was doing. I simply said, "It would take too long to explain this to you, so sit down with me and I'll show you." To my surprise, they actually did sit down and completed the kriya with me.
>
> They were blown away.

They asked if they could return the next day to do this again. They did indeed come the next day, then the next. They began to bring friends. Within a month, I had outgrown my room, and we were able to utilize the mini-gym. Between 35 and 60 students consistently gave up their lunch to participate. The work received the attention of my principal, and she called me to her office. I thought I was in trouble . . . but she encouraged me to expand my efforts for schoolwide programs that could serve more students. This was the beginning of a mindfulness school model that would prove to be wildly successful.

All school districts collect data that measure success or failure in several ways. The school where Jeff worked saw all the data moving in the right direction for several years in a row, which received the attention of central office personnel. *What are they doing in that school?* They asked if Jeff could duplicate this model in other schools. Jeff emphatically said *yes!* Now, his job is to re-create the mindfulness school program in targeted schools. As Jeff says, "I have the best job on earth!"

MOVING THE PROGRAM FORWARD

Throughout this book, we have emphasized how our own personal practice has positively impacted our lives and our results. Jeff explains the importance of his practice for staying steady, being ready, and moving ahead:

My yoga and mindfulness practices have been instrumental in maintaining the high energy level and motivation required to continuously move this program forward. There are constant challenges to the validity of this science from many directions, and the inner resilience, as well as an inner reserve of spirit, required to keep moving forward is derived through my yoga and meditative practices. I rise every morning very early for a sadhana (regular, intentional) practice to set the tone of the day, I practice short mindfulness activities during the day when I'm not feeling my best, and I always end my day in a reflective meditation. These practices have defied the compassion fatigue commonly associated with dealing in others' trauma. I also have the supreme benefit of having teachers who have mentored me to "keep up." Satwant Singh Khalsa and Krishna Kaur (another author of this book) have steadily and "quietly had my back the entire time in support."

Through this journey I have learned two things since the inception of this program:

- As the doors of opportunity open, boldly walk through them.

- Be fearless.

Mindfulness in a Maryland School District

All in all, the mindfulness program Jeff started in Maryland evolved from teaching students and preparing teachers at his school to a districtwide program over the course of 24 months. To date, over 1,400 teachers from 168 of the district's 208 schools have been prepared to teach mindfulness classes. In the summer of 2018, the district offered its first Mindfulness Teacher Preparation Program, a program with modules on self-knowledge, science-based explanations of yogic principles, personal practice, and deliverables for classroom use that was completed over a 2-day (16-hour) workshop. The courses are experiential, and teachers are expected to develop their own daily mindfulness practices. When teachers complete the course, they receive credits for recertification of their teaching certificate. The program is completely voluntary.

The Mindfulness Curriculum. In 2020, working with a team of 12 teachers, Jeff developed a curriculum for secondary teachers. During that same time, another team of teachers developed an elementary mindfulness curriculum. These curricula are based in part on Krishna Kaur's Y.O.G.A. for Youth program, as well as the *Mindfulness Practices* book authored by Christine Mason, Michele Rivers Murphy, and Yvette Jackson (2019). Jeff also relied on the yoga-mindfulness-meditation training of the district's curriculum development teams and incorporation of the most effective practices of multiple styles and schools from the yogic/mindfulness traditions such as Tara Brach, Insight Meditation, Mindful Schools, and others with the idea that any practice that gained "traction" with students was invaluable.

A key concept in the development of these curricula was the realization that not all populations had access or opportunity to this science of self-development and transformation; therefore, whatever was created had to be free and easily accessible to all. Staff also created a series of Mindful Moment archived videos of sessions, so they now have an online library of over 95 videos covering many components that are described in this book, including such basic exercises as spinal flexes, frogs, and many more.

Key aspects of the mindfulness curriculum Jeff implemented include the following:

- A graphic organizer that serves to connect the academic curricular timeline and context to the mindfulness program in a traditional lesson plan format.

- The inclusion of restorative practices, restorative circles, and trauma-informed care (see Chapters 2 and 3). These practices constantly overlap the others, and the practical inclusion of these practices expands not only the base of receptivity among staff, but the effectiveness and scope of the mindfulness program.

- Yoga games specifically created to capture the attention, imagination, and creativity of elementary students, while teaching foundational yogic principles.

- How to use mindfulness in lieu of traditional discipline practices, essentially building the "whole teacher" model of teaching social, emotional, and mental health as well as academics.

- Embedding mindfulness practices during the school day as a part a regular day. Staff who have already implemented this strategy have seen dramatic upswings in attention span, focus, and classroom culture.

- Using mindfulness both during the lunch hour and in after-school programs as extracurricular activities. These offerings are essential to school- and communitywide cultural shifts that come with time and repetition.

Adaptations During 2020 With Virtual Learning

In the spring of 2020, in response to the COVID-19 pandemic, the mindfulness program went virtual. With a virtual platform, district leaders were able to provide both synchronous and asynchronous teacher preparation and also offer direct instruction to students, reaching up to 300 students simultaneously. Because of their archived materials, they also offer asynchronous sessions.

Many of the hints provided earlier in this book for virtual instruction apply to districtwide teacher preparation and student instruction. Here are some other considerations:

- Use breakout rooms to keep participants engaged.

- Get help managing technology through staff content experts or experienced colleagues.

- Build teacher competence and confidence through creation of practicums, cohorts, and professional learning communities.

- Emphasize the neuroscience behind the practices, as well as the relationship between positive self-care and teacher effectiveness and student learning (see Chapters 1 and 2).

- Be available to answer questions and guide practices.

Because our mindfulness program was already up and running when the pandemic hit, by April 2020, staff were adapting their plans and practices to consider some of the needs that are specific to these times. This includes both the necessity for instruction and delivery of these practices as a vital tool for self-regulation and de-escalation in unprecedented times, and relationship building through virtual teaching—which is very difficult.

Staffing and Scheduling

Today, after two years of operation, our mindfulness program is staffed by a mindfulness educator based at each target school and two administrative support staff. These individuals sustain and offer continuous professional development with local yoga and meditation teachers who are providing related services through additive programs.

Jeff's role continues to evolve; however, with a staff of five, Jeff is no longer the sole mindfulness trainer. He meets weekly with a team of dedicated teachers to plan and problem solve together. The mindfulness curriculum is funded by several sources, which include budgeted dollars, Title I, Title IV, and private grant funding.

HOW MY ROLE AS MINDFULNESS COORDINATOR EVOLVED

Jeff explains his role and advice for leaders.

As my role has evolved from offering multiple classes and trainings per week in a single school to sitting in planning meetings for the next school year, I have had to adjust my mindset. Whereas I deeply miss the intimate connection and energy of direct contact from group yoga and mindfulness classes, I now must focus more on visioning for future growth and inclusion of these practices in all facets of school settings (discarding the kurta for a dress shirt and tie has been a bit of an adjustment as well). The direct work is now completed by the team of mindfulness educators and deeply committed staff members within schools. I continue to maintain contact with staff through continuous offerings of foundational mindfulness professional learning, building relationships and mindful community partnerships.

The most important challenge in this role is to confront protectionist mindsets in staff. There are many educators who continue to believe, despite all that 2020 brought to our educational system, that teaching social, emotional, and mental health as part of a "whole education" is simply not a part of their job. Many educators continue to believe that taking the role of the trusted adult and mentor in a child's life is inappropriate; they are only responsible for the delivery of academic content. The emotional drain of loving all of one's students can seem overwhelming to many educators I have spoken with over the years, and insulating themselves as a method of self-protection or longevity is far easier than opening their hearts and becoming vulnerable. This mindset is the largest hurdle to mindful practices in education today.

My typical response to this philosophy is to remind these individuals of why they entered into education in the first place. It was not because they wanted a vast salary or summers and holidays off, but because they wanted to make a difference; they were on a mission. When did they lose that? When did they allow disillusionment to take the lead?

My only tip for mindful leadership is very simple: Become absolutely fearless, knowing what you are doing is best for students, families, and communities. Never hesitate to put forward a bold idea or vision regardless of the situation. Remember, you are most likely the only person in the boardroom who is looking at your business through a mindfulness lens; if you never bring it up yourself, it will never come into reality. I have seen many ideas initially be casually swept aside, yet the seeds of the idea were planted, and as months or years went by, it would resurface as the best course of action.

STUDENT LEADERSHIP

Marley Mckind, one of the first students Jeff taught, shares the impact that yoga-mindfulness-meditation has had on her life.

[The year] 2017 was one of the biggest transitions I had yet to experience at that time. After living a comfortably known life, I was preparing to embark on a new challenge. College. At the ripe young age of 17, this was big, HUGE. And so stressful. I was not accustomed to rejection just yet, so the letters rejecting me from internships and scholarships had gotten overwhelming.

I had become interested in meditation the year before, practicing deep breathing in a dark room a few times a week, but it lacked depth of understanding and connection. It felt more as though I was pretending to be someone who meditated rather than a real, mindful entity.

Then one day, I saw a wonky-looking ad on the school news inviting us all to lunch meditations, and I was so pumped! Finally a larger group to meditate with! I walked into the photography classroom that Thursday after the lunch bell . . . aaaannnd it was just me, and Jeff Donald, of course. He took it in stride though, and told me to plop down and start breathing. I actually am grateful it was just the two of us that day, as Jeff decided to get more in depth into the different breathing techniques we were using, like how alternate nostril breathing balances the hemispheres of your brain, or how many box breaths we were taking each minute. And although my lower back was killing me, it felt magical. As I opened my eyes at the end of that first class, I felt more Zen than I had in a really long time.

Soon after this I was able to watch the group grow, and came back every week like clockwork, finding 30 minutes of calm in the sea of my freak-outs.

(Continued)

(Continued)

Thanks to the meditation and yoga manual Jeff made later that year, I was able to continue these practices after I graduated and left Northwood. I was also able to use them for my student organization. After giving presentations on the importance of mindfulness, I would teach that week's group from what I'd learned from Jeff Donald, alternate nostril breathing, box breathing, and even chanting if I was lucky!

And even further down the road in 2021, I am pursuing my yoga teacher training, not only going in depth into the kundalini yoga and meditation I practiced in that classroom, but expanding even further.

I can say without a doubt I definitely gained the confidence I have now in leading and teaching others about meditation from the time I spent in Jeff Donald's meditation classes, and I'm so excited to see it has been able to spread from a few stressed seniors, to younger and younger ages, who can benefit just as much from a few minutes of deep, slow, breath. (Marley Mckind, personal communication, May 2021)

ACCOMPLISHMENTS

Since 2018, the mindfulness program Jeff implemented has trained and prepared over 1,400 teachers and provided workshops for school administrators, paraprofessionals, and families. To date, 168 schools (80%) have participated at various levels of involvement based on comfort level and trained staff members. How staffs implement yoga-mindfulness-meditation varies from school to school and from teacher to teacher. In the most comprehensive instances, implementation involves all of the following:

- Some schoolwide yoga-mindfulness-meditation activities. This might be a mindful moment as part of a morning meeting, providing yoga as an offering within the physical education curriculum, and providing time for teachers to network and plan together.

- Use of mindfulness intervention rooms in 51 schools as part of a restorative justice initiative in lieu of traditional punitive measures such as out-of-school or in-school suspensions.

- Offering virtual sessions not only for students, but also for community members through evening classes and parent–teacher association meetings.

- Providing students options to become student mindfulness leaders. These students are trained as student instructors to act as exemplars and mentors to younger students at their respective schools, as well as continue to teach these practices in their college careers and beyond.

- Participation from the school at a districtwide weekly mindfulness coordination meeting.

Schools implementing mindfulness have seen significant gains in student attendance, participation, graduation, and academic improvements, as well as decreases in office referrals, suspensions, and expulsions. Although these schools are also implementing other innovations, discussions with involved teachers and administrators support the efficacy of this work.

In many of our schools, about 20%–30% of the teachers are using the mindfulness curriculum. However, at some of our schools, a smaller percentage of teachers (perhaps 5%–10%) are participating.

To guide teachers, the Maryland district has created robust social-emotional learning curricula and a required SEL block within the school day. The mindfulness work is a foundational piece to this initiative, and we have opted to spend our time and resources with the teachers who are most interested in ins implementation.

As Schools Implement Mindfulness

From our collective experiences, we realize that although mindfulness is growing in popularity, it is sometimes held back by teachers who are hesitant to add one more thing to their plates and teachers who have little knowledge or experience with yoga-mindfulness-meditation.

THE COALITION FOR THE FUTURE OF EDUCATION

Jeff's story reveals how a passionate, authentic, and committed mindfulness practitioner and schoolteacher can evolve from being a leader in one's classroom, to a leader within one's school building, to a leader across an entire large school district.

Mindful leadership can extend even beyond the school district level. Recently, sensing an urgency for the need for schools to transform their practices and focus on addressing the trauma that children across America have experienced as a result of the COVID-19 pandemic, Christine founded the Coalition for the Future of Education, which is steered by a coordinating committee of 29 members representing 16 states.

The Coalition began its work with a virtual listening tour, connecting with almost 100 students and educators from around the United States to listen to their top concerns regarding the current state of education. These conversations centered on student voice and provided a space to let youth share the successes and challenges they face in schools as well as the concerns, hopes, and vision they have for the future of education.

WE ENVISION

This Coalition envisions a world that leans in with heart and compassion for self, others, and our environment, where people and institutions are dedicated to expanding conscious acts of caring, building resilience, and advancing learning, equity, and justice.

We envision safe and equitable schools with education that serves as the foundation for our humanity; it is flexible and empowering. There is room for adventure, students drive their own learning, learning and self-understanding are celebrated, and communities support their individual and collective self-care and well-being.

Inspired by these conversations, the Coalition prepared a letter to the secretary of education and to President Joe Biden's education team to advocate for much needed change. The letter shared the Coalition's vision for the future of education and outlined a series of suggested actions toward creating positive and sustainable change. Several of these action steps relate directly to increasing student access to mindfulness programming:

- Ensuring that teacher preparation programs update their understanding of the psychology of learning to reflect neuroscience, trauma, and heart–mind intelligence.

- Taking steps to simplify how we approach social-emotional learning by providing an overarching framework that addresses neuroplasticity, awakening awareness (mindfulness or consciousness), self-compassion and compassion for others, confidence and courage, and community building.

- Ensuring self-care for teachers, other school staff, students, and families.

The Coalition is one example of how educators who are passionate about yoga-mindfulness-meditation can reach out beyond their school districts to collaborate with other like-minded educators who are interested in incorporating yoga and mindfulness approaches as part of an effort to transform schools. It is important for educators who are passionate about mindfulness to know that they are not alone, and by connecting with others, we grow empowered to lead the way together.

MINDFUL REFLECTION

1. Is your district ready for a mindfulness coordinator?
2. What might a mindfulness coordinator do in your district?
3. What obstacles might the coordinator face, and how could they be handled?

ONLINE RESOURCES

Visit https://resources.corwin.com/CultivatingHappiness

Online Resource 12.1   Mindful Reflection

Sources for Yoga Breath Work, Kriyas, and Meditations

The Kundalini Research Institute guided the final review and incorporation of yoga breath work, postures, kriyas, and meditations as adapted from the sources listed in this section. All are used with permission from the Kundalini Research Institute (https://kundaliniresearchinstitute.org). These are noted in the text with an asterisk (*).

- Khalsa, G. R. (2020a). *The Aquarian Teacher level one instructor textbook.* Kundalini Research Institute.
  - Breath of Fire found on pp. 133–134 of this text and p. 95 of *The Aquarian Teacher.*
  - Left Nostril Breathing found on p. 136 of this text and p. 96 of *The Aquarian Teacher.*
  - Right Nostril Breathing found on p. 137 of this text and p. 96 of *The Aquarian Teacher.*
  - Sitali Breath found on pp. 137–138 of this text and p. 97 of *The Aquarian Teacher.*
  - U Breath found on p. 137 of this text and p. 96 of *The Aquarian Teacher.*

- Khalsa, G. R. (2020b). *The Aquarian Teacher level one instructor yoga manual.* Kundalini Research Institute.
  - Archer Pose found on p. 194 of this text and p. 155 of *The Aquarian Teacher.*
  - Breath of Fire found on pp. 133–134 of this text and p. 149 of *The Aquarian Teacher.*
  - Breath of Fire to Increase Energy (Ego Eradicator) found on p. 135 of this text and p. 162 of *The Aquarian Teacher.*
  - "I Am Happy" Meditation for Children found on p. 181 of this text and p. 89 of *The Aquarian Teacher.*
  - I Am, I Am: Meditation Into Being found on pp. 182–183 of this text and p. 106 of *The Aquarian Teacher.*
  - Kriya to Conquer Self-Animosity found on p. 165 of this text and p. 110 of *The Aquarian Teacher.*
  - Kriya for Elevation found in Corwin Online Resource 6.1 of this text and pp. 18–20 of *The Aquarian Teacher.*
  - Kriya for New Lungs and Circulation found in Corwin Online Resource 8.1 for this text and pp. 54–55 of *The Aquarian Teacher.*

- Kriya for Prana Apana Balance found on pp. 179–181 of this text and pp. 44–45 of *The Aquarian Teacher*.
- Mantra for Healing: *Ra Ma Da Sa* found on pp. 222–223 of this text and p. 88 of *The Aquarian Teacher* (as Healing With the Siri Gaitri Mantra—*Ra Ma Sa Da*).
- Meditation for a Calm Heart found on pp. 163–164 of this text and p. 107 of *The Aquarian Teacher*.
- Meditation for Inner Conflict found on pp. 165–166 of this text and p. 92 of *The Aquarian Teacher*.
- One-Minute Breath found on p. 196 of this text and p. 70 of *The Aquarian Teacher*.
- *Saa Taa Naa Maa* Meditation found on pp. 221–222 of this text and p. 94 of *The Aquarian Teacher*.
- Stretch Pose found on p. 192 of this text and on p. 171 of *The Aquarian Teacher*.
- Surya Kriya: "Sun Kriya" found on pp. 140–142 of this text and pp. 60–61of *The Aquarian Teacher*.

- Khalsa, H. K. (2001). *Owner's manual for the human body*. Kundalini Research Institute.
  - Achieving Equilibrium: Balancing Energy found on pp. 216–220 of this text and pp. 10–11 of *Owner's Manual*.

- Khalsa, H. K. (2006). *Praana, praanee, praanayam*. Kundalini Research Institute.
  - Finding Happiness and Peace Within found on pp. 220–221 of this text and pp. 40–41 of *Praana*.

- Khalsa, H. K., & Khalsa, G. (2007). *Self-knowledge*. Kundalini Research Institute.
  - Kriya for Courage: Removing Body Blocks found in Corwin Online Resource 9.2 for this text and pp. 23–24 of *Self-Knowledge*.
  - Overcoming One's Sense of Limitation found on pp. 200–202 of this text and p. 40 of *Self-Knowledge* (as Conquering One's Imagined Disabilities).

- Khalsa, S. K. (2001). *Kundalini yoga: Unlock your inner potential through life-changing exercise*. Dorling Kindersley.
  - Kriya for Balancing Head and Heart found on pp. 162–163 of this text and pp. 92–93 of *Kundalini Yoga*.

- Khalsa, S. P. (2007). *Sadhana guidelines*. Kundalini Research Institute.
  - Meditation for Mind to Follow Consciousness (also known as Amarti Mudra Kriya) found on p. 202 of this text and p. 159 of *Sadhana Guidelines*.

- ○ Yoga for Tolerance and Compassion found on pp. 160–161 of this text and p. 118 of *Sadhana Guidelines*.

- Khalsa, S. P. (2009). *I am a woman: Creative, sacred & invincible*. Kundalini Research Institute.
  - ○ Meditation to Heal a Broken (or Sad) Heart found on p. 182 of this text and p. 82 of *I Am a Woman*.
  - ○ Tranquilize the Mind found on pp. 149–150 of this text and p. 107 of *I Am a Woman*.
  - ○ Yoga for Complete Workout for the Elementary Being found on pp. 196–198 of this text and pp. 120–121 of *I Am a Woman*.
  - ○ Yoga Movement Lesson: Becoming Crystal Clear found on pp. 142–143 of this text and p. 124 of *I Am a Woman*.

- Khalsa, S. P. (2010). *Transformation: Volume II. Serving the infinite*. Kundalini Research Institute.
  - ○ Self-Care Breath Kriya found on p. 216 of this text and p. 128 of *Transformation*.

- Khalsa, S. P. (2013). *Kriya yoga sets, meditations & classic kriyas*. Kundalini Research Institute.
  - ○ Meditation on Change found on p. 195 of this text and p. 139 of *Kriya*.
  - ○ Meditation for Good to Come to You found on p. 200 of this text and p. 186 of *Kriya*.

- Khalsa, S. P. K. (2009). *Kundalini yoga: The flow of eternal power*. The Berkley Publishing Group.
  - ○ Healing Hands found on p. 220 of this text and p. 73 of *Kundalini Yoga*.

References

AASA—The School Superintendents Association & Children's Defense Fund. (2014, September). *Restorative justice overview.* https://www.aasa.org/uploadedFiles/Childrens_Programs/RJ_Overview_9.15.14.pdf

Aguilar, E. (2018). *Onward: Cultivating emotional resilience in educators.* Wiley.

Allegretto, S., & Mishel, L. (2018, September 5). *The teacher pay penalty has hit a new high.* Economic Policy Institute. https://www.epi.org/publication/teacher-pay-gap-2018/

Allen, K. J. (2017, December 27). *The vagus nerve and why it matters.* Sonima. https://www.sonima.com/yoga/yoga-articles/vagus-nerve/

Allina Health. (2014, May). *Create the state you want* [Worksheet]. https://www.changetochill.org/wp-content/uploads/2014/05/Create-the-State-You-Want-worksheet.pdf

Allina Health. (2015a, August 10). *Guided imagery: Create the state you want* [Video]. YouTube.https://www.youtube.com/watch?v=BD3ubF-5KCg&t=279s

Allina Health. (2015b, October). *Self-guided inquiry activity* [Worksheet]. https://www.changetochill.org/wp-content/uploads/2015/10/Self-Guided_Imagery_worksheet.pdf

American Federation of Teachers. (2017). *2017 educator quality of life survey.* https://www.aft.org/sites/default/files/2017_eqwl_survey_web.pdf

Amato, N. (2015, March 26). A lack of resources for many classrooms. *The New York Times.* https://www.nytimes.com/roomfordebate/2015/03/26/is-improving-schools-all-about-money/a-lack-of-resources-for-many-classrooms

American Psychiatric Association. (2013). *Diagnostic and statistical manual of mental disorders* (5th ed.). American Psychiatric Association.

American Psychological Association. (2015, February 4). *Stress in America: Paying with our health.* https://www.apa.org/news/press/releases/stress/2014/stress-report.pdf

American Psychological Association. (2020a, May 1). *Learning at home during COVID-19.* https://www.apa.org/topics/covid-19/children-self-regulation

American Psychological Association. (2020b, October 20). *Stress in America 2020 survey signals a growing national mental health crisis.* https://www.apa.org/news/press/releases/2020/10/stress-mental-health-crisis

Ansley, B. M., Meyers, J., McPhee, K., & Varjas, K. (2018, March 2). The hidden threat of teacher stress. *The Conversation.* http://theconversation.com/the-hidden-threat-of-teacher-stress-92676

Archer, C. (2020, June 1). Guided meditation for courage: You are capable. *Light in the Dark.* https://lightenthedark.com/guided-meditation-for-courage/

Arnsten, A. F. (2009). Stress signalling pathways that impair prefrontal cortex structure and function. *Nature Reviews Neuroscience, 10*(6), 410–422. https://doi.org/10.1038/nrn2648

Avery, H. (n.d.). 108: Yoga's sacred number. *Wanderlust.* https://wanderlust.com/journal/108-yogas-sacred-number/

Bailey, R. A. (2015). *Conscious Discipline: Building resilient classrooms.* Loving Guidance.

Beauchamp, T. L., & Childress, J. F. (2001). *Principles of biomedical ethics.* Oxford University Press.

Belluomini, E. (2019, October 28). *Happify: A professional review.* One Mind PsyberGuide. https://onemindpsyberguide.org/expert-review/happify-an-expert-review/

Benson, Peter L., Roehlkepartain, E. C., & Rude, S. P. (2003). Spiritual development in childhood and adolescence: Toward a field of inquiry. *Applied Developmental Science, 7*(3), 205–213. https://www.tandfonline.com/doi/abs/10.1207/S1532480XADS0703_12

Berger, A. (2011). *Self-regulation: Brain, cognition, and development.* American Psychological Association.

Berta-O Freedom, R. (2019). *Dragon yoga: Contact your inner muse.* Berta-O Design.

Beswick, E. (2020, January 12). "It's the most stressful environment I've ever worked in"—How COVID is affecting Europe's teachers. *EuroNews.* https://www.euronews.com/2020/12/01/it-s

-the-most-stressful-environment-i-ve-ever-worked-in-how-covid-is-affecting-europe-s-te

Bezdek, K. G., & Telzer, E. H. (2017, December 20). Have no fear, the brain is here! How your brain responds to stress. *Frontiers for Young Minds.* https://doi.org/10.3389/frym.2017.00071

Borges, H. (2020, June 24). *Awareness based systems change: Deep resonance.* Presencing Institute. https://medium.com/presencing-institute%20-blog/awareness-based-systems-change-deep-resonance-bef9ca451749

Bose, B., Ancin, D., Frank, J., & Malik, A. (2016). *Teaching transformative life skills to students: A comprehensive dynamic mindfulness curriculum.* Norton.

Brach, T. (2020). *Radical compassion: Learning to love yourself and your world with the practice of RAIN.* Penguin Books.

Bradt, S. (2010, November 11). Wandering mind not a happy mind. *The Harvard Gazette.* https://news.harvard.edu/gazette/story/2010/11/wandering-mind-not-a-happy-mind/

Breathe for Change. (n.d.). *Breathe for change foundations course.* https://www.breatheforchange.com/foundations-course

Brown, B. (2010, June). *The power of vulnerability* [Video]. TEDxHouston. https://www.ted.com/talks/brene_brown_the_power_of_vulnerability?language=en

Brown, B. (2015). *Daring greatly: How the courage to be vulnerable transforms the way we live, love, parent, and lead.* Penguin.

Brown, V., & Olson, K. (2015). *The mindful school leader: Practices to transform your leadership and school.* Corwin.

Bunting, M. (2016). *The mindful leader: 7 practices for transforming your leadership, your organisation and your life.* Wiley.

Butzer, B., Ebert, M., Telles, S., & Khalsa, S. B. S. (2015). School-based yoga programs in the United States: A survey. *Advances in Mind-Body Medicine, 29*(4), 18. https://www.ncbi.nlm.nih.gov/pmc/articles/PMC4831047/

Calhoun, Y., & Calhoun, M. R. (2006). *Create a yoga practice for kids.* Sunstone Press.

Camera, L. (2019, April 29). Teacher salaries fell 4.5% over the last decade. *U.S. News & World Report.* https://www.usnews.com/news/education-news/articles/2019-04-29/teacher-salaries-fell-45-over-the-last-decade

Carter Avgerinos, J. (2018). *Kids yoga adventure card deck.* U.S. Games Systems Inc.

Cassie. (2021, July 13). Mindfulness activities for kids in the classroom. *Teach Starter.* https://www.teachstarter.com/us/blog/classroom-mindfulness-activities-for-children-us/

Chambers, R., Lo, B. C. Y., & Allen, N. B. (2008). The impact of intensive mindfulness training on attentional control, cognitive style, and affect. *Cognitive Therapy and Research, 32*(3), 303–322. https://doi.org/10.1007/s10608-007-9119-0

Center for Educational Improvement. (2012, July 26). *Yoga for children: A good idea?* https://www.edimprovement.org/blog/search/yoga-for-children

Center for Educational Improvement. (2018). *S-CCATE.* https://www.s-ccate.org/

Center for Educational Improvement. (2020, December). *Welcome to our HeartMind Adventure!* https://lp.constantcontactpages.com/cu/slJ5xxe

Center for Educational Improvement. (2021a). *S-CCATE: Online technology designed to enhance social emotional learning.* https://www.edimprovement.org/s-ccate-online-technology-designed-to-enhance-social-emotional-learning

Center for Educational Improvement. (2021b, April 16). *Executive functioning, mindfulness, and heart centered leadership* [Webinar]. YouTube. https://www.youtube.com/watch?v=puVHFCNbb_c

Center for Responsive Schools. (2015). *The first six weeks of school.* Center for Responsive Schools.

Centers for Disease Control and Prevention. (2019). *Protecting school staff.* https://www.cdc.gov/coronavirus/2019-ncov/community/schools-childcare/k-12-staff.html

Centers for Disease Control and Prevention. (2021, July 9). *Schools and child care programs: Plan, prepare and respond.* https://www.cdc.gov/coronavirus/2019-ncov/community/schools-childcare/

Charnas, D. (2007, August 28). The teacher's guide to sadhana. *Yoga Journal.* https://www.yogajournal.com/teach/the-teacher-s-guide-to-sadhana/

Cherry, K. (2020, September 1). What is meditation? *Verywell Mind.* https://www.verywellmind.com/what-is-meditation-2795927

Chon, M. (2020, March 17). 9 best yoga apps for your at-home workout. *The Oprah Magazine.* https://www.oprahmag.com/life/health/g31672490/best-yoga-apps/

Chou, C. C., & Huang, C. J. (2017). Effects of an 8-week yoga program on sustained attention and discrimination function in children with attention deficit hyperactivity disorder. *PeerJ, 5*, e2883. https://doi.org/10.7717/peerj.2883

Cipriano, C., & Brackett, M. (2020, April 7). Teachers are anxious and overwhelmed. They need SEL now more than ever. *EdSurge.* https://www.edsurge.com/news/2020-04-07-teachers-are-anxious-and-overwhelmed-they-need-sel-now-more-than-ever

Cohen, S. C., Harvey, D. J., Shields, R. H., Shields, G. S., Rashedi, R. N., Tancredi, D. J., Angkustsiri, K., Hansen, R. L., & Schweitzer, J. B. (2018). The effects of yoga on attention, impulsivity and hyperactivity in pre-school age children with ADHD symptoms. *Journal of Developmental and Behavioral Pediatrics, 39*(3), 200. https://doi.org/ 10.1097%2FDBP.0000000000000552

Cook-Cottone. C. P. (2017). *Mindfulness and yoga in schools: A guide for teachers and practitioners.* Springer.

Csikszentmihalyi, M. (2013). *Flow: The psychology of happiness.* Random House.

Davis, M. (2015, October 29). Restorative justice: Resources for schools. *Edutopia.* https://www.edutopia.org/blog/restorative-justice-resources-matt-davis

Dawson, P., & Guare, R. (2010). *Executive skills in children and adolescents: A practical guide to assessment and intervention* (2nd ed.). Guilford Press.

Dellitt, J., & Barajas, C. F. (n.d.). *6 most common yoga injuries and how to avoid them.* Aaptiv. https://aaptiv.com/magazine/common-yoga-injuries

Denver School-Based Restorative Practices Partnership. (2017, September). *School-wide restorative practices: Step by step.* http://educationvotes.nea.org/wp-content/uploads/2017/09/Implementation-Guide-2017-FINAL.pdf

Desbordes, G., Gard, T., Hoge, E. A., Hölzel, B. K., Kerr, C., Lazar, S. W., Olendzki, A., & Vago, D. R. (2015). Moving beyond mindfulness: Defining equanimity as an outcome measure in meditation and contemplative research. *Mindfulness, 6*(2), 356–372. https://doi.org/10.1007/s12671-013-0269-8

Domenech, D., Sherman, M., & Brown, J. L. (2016). *Personalizing 21st century education: A framework for student success.* Wiley.

Dunin, D. (2019, May 31). *Making postures fun. Yoga in schools: Specific postures, sequences, and lesson plans.* Center for Educational Improvement. http://www.edimprovement.org/2019/05/yoga-in-schools-specific-postures-sequences-and-lesson-plans/

Dweck, C. S. (2015, September 22). Carol Dweck revisits the "growth mindset." *Education Week.* https://www.edweek.org/leadership/opinion-carol-dweck-revisits-the-growth-mindset/2015/09

Ellis, P. (2020, October 19). Teacher burnout and COVID-19 stress. *HR Exchange.* https://www.tasb.org/services/hr-services/hrx/hr-trends/teacher-burnout-and-covid-19-stress.aspx

Fagin, C. (2020, December 8). *"My incredible talking body" book read aloud* [Video]. YouTube. https://www.youtube.com/watch?v=nKhsFeQXGJc

Farrise, K. (2019, July 8). *Apps and videos to bring to your classroom.* Center for Educational Improvement. http://www.edimprovement.org/2019/07/yoga-in-schools-apps-and-videos-to-bring-yoga-to-the-classroom/

Farrise, K. (2021, February 27). *How teachers can implement anti-racist practices in the classroom.* Center for Educational Improvement. http://www.edimprovement.org/2021/02/how-teachers-can-implement-anti-racist-practices-in-the-classroom/

Ferlazzo, L. (2020, January 9). Ways to implement restorative practice in the classroom. *EdWeek.* https://www.edweek.org/teaching-learning/opinion-ways-to-implement-restorative-practices-in-the-classroom/2020/01

Figley, C. R., & McCubbin, H. I. (Eds.). (2016). *Stress and the family: Coping with catastrophe.* Routledge.

Fitzgerald, T., Melkonian, C., & Kotler, A. (2021). *The bell of mindfulness.* https://www.mindfulnessbell.org/archive/2016/03/the-bell-of-mindfulness

Flook, L., & Pinger, L. (n.d.). *Lessons from creating a kindness curriculum.* University of Wisconsin-Madison. https://centerhealthyminds.org/join-the-movement/lessons-from-creating-a-kindness-curriculum

Flook, L., Smalley, S. L., Kitil, M. J., Galla, B. M., Kaiser-Greenland, S., Locke, J., Ishijima, E.,

& Kasari, C. (2010). Effects of mindful awareness practices on executive functions in elementary school children. *Journal of Applied School Psychology, 26*(1), 70–95. https://doi.org/10.1080/15377900903379125

Flynn, L. (2018). *Yoga for children—Yoga cards: 50+ yoga poses and mindfulness activities for healthier, more resilient kids.* Adams Media.

Frank, J. L., Kohler, K., Peal, A., & Bose, B. (2017). Effectiveness of a school-based yoga program on adolescent mental health and school performance: Findings from a randomized controlled trial. *Mindfulness, 8*(3), 544–553. https://doi.org/10.1080/15377903.2013.863259

Freire, P. (2018). *Pedagogy of the oppressed* (50th anniversary ed.). Bloomsbury. (Original work published 1970)

Gaiam Staff. (n.d.). *Gaiam gives back to local communities.* https://www.gaiam.com/blogs/discover/gaiam-gives-back-to-local-communities

Gasson, S., & Donaldson, J. (2018, January). Peer and vicarious framing, problematization, and situated learning in online professional masters courses. In *Proceedings of the 51st Hawaii International Conference on System Sciences,* Hawaii.

Geisler, F. C., Kubiak, T., Siewert, K., & Weber, H. (2013). Cardiac vagal tone is associated with social engagement and self-regulation. *Biological Psychology, 93*(2), 279–286. https://doi.org/10.1016/j.biopsycho.2013.02.013

Gilbert, P. (Ed.). (2005). *Compassion: Conceptualisations, research and use in psychotherapy.* Routledge.

Give Back Yoga Foundation. (n.d.). *Yoga can change a life.* https://givebackyoga.org/

Go Go Yoga for Kids. (n.d.). *Got props?! Find out kids yoga teacher favorite resources.* https://www.gogoyogakids.com/favorite-props/

Goleman, D., & Senge, P. (2014). *The triple focus: A new approach to education.* More Than Sound.

Greater Good in Education. (2019a). *Gratitude circle for staff members.* https://ggie.berkeley.edu/practice/gratitude-circle-for-staff-members/

Greater Good in Education. (2019b). *Making families feel welcome.* https://ggie.berkeley.edu/practice/making-families-feel-welcome/

Greater Good in Education. (2019c). *SOBER breathing space for teens.* https://ggie.berkeley.edu/practice/sober-breathing-space-for-teens/

Guber, T., & Kalish, L. (2005). *Yoga pretzels: 50 fun activities for kids & grownups.* Barefoot Books.

Gustafson, B. (2017). *Renegade leadership: Creating innovative schools for digital-age students.* Corwin.

Hagen, I., & Nayar, U. S. (2014). Yoga for children and young people's mental health and well-being: Research review and reflections on the mental health potentials of yoga. *Frontiers in Psychiatry, 5,* 35. https://www.frontiersin.org/articles/10.3389/fpsyt.2014.00035/full

Hanson, R. (2016). *Hardwiring happiness: The new brain science of contentment, calm, and confidence.* Harmony.

Hanson, R. (2020). *7 facts about the brain that incline the mind to joy.* MentalHelp.net. https://www.mentalhelp.net/blogs/7-facts-about-the-brain-that-incline-the-mind-to-joy/

Harris, A. R., Jennings, P. A., Katz, D. A., Abenavoli, R. M., & Greenberg, M. T. (2016). Promoting stress management and wellbeing in educators: Feasibility and efficacy of a school-based yoga and mindfulness intervention. *Mindfulness, 7*(1), 143–154. https://doi.org/10.1007/s12671-015-0451-2

Harvey, A., & Erickson, K. (2010). *Heart yoga: The sacred marriage of yoga and mysticism.* North Atlantic Books.

Haug, N. A. (2016, August 1). *Headspace: A professional review.* One Mind PsyberGuide. https://onemindpsyberguide.org/expert-review/headspace-professional-review/

Haug, N. A. (2017, January 6). *Calm: A professional review.* One Mind PsyberGuide. https://onemindpsyberguide.org/expert-review/calm-professional-review/

Hawn, F. (2011). *The MindUP curriculum: Brain-focused strategies for learning and living.* Scholastic.

Headspace. (2016, September 1). *Headspace for sport: Peak performance starts with your mind* [Video]. YouTube. https://www.youtube.com/watch?v=lbEat6qiumQ

Hunter, J. (2021, August 11). *Finding your way forward when the path is not clear.* Mindful. https://www.mindful.org/the-scary-winding-road-through-change/

JadeYoga. (n.d.). *Giving programs.* https://jadeyoga.com/pages/giving-programs

Janz, P., Dawe, S., & Wyllie, M. (2019). Mindfulness-based program embedded within the existing curriculum improves executive functioning and behavior in young children: A waitlist controlled trial. *Frontiers in Psychology, 10,* 2052. https://doi.org/10.3389/fpsyg.2019.02052

Journal Buddies. (2021). *Journal prompts for anxiety and free printables.* https://www.journal-buddies.com/journal-prompts-writing-ideas/journal-prompts-for-anxiety/

Juneau, C., Pellerin, N., Trives, E., Ricard, M., Shankland, R., & Dambrun, M. (2020, July 7). Reliability and validity of an equanimity questionnaire: The two-factor equanimity scale (EQUA-S). *PeerJ, 8*, e9405. https://doi.org/10.7717/peerj.9405

Kabat-Zinn, J. (1994). *Wherever you go there you are: Mindfulness meditation in everyday life.* Hyperion.

Kaufman, J. (2011). Deepening presence and interconnection in the classroom. In A. Johnson & M. Neagley (Eds.), *Educating from the heart* (pp. 81–90). Rowman & Littlefield.

Kaur, K. (2006). *Y.O.G.A. for Youth teacher's manual and curriculum guide.* Y.O.G.A. for Youth. www.yogaforyouth.org

Kendi, I. X. (2019). *How to be an antiracist.* One World.

Khalsa, D. S., Amen, D., Hanks, C., Money, N., & Newberg, A. (2009). Cerebral blood flow changes during chanting meditation. *Nuclear Medicine Communications, 30*(12), 956–961.

Khalsa, G. R. (2020a). *The Aquarian Teacher™ level one instructor textbook.* Kundalini Research Institute.

Khalsa, G. R. (2020b). *The Aquarian Teacher™ level one instructor yoga manual.* Kundalini Research Institute.

Khalsa, H. C. K. (2020). *Reaching out in leadership.* Sikh Dharma Ministry. https://sdministry.org/reaching-out-in-leadership

Khalsa, H. K. (2001). *Owner's manual for the human body.* Kundalini Research Institute.

Khalsa, H. K. (2006). *Praana, praanee, praanayam.* Kundalini Research Institute.

Khalsa, H. K., & Khalsa, G. S. (2007). *Self-knowledge.* Kundalini Research Institute.

Khalsa, S. (2003). *The self-sensory human.* IKYTA Teachers Curriculum.

Khalsa, S. (2021). *Yoga to balance the head and heart.* 3HO. https://www.3ho.org/articles/yoga-balance-head-and-heart

Khalsa, S. B. S. (2004). Treatment of chronic insomnia with yoga: A preliminary study with sleep–wake diaries. *Applied Psychophysiology and Biofeedback, 29*(4), 269–278.

Khalsa, S. K. (2001a). *KISS guide to yoga.* Dorling Kindersley.

Khalsa, S. K. (2001b). *Kundalini yoga: Unlock your inner potential through life-changing exercise.* Dorling Kindersley.

Khalsa, S. K. (2016). *The yoga way to radiance: How to follow your inner guidance and nurture children to do the same.* Llewellyn Publications.

Khalsa, S. P. (2007). *Sadhana guidelines.* Kundalini Research Institute.

Khalsa, S. P. (2009). *I am a woman: Creative, sacred & invincible.* Kundalini Research Institute.

Khalsa, S. P. (2010). *Transformation: Volume II. Serving the infinite.* Kundalini Research Institute.

Khalsa, S. P. (2013). *Kriya yoga sets, meditations & classic kriyas.* Kundalini Research Institute.

Khalsa, S. P. K. (2009). *Kundalini yoga: The flow of eternal power.* The Berkley Publishing Group.

Khalsa, S. S. (2012). *Healing ourselves, healing the world: A manual of mystic meditation practice for absolutely everyone.* CreateSpace.

Kirk Chang, M. (2020). Trauma-informed yoga: What beginners should know. *InsightTimer Blog.* https://insighttimer.com/blog/trauma-informed-yoga-what-beginners-should-know/

Kundalini Yoga Wageningen. (1985, August 21). *Glandular system tune-up: Owners manual for the human body.* https://kundaliniyogawageningen.nl/wp-content/uploads/2016/09/Glandular-System-Tune-Up.pdf

Kuykendall, K. (2021, March 19). *Cultivating mindful self-care to bolster confidence.* Center for Educational Improvement. http://www.edimprovement.org/2021/03/cultivating-mindful-self-care-to-bolster-confidence/

Lander, J. (2018, September 26). *Helping teachers manage the weight of trauma.* Harvard Graduate School of Education. https://www.gse.harvard.edu/news/uk/18/09/helping-teachers-manage-weight-trauma

Lantieri, L. (with Goleman, D. P.). (2008). *Building emotional intelligence: Techniques to cultivate inner strength in children.* Sounds True.

Latif, S. (2015). *Naiya in nature: A children's guide to yoga.* Prolance.

Lieberman, A. F., & Knorr, K. (2007). The impact of trauma: A developmental framework for infancy and early childhood. *Pediatric Annals, 36*(4), 209–215. https://doi.org/10.3928/0090-4481-20070401-10

Magee, R. V. (2019). *The inner work of racial justice: Healing ourselves and transforming our communities through mindfulness.* TarcherPerigee.

Mahajan, A. S. (2014). Role of yoga in hormonal homeostasis. *International Journal of Clinical and Experimental Physiology, 1*(3), 173–178.

Mak, C., Whittingham, K., Cunnington, R., & Boyd, R. N. (2018). Efficacy of mindfulness-based interventions for attention and executive function in children and adolescents: A systematic review. *Mindfulness, 9*(1), 59–78. https://doi.org/10.1007/s12671-017-0770-6

Malin, H. (2018). *Teaching for purpose: Preparing students for lives of meaning.* Harvard Education Press.

Mallinson, J., & Singleton, M. (2017). *Roots of yoga.* Penguin Classics.

Mason, C., Asby, D., Wenzel, M., Volk, K., & Staeheli, M. (2021). *Compassionate school practices: Fostering children's mental health and well-being.* Corwin.

Mason, C., & Banks, K. L. (2014). *Heart beaming.* Center for Educational Improvement. https://www.edimprovement.org/heart-beaming

Mason, C., Liabenow, P., & Patschke, M. (2020). *Visioning onward: A guide for all schools.* Corwin.

Mason, C., Rivers Murphy, M., Bergey, M., Sawilowsky, S., Mullane, S., & Asby, D. (2018). *School compassionate culture analytic tool for educators (S-CCATE) and S-CCATE supplement user manual, instrument development, psychometrics.* https://www.s-ccate.org/static/media/manual.782a06fb.pdf

Mason, C., Rivers Murphy, M., & Jackson, Y. (2019). *Mindfulness practices: Cultivating heart centered communities where students focus and flourish.* Solution Tree.

Mason, C., Rivers Murphy, M., & Jackson, Y. (2020). *Mindful school communities: The Five Cs of nurturing Heart Centered Learning.* Solution Tree.

Matsuba, M. K., Schonert-Reichl, K. A., McElroy, T., & Katahoire, A. (2020, May 22). Effectiveness of a SEL/mindfulness program on northern Ugandan children. *International Journal of School & Educational Psychology.* Advance online publication. https://doi.org/10.1080/21683603.2020.1760977

McCraty, R., & Zayas, M. A. (2014). Cardiac coherence, self-regulation, autonomic stability, and psychosocial well-being. *Frontiers in Psychology, 5,* 1090. https://doi.org/10.3389/fpsyg.2014.01090

McCreary, C. N. (2021). *Little yogi deck: Simple yoga practices to help kids move through big emotions.* Bala Kids.

Mehta, A. (n.d.). *How to teach kids yoga.* https://anmolmehta.com/yoga-for-kids-children-yoga-poses/

Michie, S., Atkins, L., & West, R. (2014). *The behaviour change wheel: A guide to designing interventions.* Silverback.

Minero, E. (2017, October 4). When students are traumatized, teachers are too. *Edutopia.* https://www.edutopia.org/article/when-students-are-traumatized-teachers-are-too

Monticello Kievlan, P. (n.d.). *Stop, breathe & think kids: Focus, calm & sleep* [Mobile app]. Common Sense Media. https://www.commonsensemedia.org/app-reviews/stop-breathe-think-kids-focus-calm-sleep

Mother Teresa: Quotes. (n.d.). Goodreads. https://www.goodreads.com/quotes/6946-not-all-of-us-can-do-great-things-but-we

MyLife. (2020). *MyLife for schools.* https://my.life/mylife-for-schools/

Namaste Kid. (2021). *How to bring yoga into classrooms.* https://www.namastekid.com/kids-yoga-teaching-tools/how-to-bring-yoga-into-classrooms/

Naureckas, J. (2019, July 10). *Restorative justice in schools: Benefits and complications.* Center for Educational Improvement. http://www.edimprovement.org/2019/07/restorative-justice-in-schools-benefits-and-complications/

Neff, K. (2011). *Why self-compassion trumps self-esteem.* https://students.ouhsc.edu/news/article/why-self-compassion-trumps-self-esteem.

Neff, K. (2021). *Exercise 1: How would you treat a friend?* Self-Compassion. https://self-compassion.org/exercise-1-treat-friend/

Nelsen, J., Lott, L., & Glenn, H. S. (2013). *Positive discipline in the classroom: Developing mutual respect, cooperation, and responsibility in your classroom.* Three Rivers Press.

Nhin, M. (2020). *Calm ninja: A children's book about calming your anxiety featuring the Calm Ninja Yoga Flow.* Grow Grit Press.

Niles, F. (2011, August 17). How to use visualization to achieve your goals. *HuffPost.* https://www.huffpost.com/entry/visualization-goals_b_878424

Nunez, K. (2020, November 9). *The benefits of Breath of Fire and how to do it.* Healthline. https://www.healthline.com/health/breath-of-fire-yoga

Omega Institute for Holistic Studies. (2017, October 27). *What is trauma-informed yoga?* https://www.eomega.org/article/what-is-trauma-informed-yoga

Owen, R. (2019). *Learning that meets life.* Doctoral dissertation, Teachers College, Columbia University. https://academiccommons.columbia.edu/doi/10.7916/d8-0421-jx97

Palmer, P. J. (2007). *The courage to teach.* Jossey-Bass.

Patel, D. (2018, December 17). *The science of deep breathing.* Zenful Spirit. https://zenfulspirit.com/2018/12/17/science-deep-breathing/

Piper, B., & Geeves, E. (2019, February 25). Here's how we're using our experience of trauma to help others. *Yoga Journal.* https://www.yogajournal.com/practice/8-yoga-poses-to-help-heal-trauma/

Pranis, K. (2015). *Little book of circle processes: A new/old approach to peacemaking.* Good Books.

Rabiner, D. (2013). *Does yoga help children with attention problems?* Internet4Classrooms. https://www.internet4classrooms.com/exceptional_children/ADHD_attention_deficit_disorder_does_yoga_help_children_with_attention_problems.htm

Ramdesh, Dr. (n.d.). *Mantra for healing: Ra ma da sa.* Spirit Voyage. https://blog.spiritvoyage.com/mantra-for-healing-ra-ma-da-sa/

Rashedi, R. N., & Schonert-Reichl, K. A. (2019). Yoga and willful embodiment: A new direction for improving education. *Educational Psychology Review, 31,* 725–734. https://doi.org/10.1007/s10648-019-09481-5

Rashedi, R. N., Wajanakunakorn, M., & Hu, C. J. (2019). Young children's embodied experiences: A classroom-based yoga intervention. *Journal of Child and Family Studies, 28*(12), 3392–3400. https://doi.org/10.1007/s10826-019-01520-7

Rashedi, R. N., Weakley, M., Malhi, A., Wajanakunakorn, M., & Sheldon, J. (2020). Supporting positive behaviors through yoga: An exploratory study. *The Journal of Positive Psychology, 15*(1), 122–128. https://doi.org/10.1080/17439760.2019.1579364

Razza, R. A., Linsner, R. U., Bergen-Cico, D., Carlson, E., & Reid, S. (2020). The feasibility and effectiveness of mindful yoga for preschoolers exposed to high levels of trauma. *Journal of Child and Family Studies, 29*(1), 82–93. https://doi.org/10.1007/s10826-019-01582-7

Rechtschaffen, D. (2016). *The mindful education workbook: Lessons for teaching mindfulness to students.* Norton.

Ressler, K. J. (2010). Amygdala activity, fear, and anxiety: Modulation by stress. *Biological Psychiatry, 67*(12), 1117–1119. https://doi.org/10.1016%2Fj.biopsych.2010.04.027

Reynard, A., Gevirtz, R., Berlow, R., Brown M., & Boutelle, K. (2011). Heart rate variability as a marker of self-regulation. *Applied Psychophysiology and Biofeedback, 36*(3), 209–215.

Richert, K., Ikler, J., & Zacchei, M. (2020). *Shifting: How school leaders can create a culture of change.* Corwin.

Rogas, M. (2018, July 23). *Yoga games.* Center for Educational Improvement. http://www.edimprovement.org/2018/07/yoga-games/

Ross, A., & Thomas, S. (2010). The health benefits of yoga and exercise: A review of comparison studies. *Journal of Alternative and Complementary Medicine, 16*(1), 3–12. https://doi.org/10.1089/acm.2009.0044

Rubia, K. (2009). The neurobiology of meditation and its clinical effectiveness in psychiatric disorders. *Biological Psychology, 82*(1), 1–11. https://doi.org/10.1016/j.biopsycho.2009.04.003

Ruiz, D. M. (2018). *The four agreements: A practical guide to personal freedom.* Amber-Allen.

Sadhana Yoga School. (2021, April 15). *Your guide to beginning a mantra practice.* https://sadhanayoga.com/your-guide-to-beginning-a-mantra-practice/

Sadhguru. (2016). *Inner engineering: A yogi's guide to joy.* Harmony.

Salzberg, S. (2002). *Lovingkindness: The revolutionary art of happiness.* Shambhala.

Sarkissian, M., Trent, N. L., Huchting, K., & Khalsa, S. B. S. (2018). Effects of a Kundalini yoga program on elementary and middle school students' stress, affect, and resilience. *Journal of Developmental & Behavioral Pediatrics, 39*(3), 210–216. https://doi.org/10.1097/dbp.0000000000000538

Scott, S. J. (n.d.). How to make a DIY mindfulness jar with video & ingredients. *Develop Good Habits.* https://www.developgoodhabits.com/mindfulness-jar/

Sells, J. (2020, August 28). Kundalini yoga for tolerance and compassion. *Nesoteric.* https://www.nesoteric.com/blog/kundalini-yoga-for-tolerance-and-compassion

Seppälä, E. (2016). *The happiness track: How to apply the science of happiness to accelerate your success.* Hachette UK.

Shanti Generation. (2013, March 3). *Jade meadow* [Audio recording]. https://www.shantigeneration.com/wp-content/uploads/2013/03/03-jade-meadow.mp3

Shardlow, G. (2018). *Kids yoga class ideas: Fun and simple yoga themes with yoga poses and children's book recommendations for each month.* Kids Yoga Stories.

Sharma, M. (2017). *Radical transformational leadership: Strategic action for change agents*. North Atlantic Books.

Shirley, D. (2016). *The new imperatives of educational change: Achievement with integrity*. Taylor & Francis.

Sing Song Yoga. (2020). *Sing Song Yoga* (Version 2.0) [Mobile app]. http://www.singsongyoga.com/

Singer, N. (2020, November 30). Teaching in the pandemic: "This is not sustainable." *The New York Times*. https://www.nytimes.com/2020/11/30/us/teachers-remote-learning-burnout.html

Smiling Mind. (2020). *Mindfulness in education*. https://www.smilingmind.com.au/mindfulness-in-education

Smith, J. (2016, November 9). A psychologist says parents should do these 18 things to raise a more confident child. *Insider*. www.businessinsider.com/psychologist-explains-how-to-raise-a-more-confident-child-2016-11

Smookler, E. (2021, April 7). *The wisdom of loving your enemy*. Mindful. https://www.mindful.org/the-wisdom-of-loving-your-enemy/

Sodian, B., & Frith, U. (2008). Metacognition, theory of mind, and self-control: The relevance of high-level cognitive processes in development, neuroscience, and education. *Mind, Brain, and Education, 2*(3), 111–113. https://doi.org/10.1111/j.1751-228X.2008.00040.x

Sol Salute. (2021, January 1). *The best travel yoga mat 2021: 6 compact, lightweight & affordable travel mats*. https://www.solsalute.com/blog/guide-to-choosing-the-best-travel-yoga-mat

Spirit Voyage. (n.d.). *Jai Te Gang*. https://spiritvoyage.com/mantra/jai-te-gang/

Srinivasan, M. (2014). *Teach, breathe, learn: Mindfulness in and out of the classroom*. Parallax Press.

Stapp, A. C., & Wolff, K. (2019). Young children's experiences with yoga in an early childhood setting. *Early Child Development and Care, 189*(9), 1397–1410. https://doi.org/10.1080/03004430.2017.1385607

Stewart, W. (2017). *Mindful kids: 50 mindfulness activities for kindness, focus and calm*. https://www.amazon.com/Mindful-Kids-Activities-Focus-Peace/dp/1782853278/ref=sr_1_2?dchild=1&keywords=50+Mindfulness+Activities&qid=1616457109&sr=8-2

Stolyar, B. (2020, April 11). Down Dog app review: At-home yoga for people who are easily bored. *Mashable*. https://mashable.com/article/down-dog-home-yoga-app-review/

TEDx Talks. (2014, September 12). *Carol S. Dweck: The power of yet* [Video]. YouTube. https://www.youtube.com/watch?v=J-swZaKN2Ic

TFA Editorial Team. (2020, October 20). *Tackling COVID-19 fatigue as a teacher*. TeachForAmerica. https://www.teachforamerica.org/stories/tackling-covid-19-fatigue-as-a-teacher

The Conflict Center. (2018). *At the center of restorative culture*. https://conflictcenter.org/programs-training/schools/restorative-practices-program/

The Flow Station. (2017, July 1). *Kobe Bryant & Phil Jackson: Meditation* [Video]. YouTube. https://www.youtube.com/watch?v=E78y66GEPvs

The Graide Network. (2019, February 26). *Teacher burnout solutions & prevention: How to retain talented educators*. https://www.thegraidenetwork.com/blog-all/teacher-burnout-solutions-prevention

Thornapple Kellogg Schools. (n.d.). *Kindergarten students find "calm" in yoga*. https://www.tkschools.org/apps/news/article/562947

Trackit Lights. (n.d.). *Restorative practice: 6 questions that improve behaviour*. https://trackitlights.com/restorative-practice-6-questions-lead-better-pupil-behaviour/

Turner, J. S. (2021, February 17). *How is stress like a roller coaster?* The Less Stress Coach. https://www.lessstresscoach.com/2021/02/17/how-is-stress-like-a-roller-coaster/

University of Massachusetts Boston: Center for Peace, Democracy, and Development. (2021). *Restorative justice project*. https://www.umb.edu/cpdd/key_areas/law_justice_reform/restorative_justice_project

University of Missouri–Columbia. (2020, January 27). Nearly all middle school teachers are highly stressed: Education experts suggest findings indicate a need to reduce burden of teaching. *ScienceDaily*. www.sciencedaily.com/releases/2020/01/200127134722.htm

van Woerkom, M. (2018, March 12). Building community with restorative circles. *Edutopia*. https://www.edutopia.org/article/building-community-restorative-circles

Vaughn-Coaxum, R. A., Wang, Y., Kiely, J., Weisz, J. R., & Dunn, E. C. (2018). Associations between trauma type, timing, and accumulation on current coping behaviors in adolescents: Results from a large, population-based sample. *Journal of Youth and Adolescence, 47*(4), 842–858.

Viglas, M., & Perlman, M. (2018). Effects of a mindfulness-based program on young children's self-regulation, prosocial behavior and hyperactivity. *Journal of Child and Family Studies, 27*(4), 1150–1161. https://doi.org/10.1007/s10826-017-0971-6

Voris, K., & Alvarez, B. (2019). *Trauma-sensitive yoga deck for kids: For therapists, caregivers, and yoga teachers.* North Atlantic Books.

Walker, T. (2014, November 2). NEA survey: Nearly half of teachers consider leaving profession due to standardized testing. *NEAToday.* http://neatoday.org/2014/11/02/nea-gsurvey-nearly-half-of-teachers-consider-leaving-profession-due-to-standardized-testing-2/

Wallace, B. A. (2010). *The four immeasurables: Practices to open the heart.* Snow Lion Publications.

Wells, C. M. (2015). Conceptualizing mindful leadership in schools: How the practice of mindfulness informs the practice of leading. *Education Leadership Review of Doctoral Research, 2*(1), 1–23. https://files.eric.ed.gov/fulltext/EJ1105711.pdf

Wenzel, M. (2019a, January 22). *Classrooms, compassion, and contentment.* Center for Educational Improvement. http://www.edimprovement.org/2019/01/compassion-and-contentment/

Wenzel, M. (2019b, March). Fear and the brain. *Wow! Ed, Newsletter for the Center for Educational Improvement.* https://myemail.constantcontact.com/News-from-Center-for-Educational-Improvement.html?soid=1103736720061&aid=7gxdjvZoXm0

Willard, C., & Nance, A. J. (2018, May 25). *A mindful kids practice: The breath ball.* Mindful. https://www.mindful.org/a-mindful-kids-practice-the-breath-ball/

Willey, K. (2016). *Mindful moments for kids* [Audio CD]. Fireflies Records. https://kirawilley.com/mindful-moments-for-kids

Williams-Fields, J. (2020, July 9). *Yoga for kids: The yoga way to radiance—a book review.* Yoga U. https://www.yogauonline.com/yoga-for-kids/yoga-for-kids-yoga-way-radiance-book-review

YOGAaccessories. (2021). *Homepage.* https://www.yogaaccessories.com/

Yoga Activist. (2013). *Grants & features.* https://yogaactivist.org/for-teachers/awards

Yoga Ed. (2021). *Free yoga & mindfulness classes for children & teens.* https://academy.yogaed.com/p/yoga-ed-for-free-online-yoga-mindfulness-classes-for-all-ages

Your Therapy Source. (2020, July 7). *Bunny breathing and other exercises to empower, calm, and self regulate.* https://www.yourtherapysource.com/blog1/2020/07/07/bunny-breathing/

Zakrzewski, V. (2013, January 8). The case for discussing spirituality in schools. *Greater Good Magazine.* https://greatergood.berkeley.eduarticle/item/how_to_discuss_spirituality_in_school

Zakrzewski, V. (2020, February 26). Announcing a new resource for educators: Greater Good in Education. *Greater Good Magazine.* https://greatergood.berkeley.edu/article/item/announcing_a_new_resource_for_educators_greater_good_in_education

Zaltzman, H. (2017, May 5). Allusionist 55: Namaste [Audio podcast episode]. https://www.theallusionist.org/allusionist/namaste?rq=namaste

Zelazo, P. D., Forston, J. L., Masten, A. S., & Carlson, S. M. (2018). Mindfulness plus reflection training: Effects on executive function in early childhood. *Frontiers in Psychology, 9*, 208. https://doi.org/10.3389/fpsyg.2018.00208

Index

CORWIN
A SAGE Publishing Company

Helping educators make the greatest impact

CORWIN HAS ONE MISSION: to enhance education through intentional professional learning.

We build long-term relationships with our authors, educators, clients, and associations who partner with us to develop and continuously improve the best evidence-based practices that establish and support lifelong learning.

Kundalini Research Institute's Mission

The Kundalini Research Institute supports the dissemination of a comprehensive system of kundalini yoga, making it accessible to everyone through classes and publications, and trains teachers who help students find peace, health, and prosperity in today's modern age. Its mission is to uphold and preserve the authenticity, integrity, and accuracy of the Teachings of Yogi Bhajan through trainings, research, publishing, and resources. Established on February 1, 1972, the Kundalini Research Institute is a group of dedicated yogis working to help people bridge this ancient practice with modern living, allowing people to experience the empowering practical benefits.